AAT-9472
VC — Lib Studie

D0153743

Philos⬤phia

WITHDRAWN

WITHDRAWN

ANDREA NYE

Philos●phia

the thought of

Rosa Luxemburg,

Simone Weil,

and

Hannah Arendt

ROUTLEDGE New York • London

Published in 1994 by

Routledge
29 West 35 Street
New York, NY 10001

Published in Great Britain by

Routledge
11 New Fetter Lane
London EC4P 4EE

Copyright © 1994 by Routledge

Printed in the United States of America on acid free paper.

All rights reserved. No part of this book may be reprinted or reproduced or utilized in any form or by any electronic, mechanical or other means, now known or hereafter invented, including photocopying and recording, or in any information storage or retrieval system, without permission in writing from the publishers.

Library of Congress Cataloging-in-Publication Data
Nye, Andrea, 1939–
    Philosophia : the thought of Rosa Luxemburg, Simone Weil, and
Hannah Arendt / Andrea Nye.
        p.   cm.
    Includes bibliographical references and index.
    ISBN 0-415-90830-2. (HB)—ISBN 0-415-90831-0 (PB)
    1. Women philosophers. 2. Luxemburg, Rosa, 1871–1919. 3. Weil,
Simone, 1909–1943. 4. Arendt, Hanna. I. Title.
B105.W6N84   1994
190'.82—dc20   93-10223
                                                                          CIP

British Library Cataloguing-in-Publication Data also available.

for Jessica Nye
with whom I began to find my way
between past and future

Table of Contents

Labor and Work
Speaking Freely
Political Action
Thinking
A NEW FOUNDATION

Preface

Like most women philosophers, I have spent my life reading and criticizing male philosophers. I learned to read with the expectation that others' thoughts are not mine. Trained as a "professional," I found my power in analyzing arguments and denying what I read. In the course of this work on Rosa Luxemburg, Simone Weil, and Hannah Arendt, my relationship to what I read began to change. At times, it was not clear whose thought was in question, mine or the woman whose words I was reading. I developed their views beyond their explicit articulation in the texts. I dropped lines of thought that I considered unproductive.

This was not the philosophy I had been taught to faithfully repeat or hostilely refute, not the meticulous dry dissections of analytic philosophy, not the mind-bending constructions of logical semantics, not the precious feints of deconstruction or the ponderous metaphysics of phenomenology. Instead, it seemed to me to be thinking itself, unowned by any one person, never finished but willing to stay with its objects, gathering to small points of concentration to pull reality in, little by little, until ideas swell, take form, expand.

Weil, struggling feverishly with failing health to complete her plan for the reconstruction of a Europe torn apart by war; Arendt, the day before her death, putting a blank page in her typewriter to begin writing the culminating volume of her final treatise on *The Life of the Mind;* Luxemburg, finding the time to work out her critique of economics while in prison for antiwar activism: there is no blueprint for the just society here, for sure access to divinity or absolute truth or ultimate Being. These women produced no system, no philosophy to end all philosophies, as some of the great male philosophers have claimed to do. They intuited no eternal essences, discovered no law of history. One was not the disciple of another, one did not refute another. Scattered in their work are acknowledgments and recognitions, Arendt of Weil, Weil of Luxemburg, Arendt of Luxemburg. There is no one thing that they say, no one thing that they think, no grand ending, but beginnings and possibilities: of a renewed socialism, a historically relevant global economics, a nondualist metaphysics that does not assume a destructive adversarial relation between human beings and nature, a theory of knowledge that returns science to common understanding, a noncredulous religion, a linguistics that accommodates the fact that diverse people might come to understand each other.

The question at issue in what follows is not whether the masculine psychology of male philosophers accounts for the fact that philosophy has not been able to deliver these goods. Nor is it whether "phallocentric" logic regulates the deep structure of philosophic reason. Once these approaches are taken, Luxemburg, Weil, Arendt, and other women thinkers are already marginalized, interesting but isolated figures. Rather it is this conviction: once continuities in women's thought are traced out—continuities which are not discursive or psychological, but experiential and responsive to events—there will be positive agendas for future feminist scholarship and action. Once there is the possibility of reaching back in time for predecessors and progenitors, women's thought will have roots in moving relation to life as it is has been lived by women and men. If a unifying bond between male philosophers has been the interest of men in authoritative discourse which gives power over others, a unifying bond in this alternative line of thought might be an interest that women and men share: the maintenance of life in recognizably human form. Whether a thought in the service of that end is fruitful or not, whether it can lead to truth or effective action, is for us, for you, to decide as we take up the inquiry as it is left for us, on our own terms.

The Kingdom of Heaven is like
unto the leaven which a woman
took and hid in three measures of meal
until the whole was leavened

Matthew 13:33

Introduction:
Feminist Theory and the
Philosophical Tradition

In the past two decades, feminist philosophers have produced a substantial body of work critical of philosophy as it is traditionally taught and written in North America and Europe. The response of philosophers to this feminist challenge has been predictably defensive, ranging from outright hostility and ridicule to amused tolerance and selective co-optation of selected motifs. A considerable academic drama has resulted at conferences, in editorial committee and promotion hearings. The dispute, however, often goes on far from the concerns and experiences of nonacademic women, both in the West and in developing countries, struggling with unfriendly social, political, and economic institutions. Given the technicality and inaccessibility of so much philosophical discussion, traditional and feminist, given the professional concerns that are often the major source of its energy, even feminist philosophy can seem of little use in day-to-day battles against poverty, violence, and discrimination.

But there is more at stake in the confrontation between feminists and traditional philosophy than professional reputations and advancement. Philosophy, as a canon of male thinkers, stands as the conceptual resource for defining and understanding the terms of human existence in the West. In that geographical area and historical era, which now claims the title of civilization, philosophy is taken as the very prototype and model of thought. The result is that when women running for political office, bringing up children, competing with men in business, laboring in low-income service jobs, trying to make a place for themselves in science and technology look for concepts, arguments, ways of knowing, theories to inform their actions, they look to philosophy or to versions of philosophy popularized in social theory, ethics, economics, political theory. Philosophy, the "love of wisdom," the "Queen of the Sciences," provides the concepts by which truth, knowledge, and goodness are understood in the West.

Notwithstanding the now considerable body of feminist critique of philosophy, this "professional" thought has been remarkably resistant to feminist influence. Token examples of feminist social theory are added to Introduction to Philosophy courses, analytic reworkings of contemporary issues of interest to feminists are included in applied ethics, feminist critiques of major philosophical figures are used to supplement primary texts in history of philosophy; regardless of these gestures, those who define the discipline and the terrain of philosophy, both as historical figures and contemporary participants, continue to be men.

Neither conscious gynophobic malice nor unconscious assumption of privilege can completely account for the cohesiveness and resiliency of philosophy against the intervention of women thinkers. Feminist philosophers have documented a masculine identification in philosophy that goes deeper than discrimination which might be redressed in affirmative action programs, deeper than bias which might be cured in an effort to consider women as well as men when choosing texts. They have pointed to the very voices of philosophy and the idioms in which it speaks. But what stands firm even against "psychoanalysis" of that voice or "deconstruction" of its idioms is a historical fact. A particular tradition of men thinking together and successively in a specific historical period and geographical location—roughly Europe and North America from the classical Greeks to the present—has articulated the terms of "civilized" life. The philosophical tradition may be more diverse than appears from the range of authors taught in philosophy courses or noticed in commentaries—one or another line of the tradition, such as continental philosophy, pragmatism, romanticism, existentialism, may be unfairly omitted just as branches of a family fall into disrepute or are disowned—but constitutive relations of descent and influence between men define what philosophy is—Aristotle inherits from Plato the problem of universal essences, Ockham corrects Abelard's treatment of logical truth, Locke revises Descartes's rationalist grounding of scientific knowledge, and so on through the history of philosophy.

If it has been difficult for women philosophers to find a place for themselves in this genealogy, its persistent masculinity poses an even more serious problem for women who are not professional philosophers. Women must continue to try to make their way in a world in which men have most of the power and in which most institutions have been designed by men. As they attempt to move forward, women need concepts adequate to reality, arguments that establish truths, and methods of understanding that produce knowledge. But can Aristotle's syllogisms, the Stoics' consequentia, Bertrand Russell's truth tables provide arguments that justify feminist claims of institutional injustice? Can Carnap's positivism, Kripke's scientific realism, Quine's naturalized epistemology motivate a science that offers knowledge of objects of interest to women such as health, prosperity, and peace?

In feminist theory, the answer to these questions has most often been an emphatic no. In past decades that no has been carried to deeper and deeper levels of critique—from the exposure of the explicit misogyny of individual male philosophers to the gender metaphors which frame the fundamental concepts of philosophical schools, from political theories that rationalize masculine power to science's separation of a knowing male subject from the feminized object of his knowledge, from the sexist sociohistorical contexts that give meaning to philosophical theory to the supposedly deep phallic logic of any rational language. At this vanishing point, where the very language in which concepts have meaning, arguments have validity, knowledge is expressed is taken to be tainted with sexism, feminist philosophy is at an impasse. If sexism goes to the very constitution of meaning, feminism can only be disruptive, never constructive. Feminist critique, with all its power to unsettle and deconstruct, reaches its furthest limit.

Critical feminist philosophy, illuminating as it has been of the gender-laden conceptual structures and mechanisms of Western thought, cannot tell a woman how to make a new beginning or a new foundation. Unless her female body or hormones alone can be relied on to result in true statements, reliable knowledge, and wise effective action, she stands in a vacuum, unable to act on her own behalf, unable even to speak in her own name. If civilization is male in its very constitutive structures, there is no medium for women's thought but men's thoughts; revised, corrected, but still categories, methods, arguments borrowed from men. Feminist theory itself must be expressed in the terms of "philosophies of man," as *Marxist* feminists criticize liberal feminists, radical feminists draw on the existentialism of *Sartre* and *Merleau-Ponty* to criticize Marxist feminists, continental feminists turn to Hedeigger to criticize Anglo-American empiricism, poststructuralist feminists turn to *Derrida* and *Lacan* to criticize radical feminism. If anyone has seen and proclaimed the need for new ways of thinking it is feminists. In all areas of feminist scholarship the call has gone out for new methods, concepts, goals. But so heavy is the weight of male authority—Plato, Aristotle, Descartes, Kant, Marx, Derrida, Foucault—that, in book after book, paper after paper, feminist philosophers continue to analyze, criticize, and appropriate theory devised by men. This avoidance of positive theorizing itself is rationalized in philosophies of postmodernism which take any claim to truth as authoritarian and treat the conceptual structures of Western philosophy as vulnerable only to disruption and deconstruction. The retreat to an expressive, nonrational "woman's language," embraced by some "French feminists," can seem the only alternative. Thought is for men; women cannot have a politics because politics is the tactics of men; women cannot construct arguments because logic is a strategy of male domination.

At this point of exhaustion, if not of despair, I suggest that a new tack might be taken. Leaving aside the critique of masculinity, it may be possible to trace other lines of thought, not protests against male bias, not the passionate complaints of victims of injustice, but a continuing meditation by women on the human condition that develops positive concepts, arguments, and ways of knowing to inform women's, and men's, ways in the world. In order to recover such a line of thought it may be necessary to abandon the requirement that texts of interest to feminists must deal primarily with gender. It may be necessary to give up the hope that if sexism can somehow be eliminated there will be no more conflict—between rich and poor, intellectuals and workers, private and public life, physical causation and the transcendent. In Western culture, the traditional conceptualizations of these conflicts and the methods for confronting them have been framed by men; in the process, issues have often been distorted. But the conflicts were not invented by men. They are an effect of the human condition, female and male: we are physical and moral creatures; painful labor is necessary for survival; human nature is individual and social; physical causation rules the natural world at the same time as there are values that transcend material life. At these radical points of contradiction women's thought might be particularly valuable.

As part of a project of recovering an alternative tradition of women's thought, I propose the work of three women who have received only marginal attention from feminists and philosophers. Each was actively involved in the events of the twentieth century, each was pressed by violence and catastrophe to rethink the nature of reality, knowledge, and the self. Rosa Luxemburg was a leader in pre-World War I Polish and German socialist politics. At the podium of international socialist conferences or at her desk writing, she patiently, shrewdly, but always with wit, challenged the numbing bureaucratic complacency of her fellow Social Democrats at the same time as she condemned the rigid determinism of Lenin's Bolsheviks. "The Polish

woman," "Rosa, the mighty," "the little woman." Rosa, who dared
to challenge the authority of the male leadership of international
socialism, Kautsky, Bernstein, even the great Lenin himself, to defend
a revolutionary and democratic socialism. She was finally murdered,
in the midst of the failed German revolution, by protofascist troops
controlled by her own Social Democratic party.

Simone Weil was a philosophy student in pre-World War I France.
Brilliant, troubled, never content with the heavy comfort of her parents' bourgeois existence, she nursed her sensitivity to oppression in
self-denial, discipline, and study. Tormented by the endless round of
historical causation that ground out pain and violence in twentieth-
century Europe, she searched for the origins of the ill-fated "adven-
ture" of Western rationalism. In the process, she reconceived modernity, projecting a metaphysics that reconciles a world ruled by force
and reestablishes the conditions for justice. In wartime London, in
the midst of work for the French Resistance, she died at thirty-four
of starvation, exhaustion, and tuberculosis.

Hannah Arendt, Jewish by birth as were both Luxemburg and Weil,
and a philosophy student in Germany during the rise of Fascism,
watched as her celebrated teacher, Heidegger, embraced National
Socialism. She was imprisoned briefly by the Nazis, became a refugee
living from hand to mouth in Paris, and finally settled in New York,
where history, in the form of the Nazi war trials, the Civil Rights
Movement, the McCarthy trials, the war in the Middle East continued
to pose difficult questions of social justice. Energetic, intense, always
refusing an easy identification with existing political philosophies,
she followed the thread of a question: how had it happened? How
had the Holocaust been possible? What deep fault in Western culture
led to this ultimate of evils? She was not a "professional thinker," a
philosopher, she insisted, but at the end of her life, she returned to
Plato, Kant, Nietzsche to rework the heavy stuff of professional
thought in her treatise on *The Life of the Mind* unfinished at her death
from cerebral hemorrhage.

None of these women declared themselves feminists. Luxemburg
regularly brushed aside her friend Clara Zetkin's interest in the
"woman question." Weil ignored power relations between men and
women. Arendt was critical of a Women's Movement narrowly focused
on women's issues rather than larger political concerns. None of them
labeled the evil of Fascism, or capitalism, or institutional religion
patriarchal. For them, the problem was not men or masculinity but
identifying evil and error. Nor did they consider whether evil and
error would go away if women took men's places. Sexism was a
dimension of oppression virtually untouched in their theoretical work.

They used suspect generic language. They drew on no body of feminist scholarship; they relied on no supportive network of women scholars. Although they had close women friends and allies, they did not identify themselves primarily as women. If this was a weakness in their thought—and it was—it was also a strength. Bypassing the very real fact of women's oppression, they took upon themselves the authority to rethink the human condition.

The reaction of philosophers, including feminist philosophers, to their work has varied from interest, to disinterest, uneasiness, and disdain. It has been difficult to conceive how their thought can fit into philosophical categories or be made to relate to problems as they are traditionally framed in philosophy. The sense has been that they are not really philosophers, and there is justice in this claim. Their thinking does not come out of experience as academic philosophers, which is the current milieu for philosophy. If they took as their predecessors Plato, Descartes, Marx, they approached these men not as authorities in a masculine tradition but as coworkers in a line of thought defined by their own concerns. These women are not isolated mavericks, as some have argued: a non-Leninist Marxist, a mystical anorexic, a unscientific social scientist. In their work are continuities, consecutive inquiries, handed down problems, relations which mark paths and indicate future studies, research and writings.

The experience which motivated and framed Luxemburg's work in socialist theory and the epistemology of economics was the crushing failure of nineteenth-century liberatory socialism. As European workers supported the militarism and colonialism of the great powers in World War I, as Lenin fell back on elitist, dictatorial, party politics, as the Social Democrats settled for reformism and a piece of the colonial pie, Luxemburg, in despair and depression, turned to the theoretical foundations of Marxism. Meticulously tracing flaws in the economic rationalism which continues to dictate public policy in both capitalist and socialist countries, developing new forms of economic analysis that take into account the international dynamics of capitalism, she projected a democratic and global socialism which is neither the state capitalism of Lenin nor reformist social democracy.

Weil, as she suffered though the world depression of the 1930s and the global tensions that resulted in a second world war, took Luxemburg's inquiry deeper: How is the liberation promised by socialism possible if modern working methods will always be dictated by technicians and managers? If economic rationalism stands in the way of addressing this question, so does the modernist epistemology that understands science as an authoritative and inaccessible system of signs. Weil, reworking the isolation of Descartes's thinking subject, evoked an alternative modern self interactive with the natural environment and a science that is the forms of ordered methods of work. She developed materials and methods for teaching such a science to her lycée students and outlined in her philosophy lectures a nondualistic naturalistic epistemology of the thinking body. Fleeing to the United States the German occupation of France, she found substantive grounding for social ideals in a noncredulous conception of divinity. Working for the Free French in wartime London, she applied those ideals to the reconstruction of Europe.

After the war, Arendt continued the inquiry, faced with the absolute evil of the Holocaust, as well as with Hiroshima, Vietnam, war in the Middle East, violent racial conflict in the United States. Are the utopian changes in science that Weil projected possible, or must force always rule in the administration of work, making it necessary to cordon labor off from a free politics? Even more serious, is Weil's goodness in human affairs reliable protection against evil? Or is goodness in human affairs actually destructive of the political spaces in which diverse citizens can present themselves freely to each other?

The connection between these women is not that they think the same thoughts or think in the same way—there are fertile and interesting disagreements between them and significant divergences in style and method. What connects them are lines of inquiry different from those which have provided continuity in the mainstream philosophical tradition. The questions they address are not the philosopher's questions: how can we escape from the subjectivity of a thinking subject? How can we break out of the web of belief constituted by the clear and distinct representations of science? How can we assure ourselves that other minds exist or that there is an external world? The questions they address are historical, practical, and theoretical: how, in the last years of the twentieth century, are we to move on into the future from a past in which there has been the collapse of progressive social theory and the evil of the Holocaust? How, given the unbelievability of orthodox religion, are we to reconceive goodness? How, if science is increasingly inaccessible to common understanding, is science to bring about human freedom?

If it is possible to say that abstracted forms of logical argument have provided continuity in philosophy, it may also be possible to say that what holds together a search for wisdom on these questions is the very refusal of abstracted argument and an insistence on constantly returning to painful experiences which provide reference and which provoke and energize passionate thought. At the end of the twentieth century there is a great need for such a thinking, which is practical and theoretical, engaged and general. There is no mainstream social theory that provides an alternative to discredited Communist party rule and the manipulated party politics of capitalist elections. There is no theology that reconciles the medieval concept of God with modern science. There is no mainstream moral philosophy which defends nonsubjective values that are neither calculations of utility nor adherence to universal principle; no epistemology that does not waiver between a version of positivism and a relativist denial that knowledge is possible at all; no metaphysics that reconceptualizes a relation between human beings and nature consistent with preservation of the earthly environment; no theory of language that explains the fact that a person can understand what others say.

No lone woman, man, genius, out of a unitary autonomous self, can legislate values and truths for others. Questions cannot be answered or even framed by solitary thinkers. This has been the insight of postmodernism. But if it is true, it is not true for postmodernist reasons. It is true not because meaning is constituted in symbolic structures, but because meaningful speaking only goes on with others in the matrix of human relations and traditions. Those relations are not already universally there to be discovered or diverted as symbolic structure; they are *made* in centuries of copying, commenting, selection, criticism, exegesis. If the history of Western philosophy is such a tradition, told, retold, memorized, what follows is an attempt to begin to trace another tradition, a tradition of women's thought. If such a line of thought has a claim on our attention it is not for essentialist reasons. It is not because women are more caring and nurturant—these qualities can be weaknesses as well as strengths— or because women are more emotional and sensitive—these qualities can distort the truth as well as reveal it—or because women do not think logically—lack of order can rob thought of all power to convince and persuade. There is a simpler reason. The tradition of male philosophers has failed to produce an understanding of divinity, self, value, reality, knowledge viable in the late twentieth century. As long as women's thought is defined in opposition or resistance to this failed thought, as what is *not* logical, not authoritative, not rational, no redress of that failure is possible.

There is no way to know what women's thoughts are until women thinkers are studied with the attention and care given to the thoughts of men, until the various and related strains, themes, problematics of women's thought are isolated, preserved, saved, and allowed to leaven the heavy stuff of contemporary existence: Luxemburg, in Germany before the Great War, as the militarism of the Reich grew increasingly deadly, identifying a deep flaw in Marxist economics and projecting an alternative democratic socialism; Weil, in France as

Stalin took control of the Russian Revolution and the fever of National Socialism swept Germany, moving in thought beyond oppositions between mind and body to an undualist metaphysics; Arendt, in the aftermath of the World Wars, sure that there can be no certain peace until we understand the life of the mind and its relation to political action.

I

Rosa Luxemburg

Unlike so many of the leaders of the workers' movement, especially the Bolsheviks, and particularly Lenin, Rosa did not restrict her life to political activity. She was a complete being, open to all things, to whom nothing human was strange. Her political action was only the expression of her generous nature. From the disagreement between her and the Bolsheviks over the attitude of the militant in regard to revolutionary action came the great political disputes which surge among us, disputes which, no doubt, time would only have deepened had Rosa lived.

It is by grace of Rosa's profoundly human character that her correspondence will always retain a current interest whatever the course of history. We are, these days, in a situation very much worse, morally speaking, than that of the militants of the war years. Rosa believed firmly, in spite of the failure of social democracy, that the war would end by putting into motion the proletariat of Germany and lead to a socialist revolution. This hope has not been confirmed. The embryo of the proletarian revolution which was produced in 1918 rapidly suffocated in blood and dragged with it in its ruin the life of Rosa Luxemburg and of Liebknecht. Since then, all the hopes which had been able to make militants have been dashed. We can no longer have blind confidence, like Rosa, in the spontaneity of the working class; their organizations have fallen apart.

But Rosa did not draw her joy and her pious love for life and the world from false hopes, she drew them from the force of her soul and of her spirit. This is why still at the present each of us might follow her example.

> From Simone Weil's review of Luxemburg's *Letters from Prison* for *La Critique sociale* no. 10, November 1933 reprinted in *Oeuvres completes* Tome III, pp. 300–302)

1

An Intractable Comrade

The tone of socialist polemics is harsh. Ridicule, sarcasm, crude irony, personal insult are often the rule when one socialist criticizes the errors of another, but the male leaders of European social democracy in the early decades of this century were particularly venomous when it came to their intractable colleague, Rosa Luxemburg. In public, they moderated their irritation that this little Jewish woman with a limp had such a prominent place in socialist politics, but in letters to each other and in personal asides, they ridiculed her person, her sex, her ideas, her presumption. She was always "Rosa," sometimes "La Rosa," never "Luxemburg" like "Bebel," "Kautsky," "Lenin," and the others.[1] She was a phenomenon, not a person, as she disrupted accepted socialist opinion, transgressed the superior wisdom of the leaders of the party, muddied clear positions with theoretical scruples, compromised tactics with second thoughts, and, worst of all, refused to take Marxist doctrine as fixed or unquestionable.

After her death, animosity and resentment at her posthumous "meddling" continued to be vented. Bukharin, writing the official bolshevik critique of her major theoretical work, *The Accumulation of Capital* (AC), was assigned to expose her "ludicrous" mistakes. Although he began and ended with token respect for "Comrade Rosa Luxemburg," his job was to make clear that as a "critic" of Marx she had departed from the ranks of the faithful. As his diatribe against Luxemburg's revisions of the master gathered momentum, Bukharin punctuated his exposition with sarcastic asides: "Excuse me, Comrade Luxemburg, if this is 'all very well' (this 'all very well' is a forced admission since she cannot bring forward *one single* argument against the fact that it is 'all very well')" (ACAC 177); or "Splendid! What a pity, though, that Rosa Luxemburg did not search for the 'stern laws of the economic process' where they can be found" (ACAC 246). Her conceptions are "atrocious" (ACAC 179); when by "accident" she comes close to a correct solution to a problem, "like a rubber ball bouncing, she leaps away from it in fright" (ACAC 196); her arguments are a "farce" (ACAC 181); she tangles herself in a "net of contradictions" (ACAC 248); she goes round and round on a meaningless "carousel" of circular argument (ACAC 178).

Bukharin was not the only man in the communist movement who ridiculed Luxemburg's thinking. Bebel, Kautsky, Bernstein, Lenin, most of the leaders of European Social Democracy, as well as twentieth-century neo-Marxists, had occasion to attack her "confused" and "erroneous" positions. The animosity she aroused was finally deadly. During the German revolution, the restored government, controlled by her old comrades in the Social Democratic party, connived at her brutal murder by the paramilitary Freikorps, whose rhetoric had often identified the communist menace with unlicensed femininity.[2] Even after her offending person had been eliminated, her influence continued to be cited as a danger and her name was regularly given to official heresy, as "Luxemburgism" was used to label whatever was considered to be deviant from current party orthodoxy.

What was it about this woman—who devoted her life to socialist politics, whose commitment to the interests of workers could not be questioned, who was imprisoned for socialist activism for long periods of time, who never stopped thinking and writing about the prospects for socialist liberation—what was it about her that so angered these men? On the surface was her irritating willingness to question many of the necessary truths of Marxist theory: a socialist revolution was not immediately at hand but would be a long process of advance and regression; class struggle between proletariat and bourgeoisie was not the contradiction that would bring down capitalism. This was bad enough. What was more disturbing was the way in which she reached these positions. Actively involved in all aspects of socialist politics in Poland and Germany, prominent at international meetings of socialists from all countries, continually published and cited in major socialist publications, there was a style to her thought that was anathema to party leadership. Her power as a speaker could not be denied; she could take and hold the floor, answer back sharply in the heat of debate, cite socialist theory with facility. Her grasp of economics and history was more detailed and sound than most of her male comrades. Still from the standpoint of the male leadership of socialist parties she was often off the point, taking positions that were impolitic, thinking when she should have been acting, acting when she should have been theorizing, and, above all, refusing to follow the prescribed logic of party discipline.

The attempt after her death to make a package of her errors was never successful; she had produced no dogma, no system, no coherent deductive structure. She did not begin from premises which were necessarily true and then work to indubitable conclusions. The attempt by her critics to fashion from her writings and speeches a theory that was a systematic, heretical alternative to Marxism always failed to do justice to her thought. But if her thought did not take the form of a deductive structure, it was still all of a piece, the strategies she urged generating an ongoing inquiry driven by commitment and reflection. Her early interest in the question of her native Poland's independence led to her later resistance to revisionism, her stand against revisionism to her support for the mass strike, the mass strike to the importance of class consciousness, class consciousness to imperialism, and imperialism to a new understanding of the economics of capitalism.

The key to the continuity is not discursive logic but an internal relation between Luxemburg's thinking and twentieth-century European socialist experience. Always her socialism was rooted in history and currently changing conditions: archaic autocracy, national liberation movements, liberal promises of democratic participation, imperialism, and ruthless monopoly capitalism. For Luxemburg these were not abstract concepts but living experiences. Imperialism was not a stage in the necessary development of capital, but the violence of German militarism at home and aggressive conquest abroad. The proletariat was not a universal class but diverse groups of men and women with ethnic identities and specific memories and desires. Nationalism, reformism, imperialism did not originate as problems in theory but as problems in socialist practice.

She was not a theoretician like Kautsky, content to construct ideal systems and draw conclusions that might have little to do with reality. She was not Lenin, the masterful tactician, adapting just enough theory to defend whatever pragmatic actions were necessary to advance the bolshevik cause. She did not start with theory and deduce action, nor did she take action and write theory to fit. Instead, from the standpoint of commitment to working people, she continued to think and rethink what she and other socialists had been doing, were doing and should do. The questions she asked were always practical— what is to be done?—but that question for Luxemburg was never simply tactical. It was never what can we do so that we, our party, our faction, will win, but rather, what can we do that takes account of the reality of the situation. This question, in the early decades of twentieth-century Eastern Europe, required, as Luxemburg saw it, a rethinking of some of the core dogmas of socialism, a rethinking that her male colleagues were unwilling to undertake.

The press of events in Luxemburg's lifetime was relentless: the romantic fervor of Eastern European national movements, the adversarial maneuvering of parliamentary politics, the hysterical edge to German militarism, the continuing violent exploitation of colonial peoples, the stunning bolshevik victory in Russia, and finally the enthusiastic support that many German workers gave the Prussian war machine. At the center of the storm in Poland and Germany, Luxemburg refused to stop thinking. She would accept no unquestionable truths, no master whose words can be cited and quoted, no universal class whose representatives are always right. There was one fixed point to which she returned; commitment to working people. Of their well-being there could be no canonical definition, to their self-realization no sure route. Instead, at every difficult step thought was necessary, thought that takes in a whole situation as it evolves in fact, thought that does not divide a problem into autonomous tactical problems to solve one at a time, that does not find one thing necessarily true and then confidently deduce correct doctrine.

Steadied only by commitment and concern, Luxemburg responded to ongoing events with energy and passion. Her emotional involvement was criticized by Lenin, who drew back with distaste from her vivid and moving descriptions of colonialism; "The description of the torture of negroes in South Africa is noisy, colorful and meaningless. Above all it is 'non-Marxist,' " he scoffed.[3] Her passionate interest in colonialism, he charged, took attention away from the correct focus of socialist attention, the Communist party coming to power. For Lenin, emotion and response were always to be harnessed to strategy, shaped and molded to serve the cause of the party. A Marxist revolutionary could intellectually note the plight of slaves in Africa or serfs in Central America, and theoretically account for it, but his interest must be to use the phenomenon in the cause of Communism. Colonial liberation movements could stir up agitation that might undermine the strength of capitalist states and distract their leaders from the growing internal contradictions that would eventually bring about their collapse. Rebelling natives could be persuaded with the promise of military and economic support to organize in Leninist parties, allied with the vanguard in Russia.

Luxemburg's response to colonialism was not opportunistic. Her willingness to attend to the reality of colonial oppression on its own terms made her the first of the social democratic leaders to appreciate its theoretical importance. As early as 1899, before Lenin had given any thought to imperialism, she saw clearly a cyclical progression from internal economic difficulties in capitalist states, to colonial expansion, to great power rivalry and war (LRL 71–72). As the European powers struggled for global domination, she addressed this new phenomenon apart from schematic preconceptions, apart even from the fixed frame of universal class struggle between bourgeoisie and proletariat posited by Marx. The world of capital had changed. Luxemburg appreciated this fact in a way Lenin did not, and when Lenin did see it, his response was myopic. If capitalism was in a new imperialist phase, said Lenin, then tactics needed to be revised, not communist theory. If the revolution did not happen on schedule in Europe, it could be made to happen elsewhere, in Russia for example. All that was necessary was to supplement theory with a "transition stage," in which a vanguard Communist party ruled for the masses. If capitalism recovered its vigor in colonial adventures, local unrest could be fostered in the colonies, controlled by the Russian party. In contrast, Luxemburg's socialism predicated neither on Marxist dogma nor on the taking of power but committed to the interests of working people, required radical revision in the changing world of international capital.

For Luxemburg, this rethinking of theory in the light of new facts is "Marxism." Luxemburg's Marx is not the originator of a scripture to be cited and revered, but the founder of a materialist "method." Materialism is not the interpretation of all phenomena according to a fixed formula, but attention to what has happened and what is happening. Refusing to accept any suprahistorical values or ideas that have regulated or should regulate human life, Luxemburg's Marx looked for laws and principles in actual events. When previous conclusions are inconsistent with new developments, he thinks again. This human and fallible Marx was unacceptable to many of Luxemburg's colleagues; certainly it was rejected by the Bolsheviks, consolidating their control in Russia and over Communist parties outside of Russia. Marxism, reformist and Leninist, had become dogma: tired slogans, catchphrases, meaningless buzzwords that make up a propagandistic rhetoric, drilled and disciplined, oblivious to reality.

Even now, with Lenin's Marxism discredited, Luxemburg's work is seldom discussed at length. Neo-Marxist economists, many of whose updated positions have affinities with her own, devote pages to Lenin's "authoritative" views and only a footnote to Luxemburg and her "mistakes."[4] In print if not in practice, Lenin continues to exert posthumous control as the designated heir of Marx and the canonical authority on the question of imperialism. A constituent feature of orthodox

Marxist rhetoric is the claim of descent from authority, the charge of infidelity to the sacred texts, the citing of dicta to enforce loyalty. Luxemburg's most persistent sin was that she rejected this rhetoric. She understood Marx as a man, like any other man caught in changing historical situations not containable in simple schemas. Luxemburg's socialist thought poses a question. Was there a way not taken, that might be taken still, a non-Leninist, nonreformist post-Marxist socialism, neither authoritarian nor dogmatic, but historical, perspectival, democratic, progressive, a socialism that might inform a mass feminist social movement?

1. Thoughtful Political Action

Reform and Revolution

Throughout the nineteenth and twentieth centuries, Marxism has been the political philosophy which speaks to the situation of working women. Marxism understood the family as a place of women's oppression, promoted the equality of women in the work force, promised to provide the social services that make women's work outside the home possible. Even when feminist experience in socialist politics proved disappointing—Marxist labor unions refused to admit women, the Soviet Union disbanded Alexandra Kolontai's Women's Bureau, the Progressive Labor party in the United States assigned women to coffee making—Marxism, in theory if not in practice, was the progressive social philosophy that addressed women's material condition.

But the failure of socialist politics in most parts of the world in its Leninist forms, as well as its current unpopularity as social democracy in Europe and North America, has undermined socialist feminism as a practical politics. Where there seemed to be beginnings, however flawed and in need of supplementation, of a theory of activism in the service of masses of working and poor women, there is now a return to market economics with its tolerance of inequality and exploitation. In Western countries, feminist activists, under attack from conservatives eager to return women to the family, ban abortion, or curtail affirmative action programs, turn away from revolutionary visions of the future to the defense of rights already won. Socialist feminists, nurtured in the student movements of the 1960s, give up materialism for separatist lesbian theory and academic postmodern critiques of culture. Although these radical and deconstructive strategies help individual women and groups of women achieve feminine identities that are a source of personal strength and comfort, they are unlikely to be the base for a political movement that includes masses of women in Western and non-Western countries. Without socialism, the only material hope for women in industrialized countries are rights which can always be rescinded and which poor women may not be able to exercise. Without socialism, the only material hope for women in the nonindustrialized world is capitalist development which may deepen their dependence on men.

The problem Luxemburg set for herself in the opening decades of the twentieth century was to understand and repair deep flaws which, even then, she saw in socialist thought, flaws which in her view threatened the future of socialist politics. Socialist feminist philosophers have seldom been willing to take Marxism theory as they find it, but the most common approach has been to add on to Marxism a supplementary analysis of patriarchal oppression. In contrast, Luxemburg's rethinking of Marxism went to the very heart of Marxist science: its economics. In the process, she rejected both of twentieth-century Marxism's ruling paradigms: socialist/reformism and Marxist/Leninism. An effective socialism, she insisted was neither reformist—willing to settle for whatever legal concessions ameliorating the condition of working people could be won within the capitalist system, nor revolutionary in the sense of an elitist separatist organization dedicated to the taking over of power. Socialism is revolutionary only when it is a democratic mass movement of working women and men.

Luxemburg was not the only one in the years before World War I to sense that there was a crisis in socialism, but the response of many male socialist leaders was retreat and retrenchment. The precarious legality of the Social Democratic party in Germany in the years before the outbreak of World War I dictated caution to her colleagues. Finally able to organize and meet openly, as well as to run for seats in the German Parliament, tactics were adjusted. Compromise was the rule, as the party leadership participated in elections and drafted legislation, always with the fear that repressive anticommunist laws would be reinstated. Attention turned inward, away from confrontation with royalists and Junkers and industrialists, to matters of party organization and internal politics. Eduard Bernstein, a Social Democrat in exile in London, in a series of articles and a book, claimed to outline the philosophy that would reflect this new democratic socialist practice.[5]

Bernstein argued that capitalism, contrary to the belief of those misguided catastrophists who believed that capitalism would soon collapse, had learned to adjust and survive. Monopolies and international cartels, the development of credit and banking facilities, new means of communication, and protective labor legislation muted the contradictions of capitalism. In response, he argued, socialists should adjust their goals. In a stable capitalist economy, social reforms, won through the extension of suffrage and legislation, supplemented with social experiments in cooperatives and communes, would slowly evolve into socialism. The motive force behind change would be neither violent revolution nor economic collapse but moral ideals of justice and equality.

This view, articulated by Bernstein in 1896, became the majority view of reformist social democracy in Europe and North America. The choice is typically expressed in dichotomous terms. If you do not accept radical bolshevism, you must settle for Bernstein's slow, process of democratic reform. In her pamphlet, "Social Reform or Revolution" (1899; PW), Luxemburg exposed the weaknesses in Bernstein's argument. That practice and theory cannot be detached from each other, Luxemburg took as central to Marxist philosophy. There is no universal truth from which socialist practice can be deduced; there is no correct socialist practice from which theory can be read. Responsible action is action that is thoughtful; theory that grasps reality is theory that is practical. But in much of socialist thought and practice, the nexus between theory and practice was misunderstood. Either intellectual schema dictated correct practice without regard for changing realities; or expedient action was taken without regard for theoretical goals. Bernstein noted that socialist practice had become reformist and read off a reformist socialist theory to match. The result, argued Luxemburg, was that both socialist theory and socialist action lost content and meaning. Theory became a description of means to arbitrary ends. Action lost purpose, and was no longer for any clear socialist goal. No action is self-evidently socialist: not trade union activity, not social welfare legislation, not the forming of cooperatives. These can be supported in order to promote the interests of capitalists or bureaucrats, just as measures supposedly friendly to women, like state-administered welfare or protective labor legislation, can increase women's dependence and powerlessness.

Whether theory is thought to govern material events, or historical events determine theory, in both cases the separation of theory from practice results in the reduction of either reality or thought. Either there is no theory, but only events incoherently grasped—as in Bernstein's reformism, or there is no reality but only the necessary laws of history—as in determinist theories of history. Bernstein, by separating practice from the theory that informs it, and Lenin, by separating theory from the activities of workers, both end at the same place. Political players, socialist and communist, vie for power and position, and there is no guide for responsible and realistic socialist action.

Luxemburg agreed with Bernstein that a drift in socialist practice had occurred. The question remained what that drift meant. Just because a course of action is the policy of a Social Democratic party or Communist party, does not make it socialist. Without the thought that defines socialist goals, action is "worthless and aimless," directed to isolated ends that have no meaning when seen in the perspective of historical reality (PW 113).

Thoughtless actions may have totally unintended consequences. The vote can be taken away as soon as militant working-class organizations have been disbanded. Social reforms can be manipulated to increase capitalist profits. Communes and cooperatives may oppress workers more harshly than unionized corporations. Feminist reforms may lead to conservative backlash. It is not enough to agitate on specific issues: higher wages, parental leave, better work conditions, abortion rights. Without a socialist grasp of the whole from a given material position, single issues, such as equal rights, welfare legislation, increased wages, can drain energy or, worse, be manipulated by conservative forces.

In order to defend his reformist socialism, Luxemburg charged, Bernstein depended on theoretical schema rather than on concrete and complex historical understanding. He claimed democratic institutions as a characteristic element in capitalism and then argued that workers had to use those institutions to achieve economic power in higher wages and benefits before they could take power. This, said Luxemburg, showed a poor understanding of working-class experience. In historical fact, rather than schematic theory, democracy occurs in a variety of economic systems and is characteristic of capitalism only at a particular stage in its development.[6] Furthermore, the schema—those who take political power already have economic power—even if it could account for the variety of past revolutions, certainly would not fit a socialist revolution. If workers' wealth and economic power are the material base of a socialist revolution, workers only constitute a new class of oppressors.

Luxemburg did not disagree with the social democratic policy of participating in elections and parliament for welfare legislation or in the traditionally Marxist trade union activity for higher wages and better working conditions. She disagreed with Bernstein over how those actions should be understood. For Luxemburg, their socialist purpose is not reformist—to get higher wages or protective legislation to alleviate the evils of capitalism—but revolutionary—to continue the political education of working women and men as they struggle to understand and master the inherent contradictions in their situation. Without that thought and knowledge, there can be no reliable socialist values; the superior judgment of party leaders and theoreticians is no substitute.

Defining a morality that can identify socialist values and guide socialist action has been a recurring problem in Marxist philosophy. From the standpoint of historical materialism, no value or ideal can have extrahistorical standing. Systems of ethics, such as utilitarianism or Kantianism, are reflections of historically locatable capitalist interests. But this rejection of universal values leaves socialism in a moral vacuum. Does a socialist activist simply follow along in existing currents of history, hoping that progress is somehow written onto economic laws of development and change? Or does she, with Bernstein, reject the determinism of historical law which ordains against the fact that capitalism is necessarily followed by a morally superior socialism and retreat to universal, suprahistorical, moral principles of philosophers like Kant?

Luxemburg agreed with Bernstein's critique of schematic historical determinism but she also firmly resisted any reversion to idealist moral philosophy. Universal moral principles provide only a fragmentary grasp of complex realities, she thought, and are never truly universal because always there are different classes of persons with different interests and aspirations (PW 126). Nor was she willing to settle for Leninist expediency—whatever promotes the interests of our group, faction or party is right. This pragmatic principle, which she saw fast becoming the only criterion of correctness for Bolsheviks intent on achieving power, was no principle at all.

In the place of Bernstein's idealist moral principles and their counterpart of Leninist expediency masked by historical law, she proposed a socialist ethics grounded in commitment to working people. Socialist policy, if it is to successfully plot a way to a just society, has to reflect their concrete interests. This is the "political compass" that enables socialists to steer a moral course, and it had been set aside by both Social Democrats and Bolsheviks. If materialism is a historical realism that refuses to impose any abstract law or abstract principle, economic or moral, on actual material experience, then the only source for a nonidealist socialist morality is the situation and aspirations of working people. The only sure guide to socialist action is judgment based on that understanding. Only by placing oneself solidly and concretely in a particular historical circumstance with masses of working people is it possible to achieve the perspective which is an "axis of intellectual crystallization around which isolated facts group themselves in the organic whole of a coherent conception of the world" (PW 126). From such a committed standpoint, a socialist can see the world not as a group of "isolated facts" but as an "organic whole" about which sound political judgments can be made.

Reformist socialists, failing to ground themselves in historical experience, misconceived not only what socialists *should* do, but also the reality of capitalism. Bernstein, for example, saw isolated aspects of the system—for example, the way credit eases the painful business cycles cited by Marx as evidence of capitalism's instability—but he failed to see credit in the "totality of living economic context" (PW 90). He understood and accurately described credit from the limited perspective of a capitalist looking for profit and a favorable economic climate for investment, but he did not see credit from the standpoint of a working woman in an urban ghetto unable to get a loan to start a small business. The result is a false choice between Bernstein's reform and Lenin's dictatorship of the Communist party.

Reform, without a view of the whole, takes issues one at a time with the false hope of eventual substantive change. An increase in the progressiveness of the tax system to redistribute wealth, social services that support women's work, affirmative action programs in corporate hiring: these single achievements will eventually add up to socialism. From the standpoint, however, of an unemployed or underemployed woman who sees how the economic system depends on a reserve of sexually segregated, minimum-wage workers or of an African man who has been delegated servile labor, such single-issue activism can seem a futile spinning of wheels. Those in power give in on one issue only to reassert their authority elsewhere. In contrast, Luxemburg's revolutionary judgment was based on knowledge of interlocking apparatuses of power, large parts of which are only visible to those who are economically disadvantaged and struggling against the oppressive institutions that oppress them. Pornography to a middle-class woman is a degrading depiction of sexual images; to prostitutes, young runaways, unemployed women, pornography might be seen as global capitalist business unlikely to be abandoned in response to moral protest.

How is this knowledge of the whole to be achieved? Many disadvantaged women are far from making the kind of socialist judgments Luxemburg describes. Should leaders and theoreticians decide for them in accordance with correct Marxist or feminist theory? The answer, Luxemburg thought, is not in corrective or directive policy drafted by elite groups of intellectuals or activists, but in careful attention to and understanding of mass action.

Mass Action

When rebellion in Russia in 1905 brought the Tsar's regime close to collapse, German Social Democrats, used to considering themselves the leaders of socialism and protective of the precarious legality of the socialist party in Germany, were quick to pass negative judgment: mass strikes by workers, protests, demonstrations, and street fighting were only ineffectual symptoms for the hopeless immaturity of Russian socialism. Nothing truly revolutionary could happen in Russia. In contrast, Luxemburg, insisting that socialist values must come out of socialist experience, immediately went to Russia, and later to Finland with Lenin, to observe the revolution first hand.

Luxemburg's pamphlet, "The Mass Strike" (1906; PW), was written to bring the lessons of the Russian Revolution back to Germany. When it became clear that Luxemburg meant more than lip service in the name of socialist solidarity, that she meant to carry the perspectives gained from the Russian experience into day-to-day party judgment in Germany, resistance against the tactic of mass action hardened. Marx and Engels were liberally cited against her: to encourage spontaneous uprisings was "anarchism." Either workers already had power and so did not need such tactics, or they did not have power and nothing would come of the sacrifice of lives. Against these "theoretical schema," Luxemburg urged a thoroughly historical understanding of unexpected developments in Russia. In Russia, the mass strike had not been a correct or mistaken tactic of either anarchists or Social Democrats, but a spontaneous mass movement of the most diverse groups of people, workers and small business people, professional and manual workers, rural and urban groups. In such action, thought Luxemburg, is the key to revolution.

From the standpoint of dogmatic theory, it is possible to argue either for or against mass action as a tactic, depending on the choice of premises. But, for Luxemburg, reform and revolution are not alternative strategies to be chosen like hot or mild "sausages" for expediency's sake (PW 114). Mass action in Russia was a complex historical reality in which "productiveness" and "unproductiveness" did not "mutually exclude each other, but, as always, condition and complete each other" (PW 228). Attending to extraordinary events in Russia, studying their history, Luxemburg traced developments that did not fit neatly into existing socialist theory but from which a revised socialist theory might be generated.

She described the Russia of 1905 with a vividness alien to the abstract theoretical style of orthodox Marxist "science." The revolution was a colossal and constantly moving complex of explosive social forces, sparks touching off conflagrations, movement stifled and then out of nothing rekindled, small channels of political struggles and 'accidental' occurrences which flowed to a raging sea. A trickle of protest met other trickles, drew in nonrevolutionary elements like the police or domestic servants, became a river of outcry which when dammed up only flowed free somewhere else. This was a "pulsation of flesh and blood"; a "ceaselessly moving, changing sea of phenomena" (RLS 182). But, scoffed the German Social Democrats, see what came of it. The tsar was not dethroned; the Duma, the Russian parliament, returned to its old powerlessness.

In Luxemburg's judgment, they had failed to learn the lessons of history. Socialism is not won in a successful coup or parliamentary maneuver that results in a takeover of state power. A revolution takes a long time and is a complex process of small movements that gather towards the end of socialism. Only in mass political action do people begin to recover the sense of agency which allows them to be conscious of their situation; only in political action do people come to understand their aspirations as well as the mechanisms that prevent the realization of those aspirations. The revolution in Russia, properly understood, was a testing and constructing of new social realities.

German social democratic leaders, she noted, had been blind to this ongoing socialist experience. Insisting on Germany, with "the glory of almost a century of continuous victories over the strongest great powers in the world," as the place where the socialist revolution must occur, Kautsky betrayed his approval of Germany's colonial adventures (TP 21). Where were these great victories? asked Luxemburg. The brutal Hunn Campaign in China, the massacre of Hottentot women and children in the Kalahari? Even in regard to the situation in Germany, Kautsky was out of touch with reality, his "theory" of a final triumphant revolution only an "abstract schema."

> When from these aetherial heights, where theory calmly circles like an eagle, the question first plunged to the flat land of the Prussian voting rights campaign, then suddenly the brainless and planless Prussian government was transfigured into a rocher de bronze. (TP 53)

"Heaven-storming theory" on the one hand, and "attrition" in practice on the other, was the order of the day, as Kautsky and the other leaders of the party discouraged any agitation or mass movement, including even demonstrations for an extension of voting rights.

With her defense of mass action as the primary form of revolutionary struggle, Luxemburg pressed on the sensitive nerve of the role of political leadership. The party, for both Social Democrats and radical Bolsheviks, was the vanguard of the proletariat; its task was to lead, issuing directives that would lead to success. Luxemburg questioned this point of agreement between socialist right and socialist left. The business of a party or political organization, she argued, is not to

issue commands "according to one's inclinations," but to maintain
an "adroit adaptability to the given situation," keeping the "closest
possible contact with the masses" (RLS 188). This was not how either
cautious Social Democrats or calculating Bolsheviks saw their role.
It was not for them to adapt but to govern, not for them to consort
with laundresses or miners, but to manipulate the actions of party
faithful according to correct theory.

As Luxemburg defended the mass strike, immediately there was an
outcry of anarchism. She had eliminated the role of the party, called
for bloodshed in the streets. But the question, for Luxemburg, was
not whether party leaders should lead. It was how they should lead.
Should organizers plan a coup or a voting campaign? Should they
issue directives that end by either being ineffectual or miscarrying
in the complex course of human events? Should they try to calculate
costs that can never be quantified? Directive policy not in touch with
the reality of working life had to fail. Party leaders such as Kautsky
saw mass action either as a spontaneous upheaval for which the party
could only wait, or as a coup planned in secret by party leadership.
But in this they misconceived the relation between leaders and people.

Mass strikes cannot be "made" by order from the "supreme command," they:

> must arise from the masses and their advancing action. But
> *politically*, in the sense of an energetic tactic, a powerful offen-
> sive, to so lead this action forward so that the masses are
> ever more conscious of their tasks—that the party can do,
> and that is also its duty. (TP 63)

If mass action cannot be manufactured, it can be crippled by poor
leadership. Luxemburg cited example after example, including the
Social Democrat's discouragement of an aggressive voting rights campaign.

In Luxemburg's dynamic reciprocal relationship between masses
and leaders, theorists work with the aspirations and actions of actual
women and men, they "guide" diverse and often uncoordinated initiatives. When there are new developments, they meet them head-on
"with resolute, consistent tactics" (TP 63). They "push" the movement
forward, "point to new forms of agitation and praxis," "inject new
life" into radical publications and meetings (LRL 77). In most of
Western philosophy's ruling paradigms of knowledge, thought has
stood apart from experience. Thought is the province of experts, those
intellectually gifted and well-educated enough to think. Action is carried out by those less well endowed; their movements form the matter

upon which thinkers pass judgment. Both the personal ambition of some of the men who led socialism and the utopian ideals of others reinforced this separation between those who act, on the one hand, and those who know and direct them in their action, on the other. Supporting party leadership's claim to know was a rapidly expanding Marxist science that replaced worker's consciousness of their situation as the basis for socialist policy. If leaders could claim superior knowledge of their constituency's conditions and interests, then for them only to support, regulate, and give direction to a movement would be foolish. From the point of view of correct theory, they should dictate what is right, what *should* be done according to correct principles.

Knowing and Doing

In his fragmentary and cryptic *Theses on Feuerbach*,[7] Marx announced a new materialist knowledge. Whether the foundations for knowledge are claimed to be in the passive reception of sensory perceptions, as they were by empiricist-materialist philosophers, or in the intuition of rational ideas, as they were by philosophical idealists, in both cases, knowledge had been removed from "sensuous *activity*." Either we passively register impressions made by objects on our sense organs, or we contemplate abstract ideas; in neither case, suggested Marx, is knowledge understood as active engagement with a world that is itself an embodiment of sensuous activity. The choice between philosophical idealism and philosophical materialism is based on a fiction, the fiction of a separation between an active mind and its passive objects. Once that split occurs, the only alternatives are solipsistic theory building, or an equally solipsistic phenomenalism that reduces knowledge to the empty calculation of "sense data."

Concrete reality is not "objects," whether ideal or material, but "real individuals, their activity, and the material conditions of their life" (*The German Ideology* CW 5:31).[8] These individuals have no objective essence whether physical or ideal; what they are can only be understood as what they are in a "definite mode of life" (ibid.). Their ideas are interwoven with material activity, expressible in the material medium of a common language which itself embodies human relationships. Even critical theories that question existing relations, if they are not intellectual exercises, are grounded in real existing conflicts in actual material life (ibid. 45).

But, even in the same breath, Marx took a different approach. It is also possible, he announced, to *observe* "empirically, and without mystification and speculation, the connection of social and political structures with production" (ibid. 35–7).[9] This scientific data must be of real social facts, not of schema imposed on data or abstractions from token examples; it must be gathered from the meticulous study of historical events. Nevertheless, Marx seemed to suggest that theorists in the privacy of their studies can trace the structures and laws of historical processes. Although each individual is rooted in a human reality of specific relationships, institutions, and social forms, and each individual's consciousness is a product of those conditions, there are functional regularities in social processes, and the Marxist scientist is in the unique position of being able to discover them.

Already a considerable distance had opened between the fragmentary vision of embodied active knowledge in the *Theses on Feuerbach* and an emergent Marxist social science. Regardless of "sensuous activity," a Marxist economist can achieve a distance from affairs that allows him to trace objectively the connection of social and political structure with production. As Marxism was adopted as the ideology of parties and factions, the view of knowledge sketched out in *Theses on Feuerbach*—that made theory always provisional, always dependent on new movements, always rooted in emerging historical developments—played a progressively minor role. After Marx's death, under Engel's editorship, Marx's economic schema hardened into communist law.

Lenin, fighting to maintain his position as leader of the left in Russia where none of the classical conditions for Marxist revolution were present, relied not on the sensuous experience of workers, but on Engels's new authoritative consolidation of Marxist science. In his attack on empirical accounts of knowledge in *Materialism and Empiriocriticism*,[10] he cited, not the *Theses on Feuerbach*, but Engels on the nature of knowledge: material things exist and ideas exist; some ideas correspond to material things and some do not; absolute knowledge is possible. Although individual realizations of knowledge may be incomplete, Marxist science can produce theory that represents objectively law, causality, and necessity: freedom comes in understanding this necessity and mastering it (ME 187–9). Using Engels's arguments, Lenin defended Marxist orthodoxy. Describing the Russian Machists' claim that much of Marxist economics itself rests on metaphysical laws which absolutize a particular "worldview," Lenin was almost too furious even to respond. "Incredibly trivial rigmarole, quasi-scientific tomfoolery," he raged (ME 317).

This view of a sovereign and independent Marxist truth was expressed in different ways by the social democratic right and the bolshevik left. Moderate Social Democrats embraced Marx's theory of the stages of historical change, insisting that capitalism *had to be* fully developed before socialism; and refusing to condone any revolution that was not faithful to the correct developmental sequence. Lenin, in a Russia on the verge of revolution but without a proletariat schooled in economic and political struggle, argued the theoretical *necessity* of a transitional "dictatorship of the proletariat" in countries which had not passed through a capitalist stage. Neither saw the necessity for workers' conscious experience to confirm or articulate these positions. Arriving at the Finland station in Petrograd in 1917 after his long exile from Russia, Lenin did not wait for reports from committees or to hear about the experiences of striking workers. He told the waiting crowd where the revolution was to go with no first-hand knowledge of their situation. Meanwhile, in Germany, Social Democrats, fearful of losing their right to political participation and willing to concede that national interest might override class interest, insisted that, regardless of what workers might think and according to doctrine, the time was not right for a revolution and any mass movement was premature.

In contrast, Luxemburg's conviction, against both social democratic conservatives and Leninist radicals, that theory had to come from actual historical events and the active knowledge of workers was in the spirit of Marx's forgotten *Theses on Feuerbach*. An example is her position on the national question. The "right to national self-determination" was a slogan with wide popular appeal: Social Democrats, Communists, capitalists, all claimed high moral ground by calling for national independence. On this issue, even the cold tactician, Lenin, resorted to emotionally charged words like "honor" and "dignity." Luxemburg's criticism of an unthinking defense of national autonomy as a principle, and of Polish nationalism in particular was a continuing source of disagreement between her and other socialists.[11]

In a series of papers written in Polish between 1908 and 1909 she addressed the difficult and complex problem of nationalities in Europe.[12] The abstract "right to self-determination of nationalities" which was added to the program of the Russian Social Democratic Party, did not, she argued, reflect socialist knowledge but was either a schematic simplification or a reversion to metaphysical fiction (NQ 103). Specific clauses dealing with the rights of minorities, such as the right to use one's native language in schools and assemblies, self-government on the local level, equality of all citizens regardless of sex, race, religion, or ethnic origin, free speech and assembly refer to substantial, experienced realities. But appeal to an abstract right of self-determination is empty and solves no practical problems. An abstract right intuited by "pure" reason that is the subject of an absolute judgment cannot be a source of socialist knowledge. Words when used to name such abstractions have no substantive meaning. Supporters of national rights treated "nationality" as if it were a category fixed for all time. Instead, Luxemburg argued, a social category has reference only in specific historical context. When words are taken as referring to actual historical phenomena, it is clear that nothing—not rights, or democracy, or equality—is always right but each must be judged "case by case."[13]

Nor is it possible to deduce the correct position on nationalism from Marx's policy pronouncements. Marx argued in favor of Polish independence, but in Luxemburg's reading, he argued from a specific tactical position in a particular situation. At the time, given the solid block of reactionary absolutism in Russia and Germany, all that was possible was to chip away at the block to weaken it by prying Poland away from Russia. By the late nineteenth century, the situation had changed; now there was a worker's movement in Russia. Understanding and judgment had to be based on that historical fact and experience. Instead of a removed theoretical judgment on nationalism, either from reason or from Marxist science, it was necessary to recover the actual experiential context of a "right" of "nationalities" to self-determination. Attention was necessary not to abstract concepts or to theoretical schema but to both intimate textures of life and broad historical trends. No thoughtless deduction can substitute for this concrete knowledge. Always ready with perspicacious examples but never mired down in irrelevant detail, weaving the minutia of historical experience into its common features, Luxemburg described the various strands in European nationalism: the centrism of the modern nation-state, the demand for local self-determination, the necessity for provincial administration, the extension of local self-government.

The nation-state serves the interests of capital, but the success of Marxist socialism is also dependent on industrial development. Central administration can implement capitalist trade policy, but it also requires local administration in which workers begin to achieve political maturity. Local democracy has to be carefully distinguished from separatist nationalist reversions to feudal enclaves inevitably dominated by traditional authorities. In trans-ethnic nation-states there are conditions that further workers' consciousness. The capitalist state generates a "national culture" which is available to all, and a fomentation of discussion and debate provides information and debate which educate working people. This "nationality," which includes individuals from a variety of different religious and ethnic groups within territorial boundaries, is not the nationality that is typically referred to in defenses of the "right of *peoples* to national self-determination."

Luxemburg pointed to the actual regressive nature of interests which clamored for independence in Europe, an independence which often meant the freedom to oppress minority populations, preserve patriarchal family relations, and resist modernization and democratization. A particularly dangerous source of "nationality" was the romanticization of native soil and the peasantry. Utopian socialists, as well as militarists who wished to fan allegiance to the imperialist state in Germany, extolled Mother Earth and the Fatherland, praising a native peasantry close to the soil as the physical source of ethnic identity, the "treasury in which every nation deposits the threads of its thoughts and the flowers of its feelings" (NQ 260).[14] But, Luxemburg pointed out, in fact if not in theory the European peasantry is no progressive force. Out of the mainstream of cosmopolitan urban development, the peasantry typically preserves conservative social customs, defends the patriarchal family, supports the authority of church and priest. Nationality, in this sense, means literally what is "conserved," archaic remnants of traditional life in speech, dress, religion, habits, that survive modernization, and a return to prejudice, conservatism, superstition, tribal rivalries.

Outside Europe in the colonial empires, nationalism was a slogan by which Lenin promised self-determination to revolutionary elements who would ally themselves with the new soviet state. Similarly, to win the allegiance of oppressed peoples in the old tsarist empire, he promised national independence. These positions were not grounded in the experience of colonized people as a material reality, but were means to advance the interests of the Communist party. Colonial movements, Luxemburg argued, had to be evaluated one by one for their revolutionary potential. The American Revolution was of emigrants able to free local capitalists from exploitation from foreign capitalists and spur on capitalist development. In other cases, independence only meant that ruling ethnic groups could oppress local minorities, enslave indigenous populations, or establish a national base from which to annex neighboring territories. If national liberation movements in Africa or India unfettered the manipulations of traditional landlords, reinforced the subordination of women, put ruthless native entrepreneurs into alliance with international capital, or established the privilege of local bureaucracies, independence would not lead to any democratic control by "peoples" but only to further economic dependence and the crippling of indigenous progressive organizations. This could not be consistent with socialist goals no matter how expedient: "to the socialist, no nation is free whose national existence is based upon the enslavement of another people, for to him, colonial peoples, too, are human beings, and, as such, parts of the nation state" (NQ 290).[15]

Luxemburg was critical of "federation" used by Lenin as a convenient principle by which free "nationalities" would supposedly voluntarily ally themselves in larger groups for economic efficiency. She warned of the strains to come in the proposed Soviet Union. Bakunin's federation of Slavic peoples, based on autonomous nationalities, preserved most of the dangers of nationalism. Again, idealism mixed with schematic rationalism and expediency had supplanted thought to produce a "revolutionary historical caricature of reality." Like nationalism, federalism had to be evaluated not as an abstract idea but as having "definite historical content" (NQ 186). Autonomous nationalities in the tsarist empire had no "common ground for the settlement of contradictory interests" (NQ 211). Foreseeing the racial and ethnic strife that would fester in Central Asia and Eastern Europe, Luxemburg cited the differences among those who participated in the 1905 Convention of Russian National Socialist Parties—Armenians, Georgians, Bylorussians, Jews, and others. In theory, differences might be overlooked; in reality, once peasants, petty gentry, romantic nationalists, different religious cultures were forced to cooperate in a Soviet federation, there would be divisive squabbling, repression, and eventually a police state.

Reformist socialists relying on Bernstein's abstract right might call for recognition of a universal right to national autonomy for all peoples. Lenin, devising policy to consolidate soviet power, might foment rebellion in colonial spheres of interest. Both defended their policies with theoretical schema rather than with knowledge gained in working people's experience, but, Luxemburg insisted, reliable socialist knowledge must be based on experienced fact. For an abstract right to self-determination, she substituted civil guarantees. For the theoretical right to secession, she substituted the experience of local self-government with legal guarantees that liberties of speech, and press, are extended to all races, sexes, and ethnic groups. Given the historical fact of intermingled ethnic identities in most parts of the world, and certainly in Europe, given the fact that there is no way that viable homogeneous ethnic states can be formed, the only practical guarantee for the exercise of cultural rights is a multinational state in which all ethnic groups participate in self-governance.

For feminists, ethnicity has also been a difficult issue. On the one hand, official feminism in Western countries has often seemed tainted with the ethnicity of white, middle class women with little appreciation or concern for ways of life different from their own. The antidote for this "ethnocentricity" most common in current feminist debates has been a postmodern celebration of "difference" internationalist more in sentiment than in substance. But women outside the capitalist centers of Europe and North America, as well as women who are members of minority groups within Western countries, are unlikely to understand ethnicity in terms of either an ideal feminine essence or textual diversity. For them, it involves making an agonizing choice between colonial and racist domination in which limited legal guarantees for women may be forthcoming at the expense of traditional ways of life, and national autonomy or separatism in which archaic patterns of paternalism are reinforced.

Luxemburg offers the possibility of a materialist understanding of this dilemma. National autonomy is not an absolute good. The specific content of each historical situation has to be understood. Marxist schema, as well as idealist claims to rights that support independence movements, can be used to cloak attempts by unscrupulous local entrepreneurs to further exploit women's work and by local bureaucrats to more freely siphon off into their own pockets foreign aid meant for family relief. A Luxemburgian politics would be informed by a detailed and specific knowledge of women's experience in national movements and nationalism's effect on women's economic and familial autonomy.

2. The Failure of Marxist-Leninism

Bolshevik Errors

In Luxemburg's view, Lenin's new authoritarian Communist party, the Russian Revolution of 1905, and the coming to power in Russia of Lenin's Bolsheviks in 1917 made necessary a radical rethinking of socialist theory. The correct response to the complexity and difficulty of the Russian situation, she argued, was neither blanket denial of Bolshevism nor a rubber stamp of approval, but rigorous critical examination.[16] She was one of the few socialist observers, most of whom remained split between uncritical loyalty and unthinking opposition, to attempt such an analysis. In backward Russia, the last stronghold of archaic absolutism, a mass movement had begun a chain of events that would dethrone the Tsar and established what claimed to be the first communist society. In the heated debates that followed the Russian revolutions of 1905 and 1917, Luxemburg played a major role. At times, conservative Social Democrats claimed her as an ally in the struggle against "premature radicalism." Other times, she was cited by Lenin as a supporter of bolshevism. In fact, she endorsed neither the opportunism of Lenin nor the caution of the Social Democrats. What was needed in the wake of the Russian Revolution, she wrote from prison in 1918, was "not uncritical apologetics but penetrating and thoughtful criticism" ("The Russian Revolution," RLS 368).

Luxemburg began with reservations that she shared with mainstream Social Democrats. Responding to the split in 1903 in the Russian Social Democratic party between the Mensheviks and Lenin's Bolsheviks, she had been critical of Lenin's "ultra-centralism" ("Organizational Questions of Russian Social Democracy," RLS). Lenin's new Communist party organization gave the Central Committee of the party absolute power over appointments, local committees, rules and tactics. Lenin's immature masses, disciplined in the factory to obedience, were to take pleasure in surrender to the higher will of party leaders. Over them would be a closed elite of trained revolutionaries who direct them in their struggle. Lenin condemned talk about democracy as revisionist opportunism, bourgeois elements taking the opportunity to use the workers' movement for their own interests. Again Luxemburg insisted on historical understanding, this time of the well-worn charge of "opportunism." Lenin was "mechanically applying to Russia formulas elaborated in Western Europe" (RLS 129), where calls for reformist legislation *did* mask an attempt to control and neutralize the workers' movement. Given the different situation of Russian absolutism, to return Russian workers to central control was opportunistic. Luxemburg defended democracy in unequivocal terms; a socialist party must be an open party, controlled by a majority of workers whose consciousness has been developed in political struggle. If there is no such conscious majority, then there can be no revolution. This was the painful truth that Lenin was unwilling to accept.

In many ways Luxemburg approved the Russian Revolution. The Bolsheviks, unlike European Social Democrats or the Mensheviks in Russia, had been able to advance socialism in tune with the currents of change in Russia. A real social transformation had taken place as a result of mass action. She differed with Lenin sharply, however, over the question of the relation between that mass action and party leaders. Leadership should be, she argued "the spontaneous co-ordination of the conscious political actions of a body of [workers]" (RLS 119). Lenin was right to pay attention to the spontaneous actions of workers, but he was wrong to think that the masses could be made docile troops under the command of a small group of revolutionaries. She agreed that the Bolsheviks had been right in refusing to be bound to the small gains of a parliamentary revisionism; she acknowledged with Lenin that democratic mechanisms were "cumbersome" (RLS 386). But cumbersome or not, Lenin's ban on the Constitutional Assembly "stops up the living source from which alone can come the correction of all the innate shortcomings of social institutions" (RLS 387). Especially in Russia, where the proletariat was small, it would not be possible to found socialism in a system where only a few workers could vote. Luxemburg was adamant in her criticism of the Bolsheviks' curtailment of freedom of speech; no one was able to vote intelligently if there was no freedom of dissent.[17]

Given the difficulties of the Russian situation—an economy ruined by war, limited industrialization, the failure of revolution in Europe— there could only be a "distorted attempt" at socialism in Russia ("The Russian Revolution," RLS 369). Lenin temporized by seeking the support of the Russian peasantry and subject nationalities in the Tsar's empire with false promises. In fact, there was no reason to think that the interests of ethnic nationalities or peasants corresponded with socialist interests. Lenin promised that large landholdings would be distributed to peasants; he promised the nationalities the right to self-determination. Luxemburg predicted with grim accuracy the violence that would result when these promises were not honored. Socialist organization and development would ultimately demand the collectivization of agriculture. The non-Russian territories were not viable economic units and so would either be annexed by the capitalist powers or by a Russian empire. The result would be a Soviet police state ruled by terror and force, as the Bolsheviks struggled to control agriculture and diverse nationalities. Lenin correctly gauged the degree of resistance to the Tsar in the countryside and in the territories, but, to him, resistance was not there to be understood; it was to be used so that the Bolsheviks could come to power. The aspirations of the peasantry in Siberia or of religious and ethnic groups in Asia were not developing consciousnesses to be understood and fostered, but discontent to be channeled by the party. An alliance between abstract dogmatic principle and manipulative tactic had removed both thought and action from contact with reality.

Similarly unhistorical was Lenin's defense of the centrist "state." Again, for Luxemburg, no universal judgment is possible if words are to have substantive meaning. In the early stages of capitalism, the nation-state protects and regulates industrial development within national borders. At that stage, it can be defended even by workers. By the later stages of capitalism, in the late nineteenth and early twentieth centuries, with opportunities for internal expansion exhausted, the state was more and more the base for capitalist imperialist expansion in noncapitalist areas. In her antiwar *Junius* pamphlet (1915) Luxemburg added up the score: England in Egypt and South Africa, France in Tunis and Tonkin, Italy in Abyssinia, Russia in Central Africa and Manchuria, Germany in Africa and the South Seas, the United States in the Philippines (RLS 281). Myopically focused on class struggle within the nation-state, socialists had failed to grasp the enormity of what was happening in the colonial empires.

The Bolsheviks condemned her "mistakes." In their anxious tutelage of radical workers in the confusion and bloodshed of the German revolution, they deplored the caution which they saw as reluctance to adopt the Russian centrist model of party organization. A Leninist party, they argued, would have been ready to shape the mass of protesting German workers into an armed corp of militants under orders from a central committee; it would have taken over the government. Indeed, by the time of the German revolution in 1918, the separation between social democratic theorists and workers' experience was complete. There was no direction of the mass movement of German workers, only confusion, disorder, death, including Luxemburg's, and, in the end, a return to the old institutions of government in the Weimar Republic.

An End to Class Struggle

Even before the debacle of the German revolution and the reversion of Lenin's Bolsheviks to autocracy, it was clear to Luxemburg that there had been a failure of the consciousness that was the "contradiction" that was to have led to socialist revolution. In Germany, to her shock and horror, almost the entire social democrat delegation to the legislature voted for war credits and to suspend criticism of the government for the duration of the war. After Germany's defeat in World War I, the humiliating collapse of the army, the ruin of the economy, and the loss of life, when revolution broke out, German workers again were persuaded to trust the old government, vote for their stewardship, and support the flawed electoral mechanisms responsible for German policy in the past. German workers whose consciousness had been schooled in Social Democracy had not understood their situation.

Luxemburg refused the Leninist response to this failure—events in Germany only proved that you cannot rely on democracy to produce a revolutionary majority, and so revolution cannot depend on self-generated mass action. The German Social Democrats' vote for war credits in 1914 gave Lenin little pause. There would be no more votes; instead, a new autocratic Russian party would run a socialist state ruled by Communists, and a new, centrist International, dominated by the Russian party, would meet to endorse and disseminate Russian policy.[18] Luxemburg also foresaw the sorry course the reformist policies of Social Democrats would take in Germany. After the failure of the German revolution, the call would be for a return to the revisionism of Bernstein. As the Bolsheviks consolidated their power in Russia and became bosses of a new International, the remnants of the old social democratic parties would meet as a continuation of the old Second International. They would endorse a Europe separated into national units, with perhaps a League of Nations to keep peace. They would count on military alliance as a deterrent, and would perpetuate the illusion that free trade would profit all countries, including the colonies. They would endorse the policies of imperialism and proclaim the protection and development of dependent Third World countries which continued to be exploited and controlled by military force. In the European democracies, they would settle for legislation that guaranteed minimum wages, eight-hour days, unemployment insurance, and various other social welfare benefits, while abroad they would support a foreign policy that tolerated dictators and military coups when it served national interest. Such a compromised peace could not last. No alliances, federations, arms agreements, or peace movements would contain the lethal antagonisms, Luxemburg correctly predicted (RLS 250). After her death, the great depression, the rise of Fascism, and the outbreak of World War II again tore Europe apart.

Why had socialist consciousness failed so that in communist Russia there was dictatorial rule by an autocratic party apparatus, and in Europe democratic socialist workers were content with higher wages and national wars? Luxemburg was not tempted, as were many Marxist theorists in the years after her death, to patch up Marxist theory by grafting back onto dialectical materialism some of the idealism Marx had rejected: to argue that bourgeois culture and ideology survive economic change, or patriarchal social relations linger on in socialism, or that there is a lag in psychological development.[19] These additions left Marxist theory untouched in its deep structures. Luxemburg, in the first shock as German workers voted for the war credits that launched World War I, did not use the excuse of "subjective factors" that temporarily interrupt the necessary workings of Marxist economic law; she attacked the material problem directly. At the very moment when industrial worker's revolutionary class-consciousness should have appeared according to Marxist theory, it had not. It was futile to simply go on with the revolution, patching up theory and practice. Nor was it any good to pretend, with Bernstein, that a reformed welfare capitalism is socialism. Why had workers so embraced nationalism that all socialist sentiment was extinguished? Why had socialist leaders not been able to make clear to workers their situation? Had irrational passion for common blood and defense of the

Fatherland overcome Marxist logic? Or was the fault deeper, in Marxist theory itself? Had the master, Marx, in laying out the economic laws of national capitalist development, failed to capture the reality of militarism and nationalism?

Nationalism moved German socialists to vote for war credits and to suspend all revolutionary action. Nationalism fueled their response to the call for the defense of the Fatherland, the preservation of German culture, and the territorial integrity of the German peoples. Nationalism eclipsed socialist principles and socialist memory. Called to arms in "national defense," the antagonism between workers and bourgeoisie was forgotten. From prison, where she was held for anti-war activities, Luxemburg vividly described the war fever that gripped Germany:

> The patriotic street demonstrations, the chase after suspicious automobiles, the false telegrams, the cholera poisoned wells . . . the excesses of a spy-hunting populace, the singing throngs, the coffee shops with their patriotic songs . . . the violent mobs, ready to denounce, ready to persecute women, ready to whip themselves into a delirious frenzy over every wild rumor . . . the atmosphere of ritual murder . . . [the young soldiers sent off as] cannon fodder . . . the hoarse croak of the hawks and hyenas of the battlefield." (*Junius* Pamphlet 1915, RLS 161)

It was not only the past, said Luxemburg, that was about to be destroyed in the inevitable ruin that would result from world war between the capitalist powers, as "cities turned into shambles, whole countries into deserts, villages into cemeteries, whole nations into beggars" (RLS 162). The future would also be destroyed. The young men who went off in trains to be slaughtered were the educated proletariat of Europe, the socialist workers who were to have been Marx's universal class creating the new society. While Lenin tightened his elite organization for the coming struggle, and conservative Social Democrats waited out the war until parliamentary business could proceed as usual, Luxemburg despaired. This was, she said, a "world tragedy," this end of forty-five years of labor history. What was necessary, she wrote, was "self-criticism, cruel, unsparing, criticism that goes to the very root of the evil," "to measure the depths of the catastrophe" and "understand the lesson it teaches" (RLS 262).

The Economic Roots of Militarism

Long before 1914, Luxemburg had protested the Social Democrats' capitulation to the military. In "Militia and Militarism" (1899, PW

135), she argued against the Social Democrats' abandonment of their traditional opposition to a standing professional army and support for an armed citizen militia. She rejected the economist argument that militarism was a natural development of capitalism and useful for the economy, and provided jobs for workers as well as profits for capitalists. When the army expanded, workers paid taxes for weapons that would inevitably be used against them. Militarism, Luxemburg agreed, is linked to the economics of capitalism, but not just as a stimulus for increased production. Capitalism would not expand simply to use up its excess in the production of useless weaponry, making militarism only a convenient dumping ground for excess goods. The imperialism that makes militarism necessary is no accidental side-product of capitalism, but "a huge historical complex of events, whose roots reach deep down into the Plutonic depths of economic creation" (RLS 206).

Marxists had for a long time argued that the truth about capitalism could not come from the limited perspectives of capitalists. Instead, relations of production have to be understood from the standpoint of exploited laborers who create value. Luxemburg's understanding of the imperialist nature of militarism, its relation to "a competitive struggle of a fully developed capitalism for world supremacy and for exploitation of the last remnant of noncapitalist world zones" (RLS 319) pointed to a further correction of socialist perspective. The economic laws and models that Marx developed in *Capital*, just like the models of bourgeois economists, are for a homogeneous capitalist society in which there are only workers and capitalists. The referent for such a model is an almost fully capitalized economy such as the England of Marx's time. But if the perspective of a shopkeeper or an industrialist gives a distorted and limited view of national economic reality, the same may be true of the national perspective of British or German workers on international economic reality. From the standpoint of colonized people, from the standpoint of minority groups not welcome in industrial unions and excluded from well-paid jobs, exploitative relations of production are not only between capitalists and industrial workers, but between rich capitalist nations and noncapitalist territories, between white European peoples and people of color, and between multinational corporations and colonized economies.

Some of the differences between Luxemburg's emerging internationalist understanding of capitalism and Lenin's use of imperialism to further Bolshevik aims can be seen in Lenin's response to her *Junius Pamphlet* (RLS 428).[20] Following Marxist etiquette, Lenin briefly applauded Luxemburg's stand against the war before he proceeded to point out her "mistakes." First, there was their old battle over national self-determination. Luxemburg had seemed to argue that no independence movement was justified, but, said Lenin, colonial wars against imperialist powers can be justified. Lenin was particularly disappointed that Luxemburg did not criticize what he saw as the real cause of the Social Democrats' failure to stand firm against the war: "revisionism," "opportunism," and the consequent failure to organize a centralized party in the bolshevik manner.

Luxemburg, on the other hand, was not willing to explain workers' reversion to nationalism and militarism from Marxist schema as a simple intrusion of bourgeois interests. From the standpoint of a national model of capital, with only two classes, capitalists and industrial workers, "opportunism," or the intrusion of bourgeois class thinking, might be the only possible socialist deviation. If the German working class regressed, the only possible diagnosis would be that they had been contaminated by bourgeois attitudes and had relaxed their national class struggle. In contrast, Luxemburg was beginning to think beyond a national understanding of capitalism: both a national bourgeois and a national proletariat might have a distorted view of reality.

Luxemburg's reaction to German militarism was very different from Lenin's determination to change tactics to meet a new situation. She had been the first among Social Democrats to protest tolerance of the government's imperialist policies. As early as 1900, when the Germans participated in the Chinese war, and again in the Moroccan crises of 1905 and 1911, she condemned government policy. After 1911, imperialism became more and more the focus of her thinking. This, it was beginning to come clear to her, was where German workers' consciousness had failed. Marx's proletariat, the source of revolutionary knowledge, had not understood their situation. They had been persuaded to support wars that insured colonial domination. They had allowed their socialist consciousnesses to be overwhelmed by a nationalist chauvinism that degraded members of alien ethnic groups. Luxemburg confronted what few of her male comrades were willing to admit: the challenge to Social Democracy posed by the war went to the very foundations of socialism. As she struggled to regain that coherent grasp of the situation that could be the basis for renewed socialist action, she worked on her lectures on economics for the Social Democratic party's school for workers. There, as she put it modestly, she came on some "technical difficulties" in the economics of Marx's *Capital*. Marx's models for capital accumulation, the very basis for Marxist science, are flawed.

3. The Accumulation of Capital

Economic Rationalism

In *Capital*, Marx, as he himself put it, "proceeded from the premises of political economy" and "accepted its language and its laws" (*Economic and Philosophic Manuscripts*, CW 3:270). But Marx's classical economic models were reconstructed to make evident not a beneficent equilibrium of supply and demand but what Marx took as the central injustice of capitalism: the extraction of surplus value in the form of capitalist profits. The value that results from labor above what is necessary from subsistence and physical reproduction of workers is taken as profit and, after an appropriately luxurious life-style for capitalists is deducted, is added to capital. In Marxist theory, this is the essence of capitalism; capital accumulates—both the capital of individual capitalists and aggregate capital—but at workers' expense.

In London, maintaining his bourgeois household and immersed in the thought of the great British political economists, Marx turned classical economics against itself. His models, mathematical and objective like those of the bourgeois economists, and also expressing equilibrium, were to show what really results when labor is taken as the seemingly obvious determinant of economic value.[21] Instead of promoting justice and an increase in prosperity for all, as bourgeois economists claim, free markets and private property lead to the exploitation and impoverishment of a working class.

But in method, Marx was no iconoclast. Like other economists, he constructed mathematical models to represent essential economic functions and relations of production. Once a model was derived, he assumed that it could be applied to reality by introducing complications that would conveniently correspond to the complexity of actual phenomena.[22] The trouble is, as Luxemburg pointed out, that Marx was not satisfied with his models for the accumulation of capital in volume I of *Capital*. At his death, he left a chaos of supplementary and corrective notes that were later compiled and published by his collaborator Engels in two additional volumes. Even with Engels's editing, a clear resolution to Marx's perplexity did not emerge. Marx's models show how individual capitalists sell their goods for a profit, but they do not show how capitalism can work as a system: how capital accumulates in the aggregate. How can the circulation of value throughout a capitalist economy proceed smoothly and efficiently— so that capital is amassed and jobs and wealth are created, as the bourgeois economists would have it, or the way prepared for the proletariat to take over the means of production and establish a socialist economy, as Marxists would have it? This was the technical "difficulty" that troubled Luxemburg as she prepared her lectures and contemplated the failure of socialist consciousness.

Her task, as teacher, as she saw it, was to make economics intelligible, to rescue it from the empty mathematical formulas and the "hollow phraseology and pompous prattle" with which economists typically explain their "science" (RLS 221).[23] This reframing of economics in terms accessible to working people, she saw not as popularization but as a restoring of meaning and content. Precapitalist systems for organizing production and distribution might have been exploitative or unjust, but they were consciously understood. With capitalism something new happened. Dark and mysterious forces—the force of commercial crises, of cyclical unemployment, of destructive fluctuations in prices—forces that destroy lives and cannot be controlled are put into play. Officiating is an economic priesthood chanting ritualistic formula and obfuscating theory. What is needed, said Luxemburg, is strenuous research and deep analysis that results in an economics that working people can understand as reflective of their experience (RLS 236).

Marx was able to construct unproblematic models of the simple reproduction of capital in which all the surplus extracted went to capitalist consumption. He could also account for "primitive accumulation" in which productive property was appropriated by force or by semilegal strategies from the remnants of feudal landed property in Europe or in colonial spheres of influence. The problem was with his models for internal capital accumulation. If capital was to accumulate within capitalist economies, the accumulated portion had to be used productively, so that accumulation would continue. But when production increases there is no one to buy the increase in goods so that the next wave of profits can be realized. If rich capitalists consume all the excess goods, accumulation stops. Workers are limited in what they can consume by the level of their wages.

The problem is not in production, the usual object of economic modeling, but in distribution.[24] In capitalism, production increases at a rapid rate—this is its benefit; at the same time, distribution of goods is not based on any rational plan to fill people's needs, but on ability to buy. Classical economists, including Marx, ignored the reality of the social environment of production which restricts distribution to those with wealth.

> [The consuming power of society] is not determined either by the absolute productive power or by the absolute consuming

power, but by the consuming power based on antagonistic conditions of distribution, which reduces the consumption of the great mass of the population to a variable minimum within more or less narrow limits. (AC 344)

An individual factory owner may concentrate on production and assume that with diligence he will be able to find a market for his goods. But in the accumulation of aggregate capital, there are objective limits to what the market can absorb. If the problem is solved by paying workers more or by increased capitalist consumption of luxuries, the rate of profit falls and capital does not accumulate. What capitalists need is buyers who do not take the money for payment out of capitalist pockets, but these cannot be found anywhere within capitalism. This was the puzzle which troubled Marx at the end of his life, the puzzle which he had not been able to solve.

Marx's notes for later volumes of *Capital* contain mathematical formulas that show the relations between the quantities of fixed capital, wages, and reinvested capital that, in theory, are necessary for accumulation. Ignoring Marx's apparent dissatisfaction with these formulas, Marxists settled on them as the authoritative account of capital accumulation. Luxemburg, struggling for a coherent grasp of reality she could offer workers in the agonizing perplexities of prewar socialist politics, turned to Marx not for authoritative dicta but for thought about a pressing problem. Marx, she noted, had continued to work on the problem of accumulation to his death, finally proposing only the provisional and, for her, inadequate, solution of an expanded money supply generated in gold production to introduce new value into the schema not produced by labor.[25] It was obvious that Marx had not intended his schema to be taken as gospel, but assumed that future socialists would continue work on the problem.

From the standpoint of the Bolsheviks, claiming to be the heirs of Marx, to say that Marx had failed to explain the central mechanism of capitalism was sacrilege. Any indication that Marx was troubled by an unsolved problem was denounced. The suggestion that the master had failed to construct a model for capital accumulation was particularly dangerous. If a model for accumulation is impossible, so is Marxist science: it may not be possible to prove that capitalism will fall to a revolt of organized workers, or that the exploitative relations maintained in capitalism will inevitably be overcome by those who represent the proletariat. The impossibility of accumulation might show, instead, that capitalism will eventually fail regardless of the revolutionary action of the proletariat, or that the mechanisms that will destroy it are not in national class struggle. For the

Bolsheviks, defending their right to rule, this was hardly possible as a conclusion.

For Luxemburg, the catastrophic capitulation of German Social Democracy to the imperialist militarist policies of the German Reich meant that all dogma had been put into question. As she worked on Marx's models, she observed with despair the rising tide of militarism in Germany. Was there a connection? Could the key to workers' enlistment in the war effort be the "technical difficulties" she had found in Marx's models for capital accumulation? Was it because Marxists relied on economic models that did not adequately explain capitalist accumulation that social democratic leaders had not been able to help workers to a coherent understanding of their situation that would have allowed them to resist militarism and racism?

In 1913, in jail for antiwar activities and deeply depressed at the tragic course of events as Europe went to war, Luxemburg sat down to write her major work, *The Accumulation of Capital*. In 1915, again in prison, surprised by the storm of criticism her first book had aroused, she responded to critics in a second volume, *The Accumulation of Capital—An Anti-Critique*. The hostile attention given to both these books even after her death is testimony to the challenging nature of her thesis. She was challenging not only Marxist explanations of capital accumulation but the very foundations of economic science.

The Use of Economic Models

The material lives of women and men in any historical period have an overwhelming richness of detail. Thought must organize and simplify this detail so as to get a grip on it. The theories of eighteenth-century political economics, inspired by the success of Newtonian physics and infused with the ideals of the Enlightenment, took a particular rationalist form. They began not with observations but with simplified concepts that had intuitive validity, that could be stated quantitatively, and that, in principle, would result in measurable quantities. From this rational base, economists mapped out functional relationships between various economic variables. To derive such models, it is necessary to make assumptions that cannot be realized in reality. In this way, economics claims to abstract the pure economic functioning underlying economic behavior that is the subject of a universal science. Marx's models for capital accumulation were in the same style. He also made the economist's counterfactual assumptions: labor is homogeneous, workers' wages are all the same, technical advance is slow and steady, there is no government interference, everyone knows how to compete, there are no discrepancies caused by time lags, and, most important, the economic universe is homogeneously capitalistic.

Luxemburg did not reject theoretical simplification *per se;* abstraction is necessary in economics as in any study of complex phenomena. But the phenomenon to be studied, in this case the accumulation of capital, cannot be factored out in the very assumptions of a theory. This, in Luxemburg's view, was exactly what had happened in both bourgeois and Marxist economic modeling. These were not abstractions from complex reality, but were framed on the basis of assumptions counter to the actual fact of capitalist development. In none of its history, Luxemburg observed, had capitalism been a homogeneous system alone in the world. From the plunder of America for gold, to the slave trade in Africa, to unequal trade relations, to emigrant plantation owners, to the sale of expensive manufactured goods and purchase of cheap raw materials abroad, capital accumulation depends on noncapitalist economies.

Marxist economic models, like other economic models, do not work for any conceivable reality. They are meant to show that, as the proportion of wages to fixed capital decreases with automation, the rate of profits extracted declines. More and more is squeezed out of wages; eventually workers rebel. Marx's models confirmed his belief in the liberatory role of an industrial proletariat whose impoverishment forces them to take over the means of production, just as bourgeois models project the illusion that capitalism is to the benefit of all. But because economic processes occur in time, the accumulation of capital on which both capitalist prosperity and socialist revolution depend cannot proceed. There is an unresolvable contradiction between the productive capabilities of capitalism and consumption. The increase in production must be sold before it can become profit and put to productive purposes, but it must be sold before there are new workers with wages to buy an increased stock of goods. Although Marx revised his early schema for expanded reproduction to accommodate a steady rate of technical progress, technological development is neither even throughout various spheres of production, nor steady, again causing excesses in production before there is anyone to buy. For confirmation, Luxemburg cited the cyclical business crises caused by gluts on the market in the nineteenth and twentieth centuries. The assumption of classical economists that the market would follow along with production, and that there would be, as in Say's Law of Markets, a balance between supply and demand cannot be maintained either in theory or in fact.

Economists attempt to deal with the problem of accumulation in a number of ways, many of which Luxemburg reviewed in *The Accumulation of Capital*. External disturbances are blamed for interrupting equilibrium, such as weather or plague. Nonproductive consumers—servants, professionals, government officials, clergy—are cited as buyers of excess production. Workers are given higher wages with which to buy more goods. But none of these explanations is adequate. There is not always a natural cause for economic depression; nonproductive consumers' salaries have to come out of the pockets of the capitalists and therefore out of profits. If workers are paid more, once again profits drop.[26]

Continually, as Luxemburg studied the failure of economics to capture the reality of capital accumulation, she came back to the status of economic models. What were they meant to do? Mathematical formulas by themselves prove nothing. Anyone can write down numbers on paper that show the proportions necessary if capital is to accumulate. Mathematical formulas can even be used to prove what is clearly false.[27] Economic models, she argued, are useful tools, but only if the *purposes* for which they are constructed are understood and evaluated. Models like those of Adam Smith can be constructed so as to make the problem of profit and the extraction of surplus value from workers disappear. In turn, Marxist models bring out the role of profit in capitalist production, but obscure the conditions for the aggregate accumulation of capital. If models are to advance knowledge, their use, their relation to thought must always be made clear. Most important, models cannot replace observation of economic experience or thought about that experience. Marx's classical models show how the relation between production of producers' goods and production of commodities has to be regulated if accumulation is to proceed. But they cannot prove that such an equilibrium is possible (ACAC 65). Just because a schema can be written down does not mean that it says anything about reality.

> The main doubt of my critique is directed towards the fact that, on the question of accumulation, [Marx's] mathematical models can prove absolutely nothing, since their historical premise is untenable. The reply: but the models work out exactly, so the problem of accumulation is solved—[i.e., the problem] simply doesn't exist. (ACAC 65)

Economic models do not prove anything; they are useful as illustrations of thought, like "maps or diagrams" (ACAC 69). They cannot replace thought, cannot be a substitute for thought. Once a model is derived, thought cannot not stop because a supposedly absolute truth has been achieved. Luxemburg satirized her Marxist opponents:

> In olden times people believed in the existence of all kinds of fabulous creatures: dwarfs, people with one eye, with one arm and leg, and so on. Does anyone believe that such creatures ever really existed? But we see them drawn in precisely on the old maps. Is that not proof that those conceptions of the ancients corresponded exactly with reality? (ACAC 69)

Marx did not explain capital accumulation. He could not, Luxemburg argued, because the assumptions made in constructing his classical models already factored out the mechanism of accumulation. Capitalism has never existed as a homogeneous or universal system. There has never been a time when there were only capitalists and industrial workers. What Marx's models show is not how such a counterfactual universal capitalism operates, but that there can never be such a system. Economic models are useful for showing how capital accumulates within a nation such as England at the level of the individual factory owner, but instead of showing how aggregate capital accumulation is possible, they show the opposite. In an isolated capitalist system, accumulation is impossible because the artificial conditions necessary for the economic model of accumulation to apply are not obtainable in fact. If communism is not possible in one country, neither is capitalism.[28]

To make more models, or to complicate existing models, cannot help if the subordination of modeling to thinking is not understood. Marx, in the process of thinking about political economy, illustrated his critical insights in revised economic models that brought out the role of surplus value in the productive process. At the same time, his thinking shared many of the limitations of classical economic thought. What makes his models useful, Luxemburg argued, even for Marx himself, is that with them Marx was able to expose contradictions in his thinking. The confused notes he left at his death are not embarrassments to be smoothed over in Engels's careful editing but evidence of his status as a thinker.

To get to the truth about economic phenomena, Luxemburg proposed an alternative critical "economic analysis" which includes a "comparison with other laws set up by Marx, consideration of the various consequences to which they lead, examination of the premises from which they proceed and so on" (ACAC 69). There can be no mechanical substitute for this interpretative process of economic analysis and understanding. Marxists had mistaken Marx's models for dogma when they should have been taken as signposts towards a more adequate analysis. When models are seen as a revealed plan for necessary relations embedded in a ideal economic reality, there is no expansion of thought and understanding. Thought stops. Economists, capitalist and Marxist, tinker with their models, use their ingenuity to factor out discrepancies, redefine variables so that data will fit schema, jealously claim immunity from criticism for their most questionable assumptions. Meanwhile, the economic lives of working men and women are unleavened by understanding and thought.

Global Economics

If the equilibrium models of classical economy are only imaginary ideals, if they have no application to fact, no one would be interested in them. If they are crass rationalizations meant to validate the amassing of wealth in a few hands, no one would believe them. Capitalism did create an accumulation of wealth in England and other industrialized countries; it might even be assumed that prosperity is to some extent shared among citizens of those nations. If Marx took the models of classical economics and used them to show what they had obscured—the exploitation of industrial workers—Luxemburg used Marx's models to show what Marx's models obscured—the matrix of imperialism and colonialism that is the underlying international condition for capitalist accumulation.

Capital accumulation cannot be explained in static, national economic models, but only as dynamic exploitative relationships between capitalist economies and peripheral economies. This was Luxemburg's insight, an insight that in her judgment made necessary a radical rethinking of both economics and socialism. Imperialism could not be simply grafted onto existing Marxist theory as a supplement. Not when it shows that the essential mechanism of aggregate accumulation is not, as Marx's models made it seem, the extraction of surplus value from European and United States workers. Exploitative as industrial labor is, extracapitalist *relations* between capitalized economies and noncapitalized economies are what drives capital accumulation, in the sale of excess goods in foreign markets, and in the extraction of value in foreign resources and cheap labor. On this understanding, when German workers supported Germany's imperialist war, they were not "defending the Fatherland," as the government would have them believe, they were infusing lifeblood into an international capitalist economy, as Germany struggled for control of foreign markets. Lenin's sentimental encouragement of national pride and national self-determination obscured the real function of nation-states as administrative units that coordinate the efforts of capitalists to accumulate wealth at the expense of increasingly impoverished noncapitalist economies with governmental policies of protectionism, free trade, banking, and taxation.

Luxemburg noted that defense expenditures play a double role in this process. Military might is necessary to maintain and control markets, while, in addition, at home, military expenditure adds a supplementary benefit in the way of a military establishment which is a new and greedy consumer of excess production. Manufacturers of arms do not have to depend on unpredictable personal consumption but can win large government contracts on advantageous terms which allow them to plan production for steady growth. The control of colonial markets, enforced by military might, insures that resources and profits are directed in a steady flow from the periphery of noncapitalist territories to the centers of capitalism in Western Europe and the United States. The impoverishment that results is not that of industrial workers at home, who can be rewarded with higher wages, but of workers abroad, their governments in bondage to foreign debt, addicted to consumer goods, robbed of their natural resources, competing for work at subsistence wages that European workers refuse.

In the powerful last chapter of the *Accumulation of Capital*, Luxemburg vividly described the terror and violence that historically accompanies the interaction between capitalist and noncapitalist economies: the American Indian populations slaughtered for gold and land and replaced with colonial settlers who imported goods from Europeans; the onslaught on primitive economies such as India's with plunder and military conquest; the violent destruction of traditional, communal forms of land ownership in Africa for private appropriation by white Europeans; south American farmers driven from their land to make way for plantations owned by foreign corporations. The result is not new capitalist states, as Marxist historical law dictates, but markets for cheap and substandard manufactured goods, sources for cheap raw materials extracted with no regard for the health or safety of local labor, permanently dependent peripheral economies burdened by debt that cannot be repaid unless more land and resources are sold to foreigners.[29]

Luxemburg reviewed the history of economic thought. The mercantilists made no secret of the international purpose of their protectionist theories. With the discovery of wealth in Asia and the Americas, there was obvious incentive for their rejection of the medieval ideal of an equal exchange of value in trade. Given a world of powerful European nation-states competing for the riches of the Orient, one country could only gain at another's expense. The mercantilists framed an economic theory that would help a nation-state like England acquire more of that wealth. Economists like Adam Smith and Ricardo continued to address the problem of increasing aggregate national wealth and achieving a favorable balance of trade at the expense of colonized people; the difference was only in strategy. Smith and Ricardo, in an England already rich with colonial possessions, argued that it was free trade, not protectionism, which was more likely to bring in wealth. With Britain's markets secured, English entrepreneurs should be allowed to buy and sell at will so that general welfare, that is to say, national wealth, would continue to increase. To prove that capitalist profit works to the benefit of all, models were constructed of smoothly functioning, autonomous, capitalist economies operating without external markets. It only remained for Adam Smith to add the reassuring, metaeconomic "invisible hand," which guaranteed that what was profitable for British traders and manufacturers was profitable for all. The fiction of an internally balanced economic system could then hold out to "underdeveloped" economies an always receding promise of wealth and prosperity.

Political economy in all its history has been the practical science of a domestic economy in equilibrium that processes most efficiently a growing influx of raw materials, and produces most efficiently large amounts of goods for internal and external markets. The external sources of incoming wealth, as well as the violence that accompanies its extraction, are made invisible in the very assumptions that make economic modeling possible. Classical economic models project a smooth progress of increasing wealth for property owners in industrialized countries. From the standpoint of London or New York, centers of international finance and trade, it is possible, using economic models, to project smooth growth in a nation growing richer and richer off foreign trade. To the English middle and upper classes, sipping port from Spain and tea from India at their comfortable firesides, what happened abroad was an exotic, even a heroic, fable. England's economy was on track. Those who served in colonial territories were forced to be more realistic, but they soon learned how to inure themselves to the violence of colonialism by racial ideologies that proclaimed the obduracy and stupidity of "primitive," "racially inferior," non-Christian peoples.

No Marxist before Luxemburg had examined imperialism and colonialism with such attention. They went unnoticed in official economic histories of the nineteenth century which focused on the benefits of science and industrialization in the Western nations. They were mentioned by Marx, but only as an aspect of "primitive accumulation." They were used by Lenin to criticize his old enemies in the German

Social Democratic party, and to harass capitalist colonial powers. For most Marxists, what happened in the colonies was inessential, a result of an inevitable clash between progress and backward people. Imperialism as the essential mechanism of capitalist prosperity and wealth remained hidden away in the assumptions that Marx inherited from classical economics.

If bourgeois economist projections of equilibrium failed with a series of economic crises in the nineteenth century; many of Marx's predictions also failed. Industrial wages did not fall but rose; there was no mass uprising of European workers. Luxemburg's internationalist economics shows why this happened. If industrial workers in capitalist centers are not the only, or even the primary, source of surplus value, they can be enlisted in the cause of capitalism, as the benefits of capitalist exploitation in foreign lands increase national wealth and make higher wages possible. Luxemburg only began to sketch out methodology for another economics that could explain the complex changing reality of a global economy and indicate points of strain at which social transformation can occur. In such an economics, there would be no law of history to guarantee the development of capitalism in the last primitive outposts of the world, or a steady progress to world socialism. Without the grand metanarratives of capitalism or Marxism, Luxemburgian economics would promise no utopian ending. In a homogeneous capitalist world, if it could ever come about, markets would immediately be glutted with overproduction. Instead, the result predicted by her economic analysis has in fact come about: peripheral economies remain dependent, drained of their resources, their populations suffering from disease and poverty.

4. Luxemburgian Socialist Feminism

Internationalist Feminism

Luxemburg did not pretend to speak for colonized people. Her concern was European workers. They had been co-opted and duped. They had let racism and ethnocentricity blind them to the fact of slave labor and brutal military rule in colonies and spheres of interest. They had been bought off by an illusion of Western supremacy that hides the crude violence that establishes and maintains that rule. They had accepted the pretext of just wars to release their frustrations. Her indictment illuminates some of the painful debate that has gone on recently between white feminists and women of color.

The issue has been understood in much academic discussion as a conflict between an essentialism that takes femininity as a constant and a postmodern refusal of universals. Meanwhile, white feminists continue to pay little attention to the material fact of racial and economic oppression. If race riots break out in the slums of Los Angeles or New York, it is seldom a feminist matter. If government policy supports dictators in developing countries, it is men's politics. In practice in Western democracies, feminist leaders, often from privileged groups, direct and ordain the course of a reformist feminist politics that helps women like themselves win elections and employment battles. International capitalism funds a comfortable existence for many of these women, siphoning wealth from capitalist spheres of influence into Western economies, and maintaining a racially segregated domestic work force, including exploited illegal aliens, which provides cheap, menial labor in support of middle-class life-styles.

Even when feminists proclaim a "radical" separatism or activism, the aim is not revolution in Luxemburg's sense. If there is no revolution when a few women manage to be elected to Congress; there is no revolution when a small group of radicals manage to take over an organization. Revolution, for Luxemburg, is in spontaneous movements of masses of people as occurred in the Russian Revolution and may even now be occurring in race riots in large cities, inchoate protests of welfare mothers, migrant or illegal labor movements, popular liberation movements in developing countries. In a feminism aspiring to revolutionary social transformation, feminist leaders would study such movements, encourage their self-organization, isolate the aspirations that motivate them. They would work to close gaps between feminist leaderships and masses of women in poorly paid service jobs, welfare mothers racially defined, women suffering debilitating, unpaid labor in non-Western countries.

Many feminists have called for contact and solidarity with non-Western women. A Luxemburgian socialism could give that sentiment a theoretical grounding which is lacking in both liberal tolerance of diversity and postmodern politics of difference. Neither the granting of minimal rights nor transgressive textual studies is likely to lead to a viable mass feminist politics. Luxemburg offers instead the committed stance with oppressed groups from which it is possible to get the coherent grasp of reality which can inform intelligent action. Because that commitment is to others in a common material world, it is necessarily shared. There are not different realities projected by different symbolic constructions, but one reality, the material world in which people live together in different but always interrelated ways. If the view is better from some positions than from others, this is consistent with the restraints of physical existence. Conflicting claims of truth can be weighed in discussion and critical analysis.

The theory of a shared material world and the basis for a Luxemburgian socialist feminism would be an economic analysis no longer veiled in mathematized mystery. It is not surprising that few feminists have wanted to take on such a formidable enemy as economic rationalism, barricaded as it is behind masculine privilege and academic discipline. Researchers whose theories promote the interests of those in power, fortified by research grants and fellowships, have strong vested interests in maintaining the authority of classical economics. At stake is the coherent view of the whole, which Luxemburg believed was necessary for revolutionary politics. No feminist peace movement, claim to abortion rights, reform of the family, or protest against male aggression taps the "Plutonian" depths of economic relations between militarism, war, capital, international monetary systems, and working lives that Luxemburg examined. No theory of women's rights, masculine aggression, or family justice can be adequate to women's knowledge of their global situation without an economic analysis of working experience.

The theory of a shared material world that might inform a mass feminist movement is a global economics that does not take as the object of interest increased production swelling capitalist profits, or the realization of the species-being of Marxist man making his mark on nature, but the satisfaction of human needs. To that end, Luxemburgian economics could address systems of distribution as well as the organization of production, could develop indexes for production that are qualitative as well as quantitative, could critically assess the covert assumptions of value that define the objects of quantitative analyses. Such an economics would *use* mathematical models in the service of an economic thought the aims and motives of which are continually critically and democratically assessed. Instead of the fiction of an abstract economic functioning divorced from family and social life, Luxemburgian economics could plot intersections between relations of production and familial, cultural, and community relations. It could develop categories and concepts necessary to represent the neglected economic function of women in both Western and non-Western countries.

Writing in support of women's right to the vote, Luxemburg identified the failure to count women's work in the home as productive with the "brutality and insanity of the present capitalist economy" (PW 221). Even more striking, she noted, is the untapped potential power of masses of working women in industrial, clerical, and service work. A feminist economic analysis would take account of structural relations between housework, part-time work, service work and mainstream industrial labor, both in the West and in developing countries, to develop new strategies for feminist action. Such analyses are impossible without knowledge of and concern for the situation of working women in industrial and nonindustrialized countries. Luxemburgian economics requires independent researchers, not in the pay of any government or corporation, directly conversant with women's work experience and postcolonial cultures, knowledgeable in global economic history, and, most important, in communication with material reality.

Luxemburg was sometimes accused of catastrophism, the view that capitalism is doomed and, therefore, no revolutionary action is necessary. In fact, she argued that, well before the point when capitalism succeeds in exhausting all external markets, economic dislocations would make life unlivable in many parts of the world. The antidote, as she saw it, was neither passive reliance on the workings of history nor desperate vanguard action, but a committed and integrated economic thought moving toward a coherent view of global reality. The stimulant that might motivate such thought is no longer likely to be the oppression of male industrial workers or the suffering of middle-class women in industrial countries, real as that suffering may be, but the global effects of capitalist expansion: violent conflict in developing countries between indigent rural populations and wealthy elites in alliance with foreign capitalists, disputes over essential resources such as oil, environmental collapse, the unrestrained marketing of drugs and arms, the almost universal unwillingness to tolerate women in positions of power. International movements, action groups, federations that form around these issues might be the source and the training ground for a new, mass, global, feminist politics.

A Mass Movement of Women

If there are obvious differences between socialist party organizations and the contemporary feminist movement, there are also commonalities. In feminism, as in Marxism, there has been an explosion of theory. Marxism and feminism both have become alternative academic establishments in some universities and departments, with vested interests and standards of political correctness. As in Marxism, much feminist theorizing is now internally generated, as feminist scholars respond to other scholars, establishing reputations and publication records. In addition, like the split between Bernstein's reformism and radical Leninism, feminists are often divided between liberals who look to the defense of rights in capitalist democracies and radicals who urge more extreme measures of exclusion, separatism, and militant action.

Most important, corresponding to the distance between well-edu-cated, theoretically sophisticated leaders of Communist parties and their constituencies, is a distance between highly visible and publi-cized feminist leaders and poor, working, radically oppressed, unem-ployed and underemployed women. For the latter, many of the issues which occupy liberal feminist politics, such as pornography and abor-tion, are peripheral to a crushing burden of poverty, crime, and drug addiction. Issues which define radical feminism such as lesbian sepa-ratism and the refusal of motherhood may be equally tangential to women whose family responsibilities are not white or middle class. If legal remedies phrased in terms of civil rights, on which so much current liberal feminist politics focuses are often beside the point for women struggling for bare survival, even more remote from their needs may be the sophisticated textual studies which now occupy the energies of many academic feminists. From the perspective of nonwhite women, official feminism can seem mired in intellectualism, tokenism, and marginalization, stalled in defensive tactics, as conser-vative forces in Western democracies become more self-confident with the proclaimed demise of socialism and the resurgence of religious fundamentalism.

Luxemburg's conception of the relation between political leader-ship and political constituency, her insistence that mass action is the only means to revolution, might inspire another kind of relationship between feminist leaderships and masses of women. Although na-tional feminist leaderships have on occasion sent out successful calls for demonstrations on issues such as abortion rights, the failure of mainstream feminism to fully engage the interest of poor women and women of color in feminist politics has been a source of general frustration. The resultant soul-searching has generally focused on feminist theorists and leaders themselves: How have *we* been inadver-tently racist? How have *we* failed to make our organization attractive to diverse women?

Luxemburg suggests another tack. The solution, as she saw it, is not to find out why feminism or socialism or any liberatory theory fails to appeal to workers or poor women, or to try to refashion white feminist goals in terms they might accept. It is to study the embryonic political activism of working people themselves, their initiatives, strikes, alliances, peaceful and violent demonstrations in ghettoes, slums, factories, depressed neighborhoods. Like reformist Social Democrats, many activist feminists have allied themselves with lib-eral political parties against conservativism. They have endorsed, at least in practice, the liberal political agenda of free markets tempered by government-provided welfare services. They have urged retrenchment as rights come under attack from conservatives. They have cited the gains of liberal feminism. The wisdom gained in a Luxemburgian mass movement of the disadvantaged clients of welfare systems and their allies might inform new feminist agendas independent of the establishment poles of liberal welfare state versus conservative free market. The locus for such a socialist feminist politics would be more local than national, revitalizing community democracy and citizens' initiatives in which the sensitive relation between Luxemburg's leaders and their constituencies can come into play. Luxemburgian leaders would not dictate, but would encourage, guide, inform, according to the "compass" of women's own developing and forming aspirations to a better life. Women participating in mass action would develop their initiatives expressing a deepening knowledge of their and other women's situations.

In recent feminist philosophy, a feminine ethical voice has been a topic of considerable discussion. Like Luxemburg, feminist philosophers have pointed out the moral deficiencies in philosophical systems of ethics such as Kantian idealism and utilitarianism. Emergent in feminist philosophy is an alternate view of ethics as contextual, affective, perspectival. The tendency however, in reaction to philosophical ethics, has been to defend such an alternative ethics as feminine, based either on feminine psychology, women's different perspective, or women's maternal instincts. Luxemburg suggests a feminist "moral compass," grounded in the aspirations and active knowledge of working women and men. Values for Luxemburg are never independent of fact, but are framed in engagement with material reality. The substance of a feminist socialist ethics, would be goals and aims that evolve in the course of feminist struggle.

In 1912, Luxemburg insisted that women's suffrage could not be a job for women alone, but was a "common class concern for women and men of the proletariat" (PW 218). Similarly, a Luxemburgian mass feminist movement would find those points of solidarity with oppressed men that could undo the "links in the chain of the reaction that shackles people's lives" (PW 218). In such an ethics of solidarity, the aspirations of women, whose poorly paid labor is vitally necessary in the work force but who also continue to be responsible for most of the work of maintaining human life in childcare, housework, and nursing of the sick, might be a source of values for both men and women. In the past few decades, feminist standpoint theories of knowledge have pointed to the necessity for knowledge from the perspective of women's lives. At issue has been not so much political action as it has been philosophical theories of knowledge which claim rational grounding independent of context or interest. Luxemburg's socialist knowledge requires more than empathetic imagination, more than a theorist putting herself in the position of women of poorer classes or racial minorities and attempting to see things from their perspective. It requires a standing with and acting with poor, racially oppressed women and a resulting coproduction of values and knowledge.

Luxemburg's support for spontaneous revolutionary action and her insistence on working-class experience as the basis for socialist knowledge suggest an approach to standpoint ethics and theories of knowledge which circumvents the relativism and political stasis that often infects perspectival theories. From the mass action of working women, as it is conceived, understood, and carried out by them and their allies, might come objective and coherent feminist understandings of the ensemble of national and international economic and political relationships that hold oppressive relations in place. Much of recent feminist politics has concentrated on single issues such as the Equal Right's Amendment, peace, abortion, pornography, welfare services. When a victory is won on one of these issues—a constitutional amendment passes, laws are blocked banning abortion—power structures that can rescind these measures and reinterpret laws and amendments are left intact. In contrast, a Luxemburgian socialist politics, informed by a coherent grasp of the system gained in the political action of masses of poor and disadvantaged women, engages the economic and cultural matrix of capitalist society. An issue like abortion can bog down in idealist debate between a right to life and a right to choose. A revived socialist feminism would relate abortion to the economics of poverty and the propagation of a marginally employed labor force that generates repressive reproductive policies. Luxemburg's socialist grasp of the whole allows evaluation of feminist action not as a means to rescindable short-term gains but as part of a far-reaching revolutionary agenda.

Essential in any recovery of a Luxemburgian socialist feminism would be the reworking of the vexed concept of democracy. Marxists, like Lenin, were quick to point out the lack of real democracy in the legislative maneuvering of interest groups and the corporate financing of elections in capitalist countries. Concentrated as they were on winning state power, democracy was hardly a priority for the Bolsheviks either. If the slogan, "socialist democracy" had concrete meaning at all, it was a euphemism for a coercive rallying of public opinion behind the decisions of the supreme Communist party. While European Social Democrats continued to participate in parliaments and legislatures as if winning elections was an end in itself, in Russia the Soviets that were to have been the basis of socialist democracy became an instrument of party control. Democracy in both cases was deferred to a distant, utopian future when workers would be mature and true Communism possible.

Like other Marxists, Luxemburg did not describe in detail what democratic institutions and practices might be like in socialism. Her Marxist materialism ruled out in principle ideals that are not generated in actual economic and historical processes; a workers' democracy would have to emerge in the course of revolution. But she grappled with problems inherent in any attempt to install a true "rule of the people." How can the unity necessary in political or social movements be achieved in a way that does not do violence to the diversity and freedom of individuals? An answer to this question, passionately and sometimes angrily discussed between feminists, is crucial for any revolutionary movement. For feminists, the question has often taken the form of the essentialist/relativist dilemma. Either some sufficiently general definition of "woman" or "femininity" must provide unity, a definition which inevitably is exclusive of some groups and perspectives, or diversity and pluralism are claimed as the basis of a unfocused politics of difference.

Luxemburg suggests an alternative. A coherence of aims that might provide a nonoppressive unity to replace doctrinal fidelity or party policy can be generated, as were Luxemburg's own theoretical positions, out of close observation and involvement in actual women's movements. Study of, participation in, and hard thought about the actions of oppressed people in times of crisis and discontent isolates directions, meanings, tendencies, common aspirations, and goals to unify policy. The politics that results is not the autonomous creation of any theorist, the intuition of any idealist essence or the application of any theory, but reflects the "sensuous activity" of social agents themselves. As she guides, facilitates, and directs, stands with a social movement, a Luxemburgian leader speaks for others without dictating, makes clear what their actions mean in the aggregate and how they might be organized, coordinated, and carried forward. Such a politics requires open channels of communication, constant reciprocity between leaders and masses, healthy grass-roots activist groups, and institutions that make each accountable to the other.

Luxemburg could not have predicted the extent to which the very possibility of action would be co-opted in capitalist production by marketing techniques and mass psychology. Citizens in capitalist countries, persuaded to limit their freedom of action to the choice of preselected candidates for office and preselected commodities for consumption, engage in little of the kind of spontaneous political activity in which a Luxemburgian socialist ethics might be developed.

Crucial for a renewed socialist feminism, therefore, would be identification of occasions and spaces for mass political struggle. These spaces, in which political action may still be possible, are no longer in the traditionally male industrial workplace, where strikes and wage disputes can be settled at the expense of foreign workers. Elsewhere— in the family, citizens' groups, welfare institutions, women's groups, environmental and peace movements, in personal relations between the sexes—women, men of ethnic minorities, and other oppressed groups in affiliation with international organizations, might find occasions for action that has reference not only to national conflicts, but also to their global setting.

Materialist Knowledge

> In the decade before the World War, German Social Democracy, as the international metropolis of proletarian intellectual life, displayed total harmony in theoretical as well as practical areas; in both areas the same indecision and ossification appeared. . . . Similarly the apparent theoretical "expert knowledge" and infallibility of official Marxism, which blessed every practice of the movement, turned out to be a grandiose facade hiding its inner insecurity and inability to act behind intolerant and insolent dogmatism. (ACAC 144)

So goes Luxemburg's indictment of the thoughtlessness of a politics that refused to engage with material reality. Luxemburg's socialism is an alternative: a thought that is referential and concrete, historical and general, critical as it constantly insists on bringing words back to experienced reality. What moves such a thought forward is not logical inconsistency or the immediate solving of practical difficulties, but an ability to think generally and concretely at the same time. In much of traditional philosophy, either the universal has been a shorthand expression for a series of facts, or facts have been taken as reflection of universal essences. To the rationalist who studies essence is opposed the empiricist who celebrates the particular. Empiricists generalize from data; rationalists manipulate concepts. In both cases, thought is a finished product: theory deductively or inductively established. What allowed Luxemburg to come to grips with social reality in the early decades of the twentieth century was an attention to concrete, day-to-day events along with attention to the most abstract of economic theories.

Thought about thought has been framed in the philosophical tradition. Either ideas are an empiricist effect of the forces that impinge on human beings through their senses and in the internal workings of their body, or rationalist cognitive structures are independent of experience. Luxemburg's thought fits neither paradigm. Thinking is neither a tabulation of private sensations nor the clear and distinct ideas of an autonomous mind, but the constant making of connections between experience and concepts and theories with which to give an account of that experience. Such connections constitute the effort of an intelligence that is neither a mechanical recording and sorting of data nor the formal manipulation of abstract ideas, but ongoing, thoughtful engagement with contradiction, resistance, and change. Required for such thought are moral as well as mental abilities, emotional as well as intellectual strengths, and, especially, a willingness to allow cherished theories to come into contact with painful reality. For many of Luxemburg's male comrades, with a vested interest in the certainty of socialist theory, and perhaps also with a masculine suspicion of emotion, there was a tendency to avoid reality in rationalization and temporization.

It was enough to say that Luxemburg had criticized Marx's economics to prove her wrong. Especially in their Leninist versions, Marx's formulas were taken as dogma, interpreted pragmatically but always given lip service as evidence of doctrinal fidelity to an infallible truth. Bukhharin's official Bolshevik response to Luxemburg, *Imperialism and the Accumulation of Capital* (reprinted ACAC 153), contains constant reference to Luxemburg's failure to respect authority. She had contradicted the "incomparable master" (ACAC 264) whom it was "dangerous" to criticize (249); Marxist teaching would "revenge" (252) this attack on its "unity" (252). Although Buhkarin admits that what makes Luxemburg's account of accumulation attractive is its economic determinism, its confirmation by empirical facts, and its "revolutionary character" (259), he nevertheless insists it is wrong "as a theory," wrong because it is not the theory of orthodox Marxism. For Luxemburg, this kind of criticism showed a fundamental misunderstanding of materialist thought. Materialism, she argued, is the study and analysis of actual material conditions which are bound to change. Certainly conditions had changed since Marx wrote in the mid-nineteenth century, when the great competition for colonial territories had not yet begun. Since Marx did not leave any final solution to the problem of accumulation, it was clear to Luxemburg that the "master" intended others to continue work. There might be no final answer; no study of society that is a science like natural science. Marxism as a critique of capitalism may be a political tool that will itself be outdated and unnecessary once capitalism is transcended (Nettl, 840).

Luxemburg describes her own "critical" materialist method of analysis in the concluding sentences of *The Accumulation of Capital:*

> Marxism is a revolutionary world outlook which must always strive for new discoveries, which completely despises rigidity in once-valid theses, and whose living force is best preserved in the intellectual clash of self-criticism and the rough and tumble of history. (ACAC 150)

Luxemburg's refusal to allow nominal definitions to hold meanings in fixed relationships helped her to avoid this "rigidity in once-valid theses." If a word is to have meaning, she insisted, it must have reference. Otherwise, reliable judgment is impossible. There can be no valid judgment on "rights," until it is clear what a right is. No study of texts or linguistic structures can provide this understanding, only historical study of the attitudes, institutions, and forms of life to which specific claims to rights refer. Claims to rights have in some circumstances served women's interests. Some women have gained the right to run for political office, to earn equal pay, to be educated along with men. In other cases, rights have not been so useful. The principle of equal rights has been used to strike down affirmative action programs designed to correct past denials of rights because they infringe the rights of men or privileged racial groups. The right to free speech has been cited in defense of a trafficking in pornography which encourages the degradation and abuse of women.

Especially problematic for women in peripheral economies has been the claim to a right to national self-determination. Again, Luxemburg's materialist understanding ruled out any universal judgment. Nationalist movements must be judged case by case, situation by situation. If nationalism in Eastern Europe means a return to aristocracy, church rule, or exclusionary racial enclaves then it is not progressive, nor likely to promote women's interests. If nationalism in Arab countries means the sequestering of women and the consolidation of the economic power of local male elites then nationalism is not in the interests of women. In such materialist judgments there is no logical division between fact and value. That the two are separate has been in many schools of modern philosophy, including Marxist science, a tenet of belief. Objects are as they are; words refer to them. The first step is to determine the truth; the next is to make a judgment according to utility, adherence to universal principle, or one's own interests. In Luxemburg's materialist thought, judgment and knowledge go together. Moral judgment cannot be made apart from a concrete grasp of material reality; the stance that allows a grasp of material reality is not possible without moral commitment. In understanding and analyzing a situation are inherent the standpoint from which judgment comes and the interests which motivate it.

Not only would a feminist materialist thought stay close to particular events and conditions in women's lives, it would place those conditions within a larger global economic context. If one of the lessons of Luxemburg's materialist thought is attention to the particular, another is the need to grasp along with particular fact the whole of physical and ideological forces that hold particulars in place. Pornography, which has occupied feminist energies, for example, is not only a local moral or social problem in capitalist countries. A materialist understanding places pornography in the context of an increasingly powerful international capitalism, with well-protected interests in the transnational sale of commodities like pornography, drugs, arms. Just as Bernstein, the reformist socialist, made the mistake of seeing credit from the narrow standpoint of easing a national monetary policy, so from one limited point of view, pornography can be viewed either as hate literature or as an exercise of free speech. Seen in the context of racist, international, economic structures, it is part of a global network that markets dangerous products and controls access to employment.

If Luxemburg's Marx saw socialism as an ongoing project and not a finished product, so Luxemburg also left unsolved problems. The problem of establishing a moral basis for social theory had not been solved. Luxemburg continued to assume the priority of working-class experience even when, according to her analysis, industrial workers in Western countries are no longer the primary "contradiction" in capitalism and have an interest in its survival. Luxemburg continued to assume the utopian core of Marxist orthodoxy: a revolutionary consciousness will bring about worker control of the means of production. Although she defined "worker" more broadly than doctrinaire Leninists—she included state employees, railroad and postal workers, farm workers, miners—Luxemburg never wavered in her belief that the trend in capitalism to economic centralization and industrialization is progressive and prepares the way for democracy in a centrally controlled, planned economy. As the great world depression of the thirties caused general despair, as Leninism degenerated into Stalinism, and German militarism hardened into Fascism, the democratization of industrial work, always honored in socialist theory if not in socialist practice, became more and more problematic. It was not only that Western workers profit from oppression abroad; if this were the only problem a new global proletariat might be formed to carry on the revolution. The very nature of modern industrial work driven by technologies to which workers have no access seems to promote apathy and dull-wittedness rather than spirit and intelligence.

Like many Marxists, Luxemburg neglected the problem of power. Power was understood by Marxists as a secondary phenomenon, an effect of property relations, needing no independent analysis. According to Marxist theory, once socialism abolishes private property, there will be no more power of one person over another. In the meantime, in Lenin's Soviet Union unchecked power mushroomed beyond anyone's control. In the midst of continued violent upheavals, constantly threatened with arrest and eventually murder, Luxemburg did not map out alternate democratic institutions or explain how they could be projected against those seeking power in a socialist state. The lack of an adequate theory of power relations and a complementary vision of a truly democratic politics was painfully evident after Luxemburg's death, as in Russia and Eastern Europe Communist governments fell into the hands of leaders who administered for their own gain.

These were the strands of thought taken up by Simone Weil and Hannah Arendt. Marxist science had taken property relations as the essential form of oppression. Faced with Stalinism, virulent racism, and Fascism, Weil and Arendt turned away from critiques of private property to specific dynamics of power and rule and their relation to liberation and freedom. In many ways, Luxemburg opened the field for this questioning. Her rejection of Marxist dogmatism opened socialist thought to an ongoing search for that grasp of the whole which would show the course a liberatory politics should take. Continuing to pursue such a materialist knowledge, Weil and Arendt thought on, past the rationalist fictions of economic modeling exposed by Luxemburg, past the shortsighted failure of socialist leaders to condemn nationalism, to the theoretical heart of Marxist philosophy: mastering nature is the original position of man the producer, material forces determine social reality, social structures define the individual. These foundational attitudes, shared by other Western philosophers, shaped Marx's view of the human condition. Going beyond Luxemburg's "technical problems," Weil and Arendt began to place social concepts and theories in the larger context of the history of Western thought.

II

Simone Weil

It is perhaps no exaggeration to say that Simone Weil's *La Condition Ouvriere* (1951) is the only book in the huge literature on the labor question which deals with the problem without prejudice or sentimentality. She chose as the motto for the diary in which she relates her day-to-day experiences in a factory a line from Homer, . . . "much against your own will, since necessity lies more mightily upon you." She concludes that the hope for an eventual liberation from labor and necessity is both the only utopian element of Marxism and, at the same time, the actual motor of all Marx-inspired revolutionary movements. It is the "opium of the people" which Marx had believed religion to be.

Hannah Arendt, The Human Condition, p. 131.

2

Suffering the World

Where does thinking go on? Where should a woman go to acquire wisdom? Since Plato, the philosopher's answer has typically involved some form of withdrawal. The philosopher retreats from the distractions and corruption of ordinary life, from the greed and materialism of commerce. He sequesters himself in compounds for rulers like Plato's philosopher kings; or, like Descartes: he removes himself from all sensory distraction in the privacy of his study, or, as the modern scholar, he retreats to the ivy-covered towers of the university. Can thinking go on in such isolation? What happens to the thought of rulers separated from their subjects, writers who see nothing of the world around them, academics obsessed by the struggle for promotion and merit that dominates university life?

Simone Weil never became a ruler, recluse, or academic. She taught briefly in provincial French lycées, with none of the protection or honors of academic tenure. For a period of time, she sought out punishing jobs in factories and agriculture, convinced that the left's understanding of alienated labor would never be complete until it came from the experience of workers themselves. She visited the front in the Spanish Civil War to see firsthand the effects of revolutionary violence. She traveled to Germany to test the mood of Fascism. In her reading she roamed widely, studying the literature of the Orient, African legends, Native American myth, Old European folklore. During World War II, with her health deteriorating, she offered herself again and again to the Resistance for active duty in occupied France.

Her vocation as a thinker, as she saw it, was not that she could detach herself from human affairs but that she could do many things, go many places, live among people in different milieus, pass as one of them and share their lives (AD 19). She could become a factory worker and know the crippling of soul that results from industrial work, she could do agricultural work and share the exhaustion and exhilaration of direct contact with physical reality, she could walk in a procession of village women on a Portuguese feast day and experience the spirituality of their ritual. Always her thought was wide-ranging and incarnate, physically rooted in activities and experiences: in labor, in political activism, in spiritual life, in her work for the Free French. Always her thought was meant to do something in the world.

She produced no system of signs: no deduction from logical intuitions, no structures or deconstructions. She condemned words that are only "signs." Wars are fought for signs, she said, against people who have another symbol on their helmets, but labels have no concrete meaning outside the realities of human life. Our lives are lived in changing circumstances, subject to the play of external necessities and modified according to specific conditions within specific limits, and yet we persist in trying futilely to act and believe according to fixed and isolated abstractions which cannot be related to one another or to any concrete facts (NR 157).

With the threat of mass violence and another world war, the intensity of Weil's attention to the suffering around her and the worse suffering to come became almost unbearable. What can justify the mass killing of war? Making the world "safe for democracy"? Always she was suspicious of mottoes, believing that it is impossible to understand the differences marked by words like "democracy" and "dictatorship" if you take words as representing "things-in-themselves" instead of points of reference from which to judge existing social structures. From her observations in Spain during the Civil War, she judged that any war fought for "democracy" was likely to defeat itself. The most idealistic of wars resulted in privation, autocracy, militarization. Because they involve retreat to an artificial world of internally consistent concepts, symbolic manipulations and abstractions, she argued, only distract us from seeing such realities and finding solutions. When we live with and attend to conflicting realities and are not content to manipulate systems of signs, it is not possible to avoid contradiction. What we take as utopian communism may turn out to be a dictatorship, what we take as exploitative capitalism may be liberatory.

Western philosophy begins with the insistence that thought must be rigorously consistent. Even the reversals and deconstructions of the rebels of the tradition, like Nietzsche or Derrida, have been carried out against a conceptual thought ordered by consistency. Weil's "intellectual honesty," her "probite intellectuelle" as she called it, required that she refuse simplistic consistence as well as the rational system-making that makes its reversal or deconstruction possible. Her honesty required that she follow "the way of what is and what is not" forbidden at the very inauguration of Western rationalism.[1]

Nowhere was this more painfully expressed than in her last letter to her would-be spiritual advisor Father Perrin, as she and her parents prepared to flee the Nazi occupation of France (May 26, 1942, WG 68–84). Replying to Perrin's rebuke of her refusal to join the church, a refusal by which she denied herself the comforts of sacrament and community for which she so much longed, she explained to him what her intellectual honesty required, as well as her suspicions that *his* honesty was impaired by attitudes that were not "impartial." Intellectual honesty demands, she told him, that we not smooth over and ignore the contradictions inherent in human life: the church is our best hope of grace and yet it can separate us from God; Christ was the savior of man but there must have been a possibility for redemption before the birth of Christ. Underlying these surface contradictions in Christian faith, Weil saw deeper contradictions ineradicable from human life: obligation is infinite, but those on earth to whom we have duties are imperfect (NR 150); natural life is ruled by blind mechanical necessity, and yet goodness also exists (OL 159); human affairs are ruled by force, but at the same time justice is sometimes done (ibid.).

For Weil, it was intellectually dishonest and dangerous to attempt to evade these contradictions. We can insist that we only owe an obligation to the infinite being who is God, allowing selfishness and greed to rule in our worldly dealings. We can find something in the world, such as pleasure or freedom, and pretend that it has absolute value, committing any crime in its name (NR 150–1). We can pretend that goodness has force and that, if we think good thoughts, all will work out well, leaving dictators and bullies to prosper. Or we can, like Marx, say that the forces of historical process themselves will have a good result. These are retreats from reality, refusals to suffer the world as it is.

From early childhood, Weil identified with the unfortunate, with those who suffer privation and violence. She would always, she vowed, try to take no more food or physical comfort than the most wretched. Reducing her parents and friends to despair, she often starved herself, lived without heat, slept on bare floors. For her, these were political acts. It was not enough to be a philanthropist, to wish the poor well; only when their suffering touched the flesh could it be understood and attended to. Like Luxemburg, Weil found no comfort in the assurances of dialectical materialism that the just socialist state was on its way, but the problem as she saw it went deeper than a flawed economics. Marx realized the impotence of "good thoughts," and determined to study only the real material forces in human affairs; in doing so he ended by leaving justice to one side. When the blind determinism that resulted became unbearable, instead of attending to the contradiction, he tacked utopianism back on in a Law of History that guarantees that productive forces will increasingly organize themselves for human good (OL 171–2). When injustice occurred it was made to disappear as collective planning instituted the dictatorship of the proletariat and dialectical materialism became the justification for inflicting suffering on "backward masses."

For Weil, thought that engages with reality has to tolerate and be patient with inconsistency; it cannot retreat into dogma and self-deception. In her youth, in regard to Christianity, she resolved not to cease to tell herself: "all this might not be true," at the same time as she told herself: "all this might be true" (WG 50). Later, she applied this method to other problems, meditating on inescapable but incompatible truths such as: "on earth all is ruled by blind necessity," and "on earth, goodness exists" (GG 93). The point, Weil said, is not to attempt to reduce or repress one or two opposing truths, but to go beyond them. We must use contradictory truths "like a pair of pincers" (OL 159) to enter into contact with an higher truth. Marx, when he calls for the opposite of the evils of capitalism, "remains on the level of that evil." If the proletariat are oppressed in capitalism then in socialism they will rule, but domination is granted to the oppressed; there still is no escape from the "oppression-domination cycle." The oppression of the capitalists becomes the dictatorship of the proletariat (GG 91). In *Oppression and Liberty*, Weil moved beyond the oppositions of Marxist class struggle to a deeper reading of the evils of capitalism. The problem with capitalism, she argued, is not so much class ownership of the means of production as it is the means of industrial production themselves, which involve alienated labor and managerial hierarchies. As long as socialist thought remains stalled at the opposition, domination/oppression, it misses this deeper truth and cannot move forward.

How is a woman to make the difficult movement to another level of understanding? How is she to take a firm hold of the "pincers" of contradiction so that they no longer limit thought but can be used to advance understanding? It cannot be done, Weil argued, by an act of will. The key to thought is not assertion, or the logical connections between assertions, but "attention": the patient holding in the mind of seemingly incompatible truths, the refusal to give in to the temptation to overlook inconvenient facts, the tolerance of uncertainty.

Attention consists in suspending thought, in making it available, empty, penetrable by the object; attention must maintain, in itself, in proximity to thought, but at a lower level and without contact with it, the diverse acquired understandings which we are forced to use. To all ideas that are particular and already formed, such a thought must be like a man on a mountain, looking in front of him, who perceives at the same time beneath him, but without looking at them, many forests and plains. Especially thought must be empty, waiting, not searching for anything, but ready to receive in its naked truth the object which will penetrate there. (WG 92–3)

Failure to pay thoughtful attention results in the "partial attitudes" of which Weil accused Father Perrin. He treated the suffering of non-Christians and Christians differently; he identified dogma with truth; he refused to recognize "implicit" faith outside church membership; he denied redemption to anyone living before the birth of Christ (WG 77–78). His allegiance to the church as an "earthly state" limited his thought. His desire for the power of the church made him "partial" and unwilling to admit the truth. He did not hold all the diverse understandings in his thought as he should, but only the ideas that serve the interests of the social institution to which he was committed. From his own center as priest of the Catholic Church, he had not been able to keep his thought in proximity to received ideas while at the same time looking on to a larger truth that would put contradictions into equilibrium.

For Weil, partiality is the necessary beginning point of human experience. Each person starts at the imaginary center of her own world, seeing things from inside her own time and space and her own hierarchy of values. She is soon forced to give up this illusion at least in regard to space; she lives also in others' space; even walking requires awareness of this fact. Giving up the center of one's own value system is harder, but when we succeed, the very sensibility changes and we become capable of a new way of seeing. We are able

to empty ourselves of this false divinity, deny oneself, to renounce being at the center of the world, to discern all the points of the world as being centers in the same title and the veritable center as being outside the world (AD 148)

Thought must be rooted in physical activity and at the same time be impartial. It must aim at the good but be without desire. It must admit contradictions at the same time as it transcends them. It must wait patiently for a solution, but long for the truth. What would such thinking be like? Can it be accorded any validity when it rests neither on the empirical verifications of science nor on the rationalizations of logicians? The only way to evaluate Weil's thought is to live it, to follow her as she prepares her lectures for her lycée classes in the philosophy of science, as she drags her aching body out of bed for another day at the factory, as, blinded by migraine, she tries to concentrate on a Gregorian chant, as, struggling for breath, she sits down at a desk in a dark, unheated, back office in wartime London to work out principles that might guide the postwar reconstruction of Europe.

1. The Rule of Force

Malheur

The situation of working people was the central concern of Rosa Luxemburg, but like so many socialist theorists Luxemburg understood working experience from a distance. She had not experienced firsthand the punishing repetition of factory work or the painful uncertainty of prolonged unemployment. Weil was not content to understand industrial labor either from the dictates of male comrades always ready to instruct her or from her own extensive reading of Marx and other socialist philosophers. Although unsuited for manual work by a sheltered, middle-class upbringing and by the always-precarious state of her health, Weil left her position as a lycée teacher to work for periods of time both in factories and in agriculture, until the war made finding a job impossible. Standing in line with other unemployed workers desperate to find a job, humiliated and bullied by foremen impatient with her clumsiness and ready to fire her at the first weakness, working machines which could cut off a finger or an arm if her attention wandered, Weil recorded her anger, her exhaustion, her pain, and her reflections in her *Factory Journal* (FW 149–227).

Already she had paid attention to the social effects of industrial production in her writings on *Oppression and Liberty*, now she described them from experience. The repetitive, numbing quality of work on machines made all thought and consciousness impossible. The worker was dehumanized, her or his situation further stressed by the global depression and the lack of employment. The lines of those wanting jobs outside factories, and pressure on managers from owners unsure of profits, meant that workers were ever more subject to the demands of their superiors, ever more abject before the humiliating and insulting scoldings and warnings to which they were continually subjected. Weil, never dexterous, and troubled with persistent and debilitating migraine, took more than her share of dressing down. Her body ached. With efficiency of output the only goal, there was no time for concern for natural movements of the body; muscles strained, fingers swelled. There was no one to turn to for sympathy, certainly not the boss, happy enough to be rid of any worker at the first insubordination, and not other workers, too tired and afraid to want to listen to anyone else's complaints. Marx's vision of a victorious proletariat was a delusion. Weil's fellow workers, worn down by worry and exhaustion, and with none of the benefits of education or culture, had no time or energy for solidarity, and could hardly manage simple kindness. The women, Weil noted, had the worst of it; not only were they victimized and abused as workers, they were also looked down on by the men (FW 203).

The physical pain of factory labor is not its only effect. Much more serious, Weil observed, is what it does to the spirit. She wrote:

> [Assembly line work] is a refinement of torture: to constrain thought, to taste continually the body's slavery. It can only be borne by mutilating the soul. Otherwise one feels as if one were delivered every day alive, to be crushed to pieces. (FLN 12)

As she went each day to the factory, she found herself losing little by little her sense of human dignity, the conviction that she had rights. Day by day subjected to the arbitrary and humiliating orders by superiors, she began to feel a mark on her soul. Sitting on the bus going home one day, she realized suddenly that she would have felt no astonishment if she had been ordered off for no reason. Numbed by abuse, when someone spoke to her with any degree of kindness she started with surprise (FW 211). Under orders for most of the day, she lost the sense of time by which we order our own movements.

> To be ruled by another's caprice is to lose the relation to time. Whoever is subjected to the arbitrary is suspended on the thread of time; he is obliged to *wait* (the most humiliating state! . . .) for what the next moment will bring; and to accept what the next moment has brought. He has no control of his passing moments; for him, the present is not a lever by which he can act upon the future. (FLN 20)

The question remained: is damage to the soul inevitable in industrial production, whether socialist or capitalist? Is it inevitable in modern societies that masses of people will be marked by punishing, mindless work, that they will be ordered around, treated like objects, made to live a life that can only lead to submission, obedience, and dehumanization? Is there a necessary link between human progress and oppression, so that the price of mastery of nature is that some human beings must be treated like things? If the answer to any of these questions is yes, then the faults in Marxist theory go deeper than Luxemburg's technical errors: the very aim and goal of socialist revolution is incoherent.

Straining to indicate a condition for which there is no name, Weil used the term *malheur*.[2] Weil's *malheur* is not just physical or even mental suffering. These are inevitable in any human life and do not necessarily cause permanent damage to the soul. What is not irreducibly physical pain can be alleviated with the right kind of attitude, and even physical pain leaves little mark on the soul once the pain itself is gone. Instead, *malheur* is an "uprooting" of life; a kind of living death. It comes not from physical pain only, but from an immediate and constant apprehension of physical pain that constrains all thought, as if one were made to contemplate continually the gallows on which one is to be hung. Some survive such a torture, but there is a threshold, different for different individuals, where suffering becomes *malheur* and the soul is crushed. The human being is broken, maimed, she can no longer express what is wrong with her. She can no longer take the steps necessary to extricate herself. All the well-intentioned charity, all the self-help programs cannot cure her. Inside, the soul is wounded or dead.

The *malheureuse* feels disgust with herself, revulsion with herself. She is overcome with sensations of uncleanness and guilt; her abject state only brings her the contempt of others. She is abused in the streets, treated roughly, spoken to without respect. *Malheur* poisons all aspects of her life, social, psychological, physical. The very aspiration to happiness is lost; even a benefactor or welfare worker is hated.[3] The *malheureux* are beyond hope, overcome with inertia. Even if they manage to extricate themselves, they are always in danger of falling back into numb despair. Just as Weil was marked for life by her factory experience, damage to the soul is never completely cured.

It is not only the destitute—beggars, homeless people, drug addicts, and the mentally disabled—who suffer from *malheur* and whose resistance to good works is explained in sensitive detail by Weil. Nor is it a simple question of poverty. *Malheur* does not disappear when industrial development increases production and brings about fuller employment, higher wages, improved working conditions as capitalism promises. Given the spiritual effects of industrial labor, even in times of prosperity there is *malheur*. The marks on the soul are made when the body is fed, as workers continue to carry out meaningless, programmed motions, subject always to orders given them by insensitive superiors with control over their livelihood. Release from physical labor does not protect from *malheur;* the numbing repetitions of much of the work done by women—computerized office work, routinized service jobs, menial temporary jobs—may be more dehumanizing and debilitating than the assembly line. Nor is equalization of wages sufficient to counteract the effects. The soul can be dead or crippled when there is energy and money left at the end of the day for leisure activities. Even that respite may not be available to working women, who are delegated in workplaces the most repetitious tasks and return home to an added burden of housework and childcare.

In his writings on capitalism, Marx pointed out the economic injustice of capitalist exploitation: a worker does not get back the full value of his or her labor because part of the value of that labor is skimmed off in capitalist profits. Theoretically this injustice can be alleviated by higher wages. Although Marx also described the alienated quality of work in capitalism, he referred that alienation to a philosophical abstraction—"species-being"—existence as part of a "human species" defined as the capability for conscious "life activity."[4] When a worker sells his labor, Marx argued, he not only gets a bad bargain, he loses his species identity and becomes an automaton carrying out the orders of others with no control over the process or the product of his labor.

Out of her experience of industrial labor, Weil understood the problem of alienated labor differently. The worst effect of industrialized labor is not the loss of an abstract human essence of man identified as the freedom to make a mark on or master nature. It is the concrete effects alienated labor has on the human soul. She agreed with Marx that work should be the most important activity of human life, but not for the same reason. She recognized no human species-being to maximize production and master nature in which all people should share. Instead, work constitutes a point of intersection with physical reality that is the most reliable source of a person's knowledge and self-identity. As such, work "must constitute for each human being what he most essentially is in need of if his life is to take on meaning and value in his own eyes" (OL 104).

The lack of feminist consciousness in working women has been explained by feminist theorists in a variety of ways: the influence of socialization, symbolic complexes that structure advertising and media images, patriarchal family roles. From a Weilian perspective, the problem is material and concrete. The kind of work many women do and that some men do in industrialized countries leads to a debased physical/spiritual condition. Given *malheur*, women's entrance into the work force may not be sufficient for their liberation. It may even increase their impotence. When a working woman suffers the conditions Weil described in her factory journal, both her self and her grasp on reality are threatened. The only hope for the sufferer, Weil concluded, is to learn to treat her masters as if they are a natural phenomenon, because then, as with disease, the torment is easier to bear. For the would-be benefactor or social worker, Weil prescribed an even more difficult attitude: a superhuman acceptance of the *malheureuse* as equals, an exercise almost impossible, given a natural human aversion to and avoidance of the unfortunate (WG 104, 136). The only substantive remedy, she concluded, is a social transformation that results in institutions in which no one is forced to damage anyone else.

The Weilian Critique of Marxism

If any philosophy had claimed to prescribe such a society it was Marxism. Like Luxemburg, Weil insisted on confronting hard facts. By the 1930s, ten years after Luxemburg's death, official Marxism had been completely compromised. Germany, where socialism had been strongest, had turned to Fascism. Revolutionaries like Luxemburg were dead and forgotten. "Fat cats" in big offices were left to direct a socialist politics that was legalist and reformist. German workers, Weil observed on her visit to Germany, were powerless, intimidated by unemployment and seduced by nationalism.[5] Even more important, Marxist-Leninism in Russia had not produced a workers' state, but its opposite—a centralized, bureaucratic, state capitalism, in structure not that dissimilar from National Socialism (OL 5).[6]

Like Luxemburg, weathering constant charges of defeatism and disloyalty from her comrades on the left, Weil persisted. It was time to rethink, not to continue blindly on with the same slogans and hopes. The very idea of socialist "revolution" as a violent overthrow of the old order was now suspect. What had revolution brought except bloodshed and a return to autocracy? Could Luxemburg's spontaneous uprising of workers ever be effective against those in power? Even if the severe economic conditions of recession or depression lead to moments of workers' solidarity, in the face of demeaning and dehumanizing labor, can that unity be maintained? After her experience in the factories, Weil could no longer share any Marxist faith in an uprising of the proletariat as a "universal class." Oppression does not result in rebellion, but in obedience and apathy. The oppressive force exerted by those in power is not progressive, but self-perpetuating. It was time to give up "empty hopes."

Marx, in his attempts to reconcile the contradiction between scientific explanations of social phenomena and social ideals, did justice to neither. He took the rigor from social science and adopted without criticism the bourgeois ideal of increased production. He exposed the surface mechanisms of capitalist production without explaining adequately how a revolution could occur, much less be inevitable. As production increased with scientific management techniques in both capitalism and state socialism, he ignored the inevitable increase in workers' alienation (OL 148ff.). Of crucial importance, he left unexplained the phenomenon of war which had so many times derailed workers' movements in the past.

Following Luxemburg's lead, Weil understood a materialist rethinking of socialism not as a dogmatic theory but as a "method of understanding and action" (OL 45). She, too, understood materialism as a study without false hopes or theoretical investment that isolates concrete mechanisms behind events. If, in all industrial production, no matter who owns productive property, there is oppression of workers, then the private ownership whose abolition is to be the key to Marxist liberation cannot be the mechanism that produces oppression. Instead industrial production itself may require a split between managers and workers and a further split between scientific theory and techniques administered by managers which results in alienated labor. If the mechanisms of oppression are inherent in industrial production; if there is, in fact, a contradiction between advanced production and liberation, then a communist revolution may make workers' lives worse and not better. The only way a socialist utopia can be projected is by imagining a technological advance which allows the total abolition of work, a recourse to which Marx often reverted. But, Weil argued, there is absolutely no reason to think that such a utopian advance is possible. As energy and raw materials become scarce, even more work may be required (OL 46–7).

Marx had only produced a more dangerous version of the economic rationalism which places capitalist production at the very center of history and human life (OL 68). Capitalist economics does not deny the existence of spheres of human activity other than the economic; when a worker finishes work, she can retreat to her family, go to church, appreciate art, activities that are separate from economic production. In the new Marxist version of political economy, there is nothing but economics, nothing but class struggle. Culture and art are superstructure, epiphenomena of economic organization, and so subject to state control. Politics as a study of just and legitimate institutions disappears and Marxism develops no categories adequate to an understanding of the similarities between Stalin's totalitarian state socialism and Hitler's Fascism. Using the universal explanation of "class struggle," Marxists can only say that Fascism is "degenerate capitalism" and Stalin's Russia is "a deformed worker's state" (OL 8).

That *malheur* would continue to cripple human lives was a possibility that Weil forced herself to face without false hopes. Much as she mourned the uprooting and dehumanization of industrial development, like Luxemburg she was never tempted to think that return to a more primitive form of economy is possible. If the only nonoppressive economies are at a low level of development, this does not mean that it is possible to go back to hunting and gathering or to handcraft. The economic skills necessary have been lost; the natural environment has been altered; without industrial production survival is no longer possible. Instead, Weil urged, what is required is thought, thought that goes deeper than either political theory or economic science to how we relate to and have knowledge of the physical world.

Luxemburg discovered technical difficulties in Marxist economics; she had not penetrated to the core of economist belief. In both Marxist and capitalist economics, "production" is taken as an elemental fact of human existence; in productive activity men and women engage in a struggle against nature to survive. History is economic history, regulated by an adversarial relation between "man" and "nature." All history leads up to a final victory of "man" as he masters that nature. As Marx put it:

> [Nature] at first confronts men as a completely alien force, with which men's relations are purely animal and by which they are overawed like beasts.
> Labour is, in the first place, a process in which both man and nature participate, and in which man of his own accord starts, regulates, and controls the material re-actions between himself and nature. He opposes himself to Nature. . . .[7]

In the course of this "historic" struggle, the economist account continues, some men inevitably grasp control of the means to the mastery of nature by asserting ownership of resources, tools, and methods, which gives to them the power to either increase productive capabilities for the benefit of all—as the capitalist would claim—or exploit others—as Marx would claim.[8]

Weil did not make the same economist assumptions. She described the origins of oppression differently. In the simplest imaginable forms of life, women and men are driven by natural necessity in the form of raw physical need and dependence on observation of nature. In all human cultures, there are simple tools and skills that allow a worker to establish a methodical relation with nature and an equilibrium with natural forces. As production becomes more complex, reserves are stored and indirect methods devised which require forethought and coordination. Natural necessity continues to assert itself, but in the need for direction. Necessity is expressed, not immediately, as when a sailor, pressed by the wind, trims her sail, but indirectly, through the imposition of force exerted by those with knowledge on workers who are told what they *must* do to accomplish certain results (OL 62–3). Although direction is not itself oppressive, it creates a further condition for oppression in the form of privilege, of priests who control the access to divinity, of a military that controls weaponry, of scientists who claim special inaccessible technical knowledge. But even this privilege is not necessarily oppressive; it becomes oppressive when it initiates a drive for power.

Weil did not locate the source of oppressive power in the private ownership of means of production which a Marxist revolution and a change to communal ownership can eliminate. Ownership, she observed, need not be oppressive any more than a religious priesthood need be; ownership can be based on a duty of stewardship and responsibility to others and not on exploitation. Instead, oppression has its source in a phenomenon rooted more deeply in human life than property rights: force exerted by one person against another, force that takes the form of power over that other. Even where there is no private ownership, even where property is held collectively, force can be exercised (OL 65).

A Natural Law of Power

After Luxemburg's death, two versions of socialism predominated— on the one hand, a liberal hope, inherited from reformers like Bernstein, that capitalism can be supplemented by laws and institutions that provide areas of freedom from oppressive power; on the other, a more radical Marxist-Leninism that understands oppressive power as a secondary phenomenon which will disappear in a communist takeover of state power. From a Weilian perspective, both versions mistake the place of power in human life. In the one case, power is ignored in favor of superficial civil liberties. In the other, power becomes a function of ownership. In both cases, the deep roots of oppression in natural life are not acknowledged. Power, Weil argued in

Oppression and Liberty, has an expansionist dynamic independent of any form of production or ownership.

Luxemburg had shown that the economic models on which both capitalist and Marxist theory are based fail to capture economic reality: to survive, capital must constantly look for new international markets and sources of cheap raw materials. But she did not explain what it is that drives on that relentless and often violent expansion. It cannot be the acquiring of more personal wealth, because for capital to be accumulated, profits cannot go to consumption. Weil provided the missing theory of power. Capitalists, like all humans, are subject to natural law: those who have power will try to expand that power. The drive toward greater and greater monopolies of resources and markets is not for profits only, but goes on beyond the point where profits have any utility. Given this expansionist drive to more power, there is no reason to think that when ownership of the means of production is no longer in private hands, state managers will not want to increase their power. Power has a momentum that need not be progressive, that may have no productive utility at all, that may lead in extreme cases to the destruction of the means of production as well as the destruction of those in power. Like Luxemburg's prediction of ethnic violence, Weil's analysis of power was prophetic of the excesses of state socialism in the Soviet Union. Not only did party officials manage for their own gain; in their drive for power they persisted to the point of environmental crisis and economic breakdown.

In the primitive balance achieved between a preindustrial worker and nature, there is stability. "The wind consents to guide to her destination the same ship which it would have sent off course if sails and rudder had not been properly adjusted" (OL 66–7). Nature does not "defend itself" against other "rules"; when a worker levers a stone, it stays in its new position; a kind of pact between worker and matter is kept in which the worker respects the natural weight of the stone and the stone yields to physics (OL 65). But when this direct thoughtful contact between worker and material is replaced by the rule of one person over another, the limit and balance inherent in natural necessity is in danger of being lost. Those in power are never secure; always there is the possibility of rebellion or dissent among those they direct and there is no limit to the force they feel called upon to exercise. To preserve and protect itself, power must always expand to become more ruthless, more excessive. Because the balance between powerful and powerless is always precarious and threatened with "an irremediable disequilibrium which is continually aggravating itself," power's drive for self-preservation has no limits (OL 67).

Those with power are driven to increase that power. A manager wants to manage more, a director to direct more, a governor to govern more (OL 16). At the same time, the instruments for the exercise of power are necessarily limited. A surplus must be produced so that those who are managed, exploited, and controlled survive; many of the power-hungry neglect this elementary fact, which shows how independent even of self-interest is the drive for power. The exercise of power must be personal, but as the empire of the capitalist, colonialist, or state manager is extended, his distance from those he controls, and therefore his ability to control, decreases; power always ends by going beyond its natural limits. What sets the boundary beyond which power will not aspire to go is not self-interest, or the threat of revolution, or the possibility of famine and economic collapse, but the fact that rulers will inevitably overextend themselves. The destruction of the empire comes not in revolution but in decay, as personal control weakens. In the meantime, people are destroyed, in wars and famines, by disease and exhaustion (OL 70ff). From the vantage point of Europe between wars, Weil saw little reason to have faith in inevitable historical progress; instead, she saw the grinding down of human beings in regime after regime, corporate, state, imperial, colonial.

Reforms and alterations may be instituted. Capitalists may manage the economy so that bankruptcies and recessions are less frequent, or institute welfare programs to alleviate poverty. Communist states may try to decentralize administration to increase efficiency or make production more responsive to needs. All of these reformist initiatives, in Weil's analysis, will have limited success. Men in power will not give it up; once in control they will be driven to extend their control beyond utility, even beyond their own desire for personal wealth or honor. They will be willing to ruin countries, populaces, even risk their own death, for more power. There will be accidents, spills, meltdowns, poisonings, reckless destruction of the environment. If history and human affairs were ordered by Adam Smith's invisible hand, which guarantees that production will move forward to greater and greater mastery of nature, it might be assumed that things will work out for the best: capitalist managers will correctly calculate their profit margins; socialist managers will plan the economy to be its most efficient; workers will obey orders. Without that invisible hand and without the Marxist faith in history a drive for power operates apart from any rational private or public calculation of utility and there is no assurance that development will be for any human good.

The exercise of oppressive and destructive power by men has been a primary topic in feminist philosophy, but the focus has been less on the dynamics of power itself than on its masculine identification.

Liberal feminists locate power in laws passed by men that discriminate against women. Marxist feminists cite men's co-option of the means of production; radical feminists blame men's aggressive masculine instincts. From none of these analyses, however, has came a completely successful feminist politics. Nondiscriminatory laws are circumvented. Socialist managers gain more oppressive power than their capitalist counterparts. Separatist enclaves of radical feminists are marginalized and threatened by the prejudices of the larger community. On a Weilian analysis, gender coding that reserves power for men and exempts women from its exercise may be a way to ensure the survival of the fabric of human life. While men are destroying each other in war and commerce, women at home preserve some semblance of human life.

In Weil's account of power, force is deep in human life, deep in the masculinist Western culture founded in the Greek and Roman empires, deep in the European-North American civilization that thrived on slave and industrial labor to become the repository of most of the world's productive wealth. In 1939, with the Germans on the move towards France, Weil translated the *Iliad*, Homer's epic account of the Trojan war; "*La poéme de la force*," as she called it. She saw in the warring factions of the *Iliad* not legendary heroes of Greek myth, not glorious warriors defending the honor of noble leaders, but the inexorable crushing power of force in human affairs: mutilated corpses, bodies dragged in the dust, a young wife raped, children taken in slavery, the contempt of victors for their captives. Just as did her contemporary, Jean Giraudoux, in his allegorical play, *La Guerre de Troie n'aura pas lieu* (The Trojan War will not take place), she tacitly compared the coming violence in Europe to the ten-year-long massacres of the Trojan War and the triumphant Greeks.

> Those who possess "la force" walk in a non-resistant milieu, as if nothing in the human material around them, or in nature, could raise [*susciter*] between the urge and the action that brief interval where thought lives. (SG 21)

In that brief interval of thought, mercy or justice might have intervened, but successful conquerors are immune. They act brutally, insanely; the sight of a suppliant only moves them to further cruelties. Any moderation is weakness; the temptation to excess is irresistible. War, the most deadly form of the drive for power, is played like a game. Possessed by power, men give up all desire to live, are incapable of mercy, blind and dumb to suffering, until finally there is an inferno of destruction. The horrors multiply. Inevitably the victors go beyond the force they can command and are crushed themselves.

Weil admired the bitterness of Homer's tone at the very dawn of the West, the tragic light the *Iliad* cast over the carnage, a tone that put into sharp relief the false optimism of socialist revolutionary theory. Given the dynamics of power, those who have it can seldom give it up, and no overturn of power relations can insure that it will disappear. In many cases, force is only defeated by itself, in an inevitable process of over-reaching in which not only lives but also living environments are irrevocably lost. The problem, for Weil, is not so much to identify the sex or race who exercise power, as it is to find the point at which its deadly automatism can be interrupted.

Liberation

Although feminist philosophers have developed powerful critiques of traditional social philosophy, the vision of a future liberated society has been more illusive. Either remedial measures are left vague, or feminist goals are redefined within established philosophical frameworks such as liberalism or Marxism. Novels such as Charlotte Perkins Gilman's *Herland* or Monique Wittig's *Les guérillères* describe visionary and surreal utopias in which women rule, but in real life feminist demands have more often been defensive or reactive: rights to abortion against the religious right, state-provided services against liberal property rights, freedom of sexual expression against compulsory heterosexuality. Weil's analysis of the problem goes deeper than gender to the very conditions of work in industrialized economies. Laws can be passed that give a woman equal rights, work conditions can be improved, women may be allowed freely to choose sexual objects and sexual identities, but if a woman is not able to think about what she is doing, understand its purpose, grasp how it is coordinated with others' activity, she is carried along in currents over which she has no control. If, on the other hand, she is able to work thoughtfully, knowing what she is doing and why, she has the sense of self and reality that allows her to make progress in the world with others. Without thoughtful work, a woman's equality with men or her sharing of their power may only make her situation worse.

Much of the work reserved for women in modern economies has been of a particularly thoughtless kind. As Weil noted, in the work force women suffer a double oppression; they are oppressed as workers, and they are oppressed as women. Invisible but often unsurmountable barriers restrict women's work to subordinate tasks, and rule out promotions and advancements that are available to men.

Responsibilities at home restrict women to interrupted or part-time work. Sexual stereotypes steer them into low-paid service jobs. The key, for Weil, is not the masculinity of their managers or bosses, but the privilege exercised by men that turns the direction necessary in any complex human endeavor into an exercise of force. If that privilege and that power can be addressed and neutralized, the situation of working women and men would change. Men's privilege to direct and manage has typically taken the form of a claim to know: the foreman knows techniques, the manager knows organization, the scientist knows what is true about reality. But if that distance between command and execution and between theory and command can be bridged, and if work is performed not as an automaton obeys commands but thoughtfully and consciously, the liberation of labor promised in socialist theory might be possible.

Luxemburg believed that socialist theory and judgement could be generated from the standpoint of working people, but she neglected the actual experience of industrial work. Obeying orders, crushed in spirit, numbed by fears of unemployment, workers may not be capable of political activism. Can a worker in nuclear energy understand the principles by which her work is ordered? Can a worker in a chemical company understand the properties and medical effects of the drugs she produces? Can a clerk who files forms understand the complexities of computer programming? If the answer is no, workers in both socialist states and capitalist states will continue to go through motions prescribed by those who command knowledge and science. The ultimate source of oppressive power is not in any class, gender, or racial ideology, but in modern production methods, driven by science and technology, that provide the material basis for capitalist and socialist economies. The problem, Weil realized, is not just political or economic; it is in science itself, the science dreamed by the first modern philosopher, Descartes, the science that Marx took as the model for his nonutopian socialism, the science whose truth, in the modern period, has become the primary, and sometimes the only concern, of professional philosophy.

2. Meditations on First Philosophy

Cartesian Beginnings

To many philosophers, especially those in English-speaking countries, politics and philosophy are only tangentially related. Questions of meaning, truth, and knowledge are taken as independent of interests in "softer" areas of ethics and social theory. Weil's interest in

philosophy was personal, political, and theoretical. As early as childhood, the inaccessibility of modern science and mathematics to ordinary understanding worried her, as she began to fear that her brother,
on his way to becoming a brilliant mathematician, was working in
areas beyond her comprehension. Her concern deepened as she involved herself in workers' causes and sharpened as she studied the
history of philosophy.

For her graduate thesis, she took as her topic what she identified
as the historical source of the contemporary problem of knowledge:
the modern, seventeenth-century, Cartesian philosophy which replaced the natural philosophy of the medieval Catholic church. An
Aristotelian physics of substances with inherent form and essences,
declared as dogma by the church, was consistent with preindustrial
production methods in which a craftsworker is a free agent striving
to realize the natural potentialities of her materials. In contrast, the
Galilean physics of force and mass which inspired Descartes's rationalism is a science of industrial development. No longer are natural
qualities to be respected, enhanced, and utilized; in Descartes's new
philosophy the material world is understood as a field of forces to be
plotted and measured in mathematical formulas. Struggling to lift
the weight of religious censorship from the mechanistic science that
he believed would enhance human life, Descartes proposed a method
of radical doubt. He would forget all he learned from his Jesuit teachers, he would ignore the evidence of his senses, he would rebuild
knowledge from the firm foundations of mathematical science.

The questions asked by Weil about this very much discussed and
celebrated moment in the history of philosophy were not the usual
philosophers' questions: is Descartes's logic valid? Can an independent mind and body interact? How can the truths of science be verified
if there are no clear and distinct ideas written on the mind by God?
Weil raised questions directly related to her social concerns. Was this
new science to be accessible only to an elite few? Had it been ordained
at the very beginnings of modernity that workers will not understand
what they are doing? Her concern was not the antinomies that have
dominated contemporary post-Cartesian philosophy, nor was it the
ensuing crises of identity as philosophers struggled to define a role
for themselves as defenders of scientific reason. Weil started from
what she took as the "most important question of our time": "Whether
I should make the conduct of my life subject to the authority of
scientific thinking, or solely to the light of my own reason," or as she
put it in other words, "Will science bring me liberty or chains?"
(FW 32).

As working method became more automated and more mechanical, science had moved further and further away from common under-standing, and shared perceptual space with Einsteinian relativity, non-Euclidean geometries, and quantum mechanics. At stake, for Weil, was not the logic of the claims of science to truth, nor was it defining the proper and limited role of philosophy; it was the link she was beginning to see between the possibility of social liberation and scientific knowledge. If the key to liberation is thoughtful work, and science makes thoughtful work impossible, no significant change in the human condition is possible without a reworking of knowledge at the most fundamental of levels.[9]

Weil's approach to Descartes, the founder of modern theory of knowledge, was similar to Luxemburg's approach to Marx. Weil read Descartes as a man struggling with a serious and important problem. Her Descartes is not the textbook rationalist of the traditional philoso-phy curriculum, eventual target for empiricist refutation, nor is he the hero who rescued philosophy from mysticism and dogmatism. He is a man thinking in a problematic historical situation, a situation that we continue to share in the twentieth century, half in the ruins of Descartes's Catholic Europe and half in science's brave new world of the future. Rather than isolate logically consistent doctrines that Descartes believed or should have believed, rather than exposing logi-cal contradictions, Weil paid attention to inconsistencies where, in her view, Descartes's thought and indeed any thought is located, inconsistencies which mark the stress lines of the continuing problem of modern science's inaccessibility to ordinary understanding.

In Descartes, Weil found conflicting tendencies. Descartes rejected the evidence of ordinary perception as unreliable, but he also referred to the work of lensmakers and seamstresses, sometimes even sug-gesting that it is workers themselves who must test the validity of scientific theories. Descartes insisted that the only beginning point for knowledge is clear and distinct rational ideas, but he also claimed that the point of understanding nature is to put it to use in workshops and studios. Descartes argued that only mathematics has the clarity and distinctness necessary for science, but he published the practical results of his scientific work in the vernacular and laid out clearly and distinctly why a proposition has to be true in proofs supposedly graspable by any woman or man who thinks and concentrates. Al-though Descartes rejected simple, possibly illusory, sensory percep-tion, he continued to speak in terms of ordinary spacial imagination and the extension of physical bodies.

But Weil was not content to simply mark out unresolved tensions in Descartes's thought. Descartes had resolved to make knowledge scientific by eliminating all that is doubtful, and beginning only with what he could know with certainty. What if she repeated the exercise? What if she tried the Cartesian experiment again, refusing to believe anything which is not certain, trusting only to her own clear and distinct understanding. If Descartes had not succeeded in doubting all that can be doubted, there might be other versions of modernity, other ways of thinking about science, not as an authoritative system of signs removed from human life and working experience, but as integrated methods of human practice.

Through all the tortured and not always intelligible turnings of Weil's youthful neo-Meditations, certain crucial differences between her "first philosophy" and Descartes's come clear, differences which suggest nothing less than an alternative starting point for modern thought. Descartes's final answer to the question, "what is it that I cannot doubt?" is "I cannot doubt that I exist as a thing that thinks"; I may be able to doubt that I exist as a body or as a man, but not that I exist as an autonomous mental substance. This Weil rejected. The primal sense of self to which she returns, the bedrock of experience to which her radical doubt reduces her, is not private mental activity or autonomous self-consciousness, but the fact that "we are living beings" in the world, subject to external forces that are subject to us in turn and can cause us either pleasure or pain. For Weil there is no primal privacy or consciousness. I may be weary, for example, but this is not a private sensation; "my weariness makes itself known to me in the form of a weight that is oppressive and ground which is slippery" (FW 56). Descartes's "idea" that body is separate from mind and that mind can exist apart from body is not "clear and distinct" as Descartes claimed. To speak of private mental objects that may or may not be marks, or effects, or images of physical objects is already to go beyond what we know and experience. What we know is human existence, an existence which is always a reciprocal interaction between body and world. I can only come to know the world as I physically encounter its resistance, as I move against it.

Descartes is often credited with inventing the modern "subject" as an autonomous consciousness, detached from the passive objects of knowledge. In the late twentieth century, this subject has been the object of many critiques. Continental postmodernists have claimed that it exemplifies the imperialism of Western culture; feminists have claimed it is gender specific; psychoanalysts have seen it as the victim of escapist fantasies of domination and unity. Weil does not criticize or undermine the certainty of Descartes's modern consciousness, so much as she replaces it in an alternative narrative of primary being-in-the-world. In her "first philosophy," in the place of Descartes's thinking thing is a new, embodied, modern person, neither escapist nor dominating but in realistic and methodical interaction with the physical world.

For Weil, there is no primal experience of detached mental consciousness. In the most private of thoughts, a person moves against the resistance of what is external even if it is only her own appetites. Not even the ability to doubt and refuse assent is autonomous; here too, we work against the resistance of passions and desires. But if a knower is not separate from physical reality, as Descartes dreamed, how is knowledge possible? If a woman cannot step back into the privacy and autonomy of her mind, how can she grasp reality, get hold of it? Weil, like Descartes, looked for something that cannot be doubted, but her indubitable beginning is not Descartes's "I think, therefore I am." It is "je puis, donc je suis" (I can, therefore I am).[10] Even Descartes's doubt is not something a man thinks about a idea, it is something he does against his inclinations, prejudices, bodily instincts, just as he *can* assent or refuse to assent to ideas and beliefs. Like any other human action, doubt is conditioned by the natural world.

Weil's "I can" does not constitute knowledge any more than did Descartes's "I think." All can still be illusion. Even apparent physical successes might be illusory. But unlike Descartes, Weil was not willing, at this crucial point in her meditations, to fall back on the certainty of a script of clear and distinct ideas provided by God. Instead, she returns to human experience; she will "read in the feeling of my own existence, in its coloring of pleasure and pain, its clothing of appearances and illusions, only the obstacle submitted to and overcome" (FW 64). Knowledge is not a passive possession or recording of an idea, stamped on the mind by any agency. There is no autonomous consciousness imprinted either by sensation or by God. Knowledge is the grasp a human being has on the world when she is able to take hold of a reality external to herself. Whether that reality is a physical thing, her own feelings, or her own action, it is something she acquires little by little as she lives in the world. A constant "intersection between mind and body" constitutes human existence. Not only is any separation between mind and body not "clear and distinct," as Descartes claimed, Weil cannot even imagine such a separation. If you try to separate mind and body, you find you must attribute to one the qualities of the other; you see passions in the world and things in the mind.

In other writings, Weil applied these insights to later versions of modernity, such as Kant's philosophical categories of transcendental reason, supposedly prior to all experience or activity: space, time, extension, matter, causation. These too, she argued, cannot be conceived apart from physical work (O 329–331). In spontaneous animal activity, there is no "matter"; action is an immediate expression of appetite. Only when a human being puts herself consciously against the resistance of material reality does she have the idea of matter as a distance between desire and its gratification. Similarly, the idea of "time" is impossible without working method. An animal's activity is not in time; time is the schema by which a series of actions is plotted. Kant's universal "natural law" is a way of speaking about restrictions imposed on desires and projects. When primitive people think that an action has an immediate effect on matter, this is magic. "All sorts of mysterious caprices, at whose mercy they believe themselves to be, henceforth interpose themselves in the manner of a screen" (OL 90). The idea of "nature" as an inert substance governed by natural law comes when an intermediate series of actions toward a desired effect, ordered according to necessity, is imagined and implemented. To achieve an effect, we *must* do this, and this; and in this order, this "must," for Weil, is the substance of natural necessity, not essences embedded in nature, or ideas imprinted on the mind, or the necessary structure of consciousness. "A paralyzed man could not give the idea of a natural law of nature" (O 378). The idea of "causality" is derived from the breaking down of tasks like shelling peas into their component ordered "events."

Painstakingly, Weil separated out the strands of Kant's critical reason. Kant's transcendental categories *are* the most general of conceptions and without them knowledge is impossible, *but* Kant's mistake was to think that time, extension, quantity, substance, "are imposed in advance on each of the projects that I can undertake, before I would wish to accomplish them by such and such work." This, Weil said, is "way too abstract" (O 329); there is no pure reason before or outside human activity. Empty abstractions do not advance understanding. When it is understood that general categories of space and time are inherent in work, however, it is clear that each category must be analyzed separately to bring out the specific way it informs methodical activity. Kant was right that reality is conformity with the "laws of reason," but laws of reason are not detached ideas; they are embodied in thoughtful productive activity.

In the accounts of philosophers, the modern scientific mind, imprinted by God or imbued with pure reason, detached itself from the natural world. Sovereign and autonomous, it entertained an illusion of rule over physical things and over the physical bodies robbed of thought who would carry out the manipulations it prescribes. But how is a grasp on reality possible if human beings are always in reciprocal relation to the natural world? How is it possible to break out of an endless flow of reaction and counterreaction? Mathematics, Weil agreed with Descartes, is the answer, but her mathematics is not Descartes's mathematics. For Descartes, innate mathematical ideas are imprinted on minds by God as the guide to a reality inaccessible to the senses. For Weil, numbering is the form of methodical encounters with the world. If its basis is divine, it is not because it is a copy of the writing of an all-powerful god. It is divine in the sense that methodical work is possible; human aspiration "can" make a way in the world. Numbering opens the passage to the world, allowing orderly progression in actions and work, and a measuring of activity.

Mathematics, mathematical sciences, and related fields such as computer science have been persistently unfriendly to women, closing off important sources of privilege and power in the form of jobs in technology and research. Recent feminist theory has explained this phenomenon in various ways: outright discrimination and prejudice have kept women out of science; sexist metaphors have identified the scientist as the male master of a feminized nature; scientific research is designed along the lines of preconceived notions of sexual difference. Again Weil took no notice of the fact that those who do mathematics and philosophize about it are predominately men; what she does offer is a positive theory of a mathematics and science in which women might participate fully. If the reason for many women's failure in mathematics is neither a feminine lack of ability nor a masculine refusal to grant equality, but the fact that women have found little interest in Descartes's script of representations removed from sensuous experience, Weil's mathematical sciences, rigorous and technical like Descartes's, but understood as paths of human activity in the world, might be of vital interest to women who are concerned with health, the environment, work conditions, and peace.

Mathematics as Method

The status of mathematical objects has been passionately debated in Western philosophy since Plato claimed mathematics as the highest form of knowledge and the proper preparation for philosophic reason. His followers have claimed that numbers are super-real ideal forms. Phenomenologists have claimed that numbers are perceptual essences; positivists have derived numbers from sense data; logicians tried to generate numbers from elementary logical principles; pragmatists have seen in mathematics useful devices; conventionalists have understood mathematical reasoning as forms of behavior arbitrarily constituted by rule. Weil accepted none of these philosophical accounts.

Certainly, she rejected the notion that there are transcendent mathematical objects. But numbering cannot come from a retrospective, empiricist tallying of perceptions either. "Sensations" are not passive data, a screen between a thinker and the physical world, but "intermediaries" for grasping work (FW 79). Phenomenological essences claimed by continental philosophers as inherent in consciousness are no more realistic. When the world is "bracketed" out so that there is no longer an interest in it, the possibility of contact with reality and therefore the possibility of knowledge disappears. Even pragmatism, closest to Weil's view, remains within the problematic inherited from Descartes: if Descartes's God is not available to guarantee that ideas are true, ideas must be validated in practice, according to standard methods of scientific verification. But for Weil the truth of a mathematical theory is not established in a practical test—such a test, if it is within the compass of the ways-of-acting-on-the-world of the theory, is bound to be self-validating. Ways in the world will inevitably cross, recross, and be at cross-purposes, and theories will have to be adjusted, but the judgment that makes this adjustment possible cannot be based on any "verification" detached from human life. The idea that there is a truth corresponding to human will that exists separately from manipulatable physical reality is as illusory as Descartes's clear and distinct ideas. We make a way in the world; values, desires, and ideas are formed in that interaction. For Weil, neither the will to enjoy or use an object, nor the drive to insure survival can stand in for the missing theological text. Use and enjoyment, subject to the destructive dynamics of power, are themselves paths to be negotiated.[11]

The alternate attempt to give mathematics logical grounding, which has been the basis for much professional philosophizing in Britain and North America, would be even more misguided from Weil's perspective. Any attempt to give mathematics foundations independent of human experience radically mistakes the nature of mathematics. Nor would she adopt the Wittgensteinian conventionalism which, once the transcendental necessity of logic is rejected, seemed, to many philosophers, the only alternative. Because mathematics is the result of the world's impact on us as well as of our impact on it, mathematics is a real grasp of reality. We cannot change the rules and produce another reality as we could another convention. Mathematics is the form of actions in the world that *must* be in a certain order. Whatever a woman constructs and imagines, the world as it necessarily is is already in her thoughts. If a craftswoman makes a table, she contributes to the design, but when she reviews the actual steps by which she will make it, she comes up against reality in the fact that she can not accomplish the design in any other way (O 231).

Perhaps Weil's view is closest to that of mathematicians themselves, who have tended to insist—at least until the discovery of non-Euclidean geometries in the nineteenth century—that mathematics rests on a bedrock of geometrical intuition.[12] But Weil's mathematician does not "intuit" an idea; she imagines abstract forms of actions in the world, the origins of which are forms of simple kinds of human work. Weil gives the example of a shepherd. He wants to feed his flock, giving each animal a ration of grain. In order to do this, he feeds them methodically one by one, so that to his left the sheep have been fed, and to his right they have not. Inherent in this work is the idea of a series or a succession and of a range of countable objects. When it comes to the point that we need to deal in the same way with objects we cannot physically move around, we begin to use numbers proper. Numbering allows a grasp of reality beyond a physical grasp, but in the physical grasp of the shepherd is already the idea of a series of numbers (O 237ff.). Weil reviews some of the specific kinds of simple actions related to elementary mathematical concepts. The straight line means we can make a line in the world by adding one action to another. To count is to know how to walk, to take one step after another. In geometry, new concepts open the world to action; as I pull at a line, a new form, a circle, results, and a new kind of action. The continued resistance of the world allows additional figures to be formed (FW 74–5).

Positivism, mathematical realism, conventionalism all have been ways philosophers have tried to solve the epistemological problems that result from Descartes's conception of a mathematical science whose validity is independent of ordinary human experience. Do clear and distinct mathematical representations describe reality? Are there mathematical objects? Do numbers exist? In Weil's view, these questions cannot be asked in the way philosophers have asked them. There is no objective reality, if that means a reality separate from human experience and action, but this does not mean that there is only an ideal reality. Neither exist. What is real is concrete interactions between the world and human agents. In those interactions both person and world act and are acted upon. To ask the questions: how can ideas match reality? or do mathematical expressions name real objects? is already to assume a dualism which, for Weil, never exists. Human experience is not of objective material reality on the one hand and, on the other, subjective thought which may or may not correspond with that reality.

Weil's neo-Cartesianism is Cartesian in that, for her, knowledge is mathematical at its very deepest roots. But her understanding of mathematics is not in the tradition of modern philosophy as it was passed on from Descartes. If Descartes's certain knowledge of mathematical physics laid the groundwork for the separation of theoretical knowledge from manual labor, and consequently for the inaccessibility of science to common understanding, it also set the terms of philosophical debate in the modern period, as thinkers attempted to solve problems resulting from that separation. Once philosophers begin to doubt that they can prove, as Descartes thought he could, that God exists to guarantee that clear and distinct mathematical and scientific ideas are not illusory, then the objective truth of mathematics and mathematical science is immediately called into question. Knowledge becomes the "*problem* of knowledge," a problem which drives philosophical inquiry in the modern period from Cartesian rationalism, to British empiricism, Kantian idealism, phenomenology, logical positivism, scientific realism and on to ever-increasing technicality and isolation from the real world of work and experience.

Weil's inquiry into modern science is differently motivated and different in form. There is no question of a choice, as it is often laid out in philosophy, between some version of objectivism and some version of subjectivism. For Weil, both are fictions that do not capture the fact of human experience, that we and the world act on each other. We may have, for example, the feeling that time is an independent "course of the world," that it exists separately from and independently of our efforts; without effort, however, without methodical work, we would have no conception of time at all. It would be equally wrong to say that time is a "course of the spirit," because spirit without effort is in a timeless present. Time only comes into being in the reciprocal interaction between effort and material force (O 331). For this reason, neither objectivism—time exists independently of what I want or think of it—nor subjectivism—time is as I think it or perceive it—captures the quality of human experience. Even more important, as soon as the world is separated from anyone's idea of it, truth also becomes problematic. Rationalists argue that some ideas are self-evident; the problem becomes how to distinguish objective validity from fallible certainty.[13] Positivists argue that there is no extrasensory source of truth, so propositions must be verified by sense impressions; the problem becomes how to define sense data in such a way that they are not tainted with subjectivity.[14] Kantians argue that the necessary structure of understanding has transcendental objectivity; contact with other cultures immediately suggests the possibility of other equally valid ways of seeing the world.[15] Scientific realists argue that scientific theories are true when verified according to the methods of the current scientific establishment, but when methods change, the validity of science is undermined.[16] In this ongoing discussion, which makes up the history of philosophy in the modern period, the "sensuous activity" of women and men has disappeared; in its place are either the impressions of scientists making observations, structures of scientists' rational thought, or the necessary validity of scientists' procedures.

Beyond Representation

However mathematical science was validated by philosophers, it was understood, after Descartes, to be a representation of reality. A representational relation between the mind and its objects is assumed in the skeptical question that initiates modern philosophy: how do I know that my ideas are not caused by myself, an evil demon, or illusory perception? It continues to be assumed in philosophical epistemologies after Descartes, whether they are Kantian, empiricist, pragmatist, logicist, or functionalist. Ideas, or their linguistic counterparts, propositions, are "representations," scripts which must be validated, if not by God then in some other way. Descartes's warrant for the truth of the representations of science was theological. God guarantees knowledge by imprinting on the mind "clear and distinct" ideas; the knower's job is to restrict beliefs to what is written there. In the subsequent history of Western philosophy, as theological warrants had less and less credibility, the idea of a script was not abandoned. When confidence waned that there is a God who reliably imprints ideas on the human mind, the problem for philosophers was to find another authoritative script in associations of simple impressions, the innate structures of the mind, experiential essences, imprinted neurological patterns. In each case the same assumption is made: there must be something that correctly forms thought but is not dependent on thought. The impasse at which philosophers inevitably find themselves is that, in reality, there is nothing that can serve; representations are not imprinted on anyone's mind by sensation, or by God, or even by one's own imagination. If they were, we would have no reason to believe them. The result is that representations eventually stand alone, as in structuralist and poststructuralist theories of meaning. In the place of Descartes's divine script are conceptual and symbolic structures whose references are inscrutable and whose validity is internally generated.

In an alternative, Weilian, modern tradition, thinking is not "representation." I may represent to myself anything I like; someone else may represent to me anything they like. Because of its remove from reality, representation is always suspect and in need of verification. Because it has little to do with making a way in the world as an embodied person, it is cut off from reality. Weil's modern thought begins in contact with reality and involves a "constructing" which must proceed in a given way because of the nature of reality. This, Weil explains, is not a constructing in the sense that one builds a building from foundations up, but to "indicate the general possibility in a strong sense of a category of actions." It is not "to construct the manner something could be done in a world we represent to ourselves but (to construct) something which could be done in this world" (O 228–9). Philosophers may represent possible worlds in which matter is not indestructible, or where water has the same appearance but a different molecular structure, but they cannot conceive them or construct them. For Weil, when it is truth that is in question and not schema or representations, there is no way to go behind or beyond a science which is irrevocably incarnate, compromised by physical contact with reality, and implicated with desirous human action in the world. Even if some God, sensation, brain structure, linguistic structure, or other agency were found to provide an authoritative script for representation, what results would not be knowledge but the role-playing of an actor in a play.

A science that can grasp reality is not representation but projected forms of methodical actions. The most abstract science, the purest of mathematics, just as with the most advanced technology in so far as it has substance or meaning, are paths of human action in the world. Weil acknowledged that there is a difference between theory and practice. Even when a thinker has made a plan of action, it is usually impossible, unless action is very simple, to have the whole theory always in mind while she works. In complex actions movements are broken down, and she concentrates on accomplishing one particular set without thinking of the theory behind the whole (OL 91–3). Similarly, in theoretical work, often there are mechanical subproblems to solve. A mathematician or scientist may need to learn to handle signs like tokens with no thought to what they mean. Science accumulates such ready-made sequences of signs which are accepted by researchers without question. These normal and necessary mechanizations of thought, once they are detached from the substance of actual thought in reciprocal relation with reality, can dangerously proliferate. Weil foresaw the "calculating machines" that might one day replace thought, as well as the possibility of a disutopia in which no one thinks about what they are doing. At this point, at which there is nothing but representation, reference becomes a relation between signs, and logical semantics replaces theory. Signs are manipulated as elements related only to each other, marks on paper—signifiers—that represent only their own reflections—signifieds.

Eventually, no matter how representational symbolic structures are mapped, remapped, unmapped, there will be no way to anchor them in any reality, an admission made explicit in postmodern philosophies. The supercerebral constructions of linguistic, discursive, rhetorical structures which have replaced the empiricism and pragmatism of the eighteenth and nineteenth centuries signal that action and theory have moved irrevocably apart. As Weil prophetically described it:

> The relation of the sign to the thing signified is being destroyed, the game of exchanges between signs is being multiplied of itself and for itself. And the increasing complication demands that there should be signs for signs. (GG 139)

Thought no longer has grounding in "the concrete terms of the relationship between effort and result of effort." There are, as Weil says "too many intermediaries" (GG 139). Removed from reality, the mind turns back on itself in endless, repetitive, ultimately meaningless movements of reflexivity.

Like any theory or method, Cartesian rationalism plotted a project in the world, a project that was transmitted both to philosophers of science and to scientific practice in the modern period. Modern science followed Descartes's "Rules of Method." Stacks of journals, mountains of articles, inscrutable formulas incomprehensible to nonscientists, are separated from human activities. In schools and universities science is textbook science, not taught as a series of ordered actions in the world, but as popularized versions of the truth about a hidden reality represented in a mathematical notation that maps occult objects. Nor does the pure mathematician in her research center supported by the Defense Department dwell on the relation between her equations and military technology. The charge that Weil brings against this supposedly "pure," value-free, and objective Cartesian science is not that it does not exist or even that it is morally irresponsible. More simply, it is self-deceiving. The pure mathematician or scientist does not understand the nature of her knowledge. No matter what illusion is maintained of the autonomy of thought, as the pure scientist works her equations, she is plotting possible ways of action in the world. Working without the burden of knowing what she is doing, her representations further whatever ends those in power conceive. Once theory loses its roots in reality, it can plot any action, no matter how useless, evil, or destructive. Once action is removed from thought, responsible action is no longer possible. Techniques multiply beyond the restraints of human aspiration, even beyond the physical necessity which may make them self-defeating.

The Thinking Body

To replace representational science, Weil developed in her philosophy lectures (*Lessons in Philosophy*) a new "materialist point of view." Weilian materialism is neither the materialism of the empiricist philosophers nor the materialism of Marx. She does not begin with the impinging of physical bodies on sense organs or with the "means of production," but consistent with her "first philosophy," with the living, thinking body, the ground of all experience in the world. The body thinks, Weil argued, even in its most physical reflexes. In responses to stimuli, the body classifies events and orders the world. In conditioned reflexes, the body responds to forms. These material processes are essential to learning and education, as are instincts, sexual or maternal, which are also reactions to forms or ideas. Perception, Weil argued, is never passive. Always it is associated with movement: with the movement of two eyes that together act as pincers to get a grip on the world; with the movement of the body as we move around what we want to see, and it moves around us. She used color as an example. We do not experience passively a red sense impression; instead we learn to make a series that has a use, we handle the colors, sort them, make a color spectrum.[17] Numbering is only a further advance in the method of action in the world, as we put one step ahead of another in a particular order.

In her analysis of embodied thought and thoughtful bodies, Weil reversed the order of traditional epistemology. Knowledge does not begin with particulars and then move by abstraction to universals. Instead, in bodily experience, a thinking woman begins from the general, from linkages and ratios discerned in the course of her actions. In so far as a thinker manages to remove herself from her body, as Descartes claimed is possible, distancing herself from her instincts and sensations and pretending to an illusory independence of thought, she is cut off from reliable meanings and valid inference. For Weil the universals between which inferences hold are no mysterious puzzle, as they have been so often in philosophy. We use concepts naturally because from the beginning we think in and respond to forms. Objects given in perception are not collections of atomized and passive sensations, but relations and ratios. Abstraction in language only strengthens a bodily ability to grasp the whole.

But if Weilian thought is embodied, how is it possible to be sure that the actions undertaken are the right ones? How are we to choose from various theories those that correctly map the world? Foundationalism, verifiability, mathematical realism, all are ways philosophers have tried to escape the unacceptable relativism that results when representational knowledge loses its original divine anchoring. Determining the truth must involve finding a substitute script in sensation, sense data, set theory to which theory can be compared. But in Weil's view, judgment on mathematical and scientific theories cannot be by comparison with any script. A question, such as is the viral theory of disease true? can be answered only in the course of medical practice on real physical bodies whose health or illness is a fact. Virology cannot be evaluated apart from the path virology takes in the world, for evil or good. It is not simply a question of whether a theory works, because it may work well enough for what is meant to do—kill viruses. But unrestrained treatment of disease by drugs may also suppress the body's immune system or encourage mutations of viruses resistant to treatment. In more general terms, neither bodies nor viruses may be grasped adequately in theories which treat them as machines. A reliable evaluation of the truth of the viral theory of disease cannot be made apart from those who work—apart from the health workers, nurses, physicians, patients who act and are acted upon. Validation of Weilian science is not in philosophical logic or in laboratory experimentation, but on the factory floor, in the power plant, the farm, the clinic, the household.

Weil's materialist philosophy is both a theory of knowledge and a social theory. It is an attempt to project what few socialists, including Luxemburg, imagined with any clarity: the liberation of work which is avowedly the aim of socialism. That liberation, for Weil, is not just enjoying a fair share of distributed goods, which might only subject women further to the tyranny of appetites and desires. Nor is it the power to mark along with men an image of Man's species-being on nature, an aggressive act which does not respect the equilibrium of methodical relations between human beings and the natural world, and which can end in rampant pollution and nuclear disaster.[18] Instead, a liberated woman is, as far as is possible, conscious of what she is doing, aware of the final aim of her work, cognizant of the ways her tasks are coordinated with others'.

Thought and actions are reunited—not as a superficial graft of worker benefits onto directed labor, or moral responsibility onto scientific research, but by bringing together those who work and those who theorize. Those who know are relieved of a false liberty of thought by coming to understand the concrete actions that they are plotting in the world. Those who work know what they are doing and can evaluate the results. Weil projected the ideal of a social transformation that involves not only a change of laws, or even of economic organization, but one that reworks the very texture of social life as it is lived by women and by men in high schools, universities, factories, hospitals, farms. Women cannot be cognizant of what they are doing in huge industrial complexes controlled by distant corporate managers. These would split into smaller, local, and sometimes rural, workshops with central assembly points where all workers take turns working. In support of production, science would be a concrete discipline in which researchers knowledgeable of applications and concerned for the quality of human life, work closely with actual spheres of production and service. Research facilities would be cooperatives of practitioners, scientists, and mathematicians.

The transformation in education Weil saw as required for such changes was massive. Current university education for an elite few who have the privileges of directive knowledge, and vocational training for the rest enriched with watered-down doses of "culture" is clearly inadequate. For Weil, such an educational system reflects the modern split between thought and programmed, thoughtless action. Instead, "It is as manual workers that workers have a right to education, first, because education is necessary so that their action be work, and second, because they alone are capable of giving to the ensemble of human thought, which up to now soars in another world, a kind of existence" (O 274). The current pedagogy, Weil thought, miserably fails by this standard. It enriches technical education by watering down to banality some supposedly timeless truths of Western culture, removed from material historical reality and therefore meaningless. Schools "shovel this garbage" into the masses at the same time as they teach obedience and the meaningless movements necessary for alienated manual or office labor in corporate complexes (NR 43–4). At the very best, general-education courses clear a little pocket of life, detached from work, for meditative thought.

Education should infuse the student's life and work with thought. To this end, Weil argued, education must be local and regional, rural schools having different curricula from city schools, introducing students to the rich literature of folklore and myth: Hesiod and Piers Plowman, for example, could be presented not as anachronistic puzzles but as poetry of rural life (NR 84); myth could be taught as giving meaning to agricultural labor. Teachers could work with the actual fabric of reproductive and social and productive life of the students' own region. Rather than teaching by rote, they would place themselves at the "center of a truth and possess it in all its nakedness"

(NR 65). Rather than drilling students on facts which can be memorized and forgotten, they would act as a "mode of transposition to people not familiar with culture" (ibid.).

Of crucial importance, thought Weil, is the teaching of mathematics and science. If the liberation of labor is to be possible, science must be demystified, taught with attention to the practical applications that make it intelligible, taught for what it is, a human grasp on reality, not as laboratory "experimental method" but with reference to the effects of technologies on the environment, on relations between persons, on concrete methods of production that involve environmental danger or bodily abuse to workers. It is not enough to supplement a medical curriculum with courses in medical ethics, or to inject a lecture on environmental concerns into a biology course. In a Weilian revolution, the very subject matter of the sciences is transformed so that scientific theory is understood as ways of acting in the world.

Weil envisioned a transformation of production and education in which working women and men become empowered agents, subject to the constraints of physical reality but free to determine the paths that they, their children, and their communities take in the world. She herself acknowledged the utopian nature of that vision. She described advanced capitalism moving in the opposite direction. Science becomes increasingly more abstract and inaccessible; production with the help of computers approaches complete mechanization; multinational corporations administer production on such a large scale that even their directors cannot know their various parts; the manipulation of global financial markets threatens catastrophic economic effects beyond the reach of any conceivable government regulation. Mechanisms control lives beyond any individual's understanding and control; the coordination of production and distribution is left to monetary manipulation; management is carried out by way of statistics and computer printouts; programs replace thought. In a world of fictions created by aggressive marketing of products and financial speculation, the drive for power in politics and commerce leads to massive corruption (OL 114–5). In such a situation, any such project of decentralization is "absurd" (OL 120).

But for Weil, existing fact is not all that there is. The problem, as she saw it, is to change facts, and for that it is necessary to find a fulcrum or point of tension from which to break into the apparatuses of scientific, economic, and political power. She agreed with Luxemburg that Marxism had lost its moral compass. Given her experience of industrial labor she could no longer rely on Luxemburg's working-class standpoint to provide it. Not only was it true, as Luxemburg had shown, that a profitable alliance between industrial workers and management can be made to exploit foreign workers. Weil added to this economic insight the fact of the sensuous experience of modern, industrial, corporate and service work. With depressions and recessions constantly threatening, with science and math understood as authoritative texts which dictate the movements of working people, masses of women and men are reduced to various degrees of *malheur*, apathy, and impotence. Where, then, is the compass that can find the lost path toward liberation, a compass based neither on the subjective, self-interested projections to which standpoint moralities, socialist or feminist, are always in danger of being reduced, nor on absolutes and universal principles in whose name violence can be done?

What is missing from social theory, Weil thought, is an aspect of reality lost back in the modernist split between mechanical nature and subjective desire: the ideal. Judged by the *ideal* of thoughtful, liberated labor, neither capitalism nor Communism is a desirable model; a craftsman in the Middle Ages or a fisherman in a traditional society may be better off than an assembly line worker in either a market- or state-controlled economy. Judged by the *ideal* of thoughtful labor, the industrial development forced on developing countries is no benefit. A society at a lesser level of growth measured in terms of commodity production, but in which work has meaning and dignity, may be more liberated and therefore preferable to a society in which there is a high rate of production for the international market.

But what can be the basis for an ideal if it is reference neither to physical fact nor to particular drives and appetites? How can an ideal be formulated so that it is neither an interested projection of desire nor a thing made into a dangerous absolute? To project a program of decentralization and workers' education as future technological or historical fact is to turn an ideal into a thing. To claim that any one economic or political system necessarily leads to human happiness is to mistake an ideal for a material situation in which good and bad must always be mixed. To complain that an ideal can never be completely realized is to mistake the status of an ideal as a point of aspiration. An ideal must be real and at the same time "a standard for the analysis and evaluation of actual social patterns" (OL 100). An ideal must point, not to a real state realizable in fact, but to a real measure by which to judge what is better or worse.

Weil's reflections on *Oppression and Liberty* ended with contradiction. On the one hand, blind mechanical forces grind down human beings; even the force exercised by those in power against those they subjugate is driven by a kind of automatism. On the other hand, it is also true that women and men are capable at times of disinterested acts of justice. In her early political writings, Weil made no attempt to reduce this contradiction between the brutal force of natural necessity and the possibility of justice. Such a contradiction meant that, as she put it, she had come up against what is real (OL 89). A philosophy that attempts to eliminate contradiction by constructing logical systems and reducing phenomena to schema "sets aside" the problem. To try to convince oneself that Stalinist repression, or Fascism, or the great depression were somehow good—to explain them away as necessary to the eventual triumph of socialism, the purification of the human race, or more efficient production—is to ignore the fact of evil. To argue conversely that goodness is a natural phenomena, like having a positive attitude or an instinct to avoid pain ignores the fact of goodness.[19] On occasion, people do sacrifice themselves for others, give without asking anything for themselves in return, renounce exercising all the power at their disposal; and in addition, events, both physical and mental, happen according to necessary processes which often result in more pain than happiness. Weil's problem now was to move past the contradiction. The key, as she saw it, is an understanding of divinity that has been lost in the West.

3. The Nature of Divinity

The Critique of Institutional Religion

As a Marxist materialist, Luxemburg took little interest in religion. Observing Christian churches in Europe with their reactionary protection of privilege, exclusion of outsiders, polemical moralizing, it seemed clear to her and to other socialists that religion was unlikely to be a progressive force. At most, religion might be tolerated in ethnically diverse nation-states as an expression of cultural identity. In this negative judgment on the Christian church as a social institution, Weil concurred. Her conclusion, however, was not that religion should be disregarded, but that a noncredulous, noninstitutional religion should be revived. The major barrier, as she saw it, is the troubled conception of divinity in Western religious thought.

The two testaments of the Christian Bible mark one of the major strains. Christianity inherits from the Old Testament the patriarchal God of the ancient Hebrews, Yahweh, whose attributes are power, sovereignty, omnipotence, and righteous judgment. In contrast to the message of the Christian gospels, which is pacifist, egalitarian, mystical, Yahweh is a creator, a ruler, a warrior, and the director of history. In his relation with his "chosen" people, he is a master of slaves: he commands, they obey or are punished; they fight and kill his enemies, he rewards them with land and protection. This places the Hebrew God solidly within the earthly dynamics of force described by Weil.[20]

The atrocities of the Old Testament—the genocides, massacres, inhuman punishments demanded and rewarded by the patriarchal war god Yahweh—survive as a strong undercurrent in Christian thought and practice. Even as the New Testament grafts onto Semitic sources elements from Greek mystery religion, the image of God as an all-powerful ruler/father remains central in Christian thought. The Near Eastern dying god, son/consort of the Great Goddess, and Sophia, the Greek's Holy Wisdom, are dissolved in the mystery of a Trinity in which the law-giving Father takes precedence over the compassionate son and the beneficient Holy Spirit. God tests believers' obedience, tries their loyalty, makes them endure pain and hardship, has them vow exclusive fidelity, commands that they wage war against idolaters. In times of relative peace, his goodness and love are stressed, but it is a goodness and love that are always conditional on his servants' fulfillment of their obligations to Lord and Master.

Weil's response was characteristically unorthodox. Taking no interest in scholastic arguments that attempt to prove or disprove such a God's existence, or that reconcile logically God's absolute power with the possibility of human agency,[21] but at the same time refusing to abandon Christianity as the native religious language of the West, Weil attempted a transformation of Christianity as radical as her transformation of Descartes's modern subject. Using the terms of the West's native Christianity, she reconceived a divinity that challenged all aspects of orthodox Christian practice and belief but preserved what she took as the core "attitudes" of Christianity. She was no loyal adherent to orthodox Christian belief, nor did she reject Christianity as escapist denial, nor did she try the reformist middle ground of revising offensive but supposedly inessential aspects of Christian belief and practice. Just as Luxemburg understood that supplementation or revision of Marxist dogma only put off confrontation with its deep contradictions, so Weil realized that faults in Western religious thought went deeper than acceptable or revisable tenets of belief.

Christian belief is typically doctrinal. Weil worked her transformation by understanding Christianity not as a sectarian set of beliefs or representations, but as a living, speakable, religious "language."[22] That language, like any religion, is imperfect, but it is also expressive of attitudes and practices that provide access to the real presence of divinity in natural life. Weil made no claim to be Descartes's "thinking thing," reading a creed from the direct dictation of God autonomous of all human influence. As with any language, no absolute break with past meanings is possible. Weil continued to use the words of orthodox Christian belief: creation, immortality, prayer, God; but she used them as indicating ideals which call orthodox Christian practice into question and not as labels for existing practice.

This conception of religion as a speakable and reinterpretable native language is in sharp contrast to institutional Christianity in which Christian devotion is understood as an expression of belief and allegiance. Weil, Jewish by birth, believed herself closest in attitude to Catholicism, but she persistently refused to join any church or religious institution.[23] She explained this refusal in letters to Father Perrin, her would-be spiritual advisor: once the church becomes a "collectivity" with territorial, fiscal, or spiritual administration, it is subject to the same necessity that governs human affairs. There are good results but there is also evil. The powerful crush the weak; holy wars are launched against nonbelievers; those in office will seek to expand their privileges and their power. She was, Weil confessed, as much or more than others, attracted to such a collectivity; she also craved the sense of belonging that was one of the psychological attractions of Fascism. She chided Father Perrin and other Christians for having "set aside" much of the evil of Christianity: they had chosen to ignore the Inquisition, the Crusades, the European witch-hunts.

Weil's indictment was not only of Christian sectarian allegiance, it was also of the Western culture which the Christian church had done so much to define. In that culture, the root Christian virtues of charity, gratitude, and compassion had disappeared (WG 162). The "white races" of the Christian West, committed to the Old Testament view of divinity, lost the access to divinity that Weil found from antiquity in China, India, Greece, and in parts of the Bible such as *Psalms, Job, The Book of Wisdom*. Even worse, white races were trying to destroy access to divinity in "all the countries where it takes its arms, its commerce and its religion." Colonization, missionaries, the Christianization of other cultures destroy customs, rituals, ways of life that are approaches to God (ibid.).

Weil was skeptical of attempts to escape the injustice of institutional Christianity or contradictions in Christian belief by pretending superficial conversion to foreign religions. Instead, as an enlightened speaker of the language of Christianity, she enriched her religious understanding and modes of expression with extended study of other non-Christian religious languages: Greek philosophy, especially Plato and the Pythagoreans, the *Iliad*, Greek myth, the Egyptian cults of Osiris and Dionysus, the Indian *Bhagavad Gita*, the ancient Egyptian *Book of the Dead*, folklore and myth from all parts of the world. In all these languages, the name of God was repeated more or less faithfully, more or less intelligibly. Discarding the Old Testament, but retaining the language and the attitudes of New Testament Christianity, Weil was in the process of recovering a noninstitutional, truly "Catholic" or universal basis for Christian devotion severed from the Old Testament tradition.

God the Master, God the Mother

The Christian patriarchal God has been under attack in recent years from many sources. Feminists point to the masculinity of God and suggest either a sex change or an androgynous divinity beyond gender. Opponents of Western colonialism cite the connection between missionary zeal and the oppression of indigenous peoples, and demand a diversion of attention from God the master to God the deliverer of slaves. Social reformers protest the identification of religion with conservative values and urge a change of focus from God the lawgiver to Christ the protector of the poor. Weil does not replace a male God with a female God, a war god with the champion of the oppressed, or a commanding god with a liberator; her reworking goes deeper to the very conception of a personal divinity transcendent to natural life.

Somehow, if there is to be a noncredulous religion, divinity must coexist with the inexorable working of physical causation in material processes and human affairs. Given the events of the twentieth century, it was clear to Weil that there can be no faith in a guiding benevolent hand in history. Faced squarely, the dynamics of power and privilege imply the absence of God. Weil rejected arguments in which Christian theologians tried to reconcile evil and faith: there is some hidden reward planned by God; violent catastrophic events must in the end turn out to be beneficial. These attempts to solve the "problem of evil" lead to evil. They require that believers become "pitiless," eyes closed to suffering, as they refuse to see *malheur* as the evil it is, and so justify all sorts of violence. All that the phrase "God's mercy" can name is painful natural existence. All that the phrase "God's love" can mean that is *real* is God's absence from the world. Weil did not turn away from the contradiction: "relentless necessity, wretchedness, distress, the crushing burden of poverty and of labour, cruelty, torture, violent death, constraint, disease—all these must constitute divine love" (GG 28). To continue to project a guiding hand of Providence only removes religion further from reality. Weil applied the pincers of contradiction: the absence of divinity, then, must be the actual trace of divinity in the world. God's absence—the pointless and cruel mechanisms of necessity and force—are God's love and God's creation. The suffering and pain that inevitably result are God's mercy.

One way to make sense of this apparent paradox is by comparing conceptions of fatherly and motherly love. A patriarch is unequivocally present; he chastises, directs, rules just like the Semitic father god. The good mother, on the other hand, steps back out of a fusional relationship with her child. Allowing the child autonomy and a separate identity, she waits for her child to renounce a false divinity, the sense of being the all-powerful center of the world. In doing so, she allows the child to become capable of love for another being. Weil's divine love, the model in her view for all love, is not a father's intervention, direction, rule, or command but a maternal renunciation of command so that there is a possibility of relation between two independent beings (FLN 140–1).[24]

A maternal divinity is consistent with Weil's revelations. Her first mystical experience occurred in Portugal, in that Mediterranean culture in which Christianity is still in many places a thin patina of allegiance over pre-Christian ritual and belief (AD 67). Just come from a punishing stint of factory work, exhausted in mind and body and convinced that all hope of a Marxist revolution was vain, Weil experienced divinity in a religious procession of Portuguese women around a village harbor, blessing boats and singing mournful songs. The Mediterranean devotion that inspired this first of Weil's revelations was not allegiance to a patristic imperial church or to a distant father God. The spirit worshipped by the Portuguese women was the ancient divinity of the pagan Mediterranean. Rooted in the rhythms of natural life, not unitary but multiple, honored in patron saints of local origin, many of them feminine, and identified with events in the history of the human community, she is Our Lady, the Mother of God. In place of the fear of punishment of a heavenly father is Our Lady's mediation. In place of strident law and commandment is silent, motherly love and concern.

In this and other revelatory experiences, Weil continued to experience divinity.[25] In these experiences, God is no figure, ghost, or personlike image. There is no illusion of any kind, no quasiphysical presence, but rather access to a different dimension of experience, Weil gave several descriptions:

> In this sudden seizing of me by Christ, neither the senses nor the imagination played any part—I had only felt through suffering the presence of a love like that which one reads in the smile of a loved face. (AD 45, WG 69)

Or another experience when repeating the Lord's Prayer while working in a vineyard:

> [I went] outside of space to where there is neither perspective nor point of view. Space opens. The infinity of the ordinary space of perception is replaced by an infinity to the second or sometimes third power. At the same time, this infinity of infinity fills little by little with silence, a silence which is not an absence of sound, which is the object of a possible sensation, more positive than that of a sound. Noise, if there is any, comes to me only after having crossed this silence. (AD 48–9, WG 72)

Although Weil used the word "God," with its complement of masculine pronouns, her God has no paternal "intentions" for man, does no miracles, does not control or rule human affairs in any way. This is no omnipotent slave master whose command must be obeyed, but who commits random acts of mercy when the spirit so moves him. To make divinity, absolutely out of the world, a thing of this world, an object or a person standing above the world who acts in the world in interested ways, for Weil is blasphemy. It is to refuse to acknowledge the truth of natural existence that necessity operates without interruption, and to mistake the nature of divinity which is altogether the other of natural necessity.

Attending to God

The various Christian editors and promoters of Weil's religious writing avoided direct confrontation with Weil's heterodoxy. Father Perrin, her friend and employer Gustav Thibon, the celebrated T. S. Eliot, all were more or less doctrinaire in their beliefs. All acknowledged the power and the spiritual authority of Weil's religious thought: all realized that what she proposed was not orthodox Christian teaching; all were intent on reclaiming her vision for orthodoxy by smoothing over what they took as a few pardonable excesses.[26] None of them was interested in projecting radical forms of Christian devotion inspired by Weil's new conception of divinity.

Christian devotion has traditionally been consistent with the understanding of God as a patriarchal master of slaves. The very first Christian duty is obedience: the Christian must do what the master commands without question, commands that were taken by dictation by Moses, and transmitted and interpreted by the fathers of the church. Christians may appeal to the master in prayer, pleading with him as with the powerful sovereign for mercy and forgiveness. Obedience to commands and humility in prayer wins for the believer the reward of salvation and immortality. Women especially, given their supposed greater propensity to sin, are exhorted to efface themselves and obey. For Weil, this is false devotion; it leads to moral weakness and bars the way to divinity. Access to God, she argued, cannot be understood as allegiance to or supplication of any ruler, master, or lord.

In orthodox Christian worship, participation in the liturgies of the church is the primary expression of allegiance.[27] Although Weil did not reject religious ritual as access to God, its value, for her, is only secondary. God, she argued, is not directly in any specific mass or liturgy; no religious service is any better an approach to God than charity or a sense of the beauty of the world. No faithful churchgoer is any closer to God than someone who loves her neighbor. The conventionality of religious ritual, and not its specific content, brings the participant closer to the divine.[28] More important by far than participation in any ritual or service, for Weil, is having the "Christian attitude" of charity and a sense of the beauty of the world.

Weil's charity is not the usual sentiment of generalized benevolence or generosity.

> To love our neighbor as ourselves does not mean that we should love all people equally, for I do not have an equal love for all the modes of existence of myself. Nor does it mean that we should never make them suffer, for I do not refuse to make myself suffer. But we should have with each person the relationship of one conception of the universe to another conception of the universe, and not to a part of that universe. (GG 129)

Charity is a tear in natural necessity that makes a gap or void through which divinity in the form of the recognition of specific others as separate centers of consciousness is possible. Instead of being drawn up into the churning of instinct and desire, manipulating others as pieces of matter, instead of venting on others natural appetites, a person is able to treat another as an autonomous, thinking being. When we are charitable, regardless of the power we have or might win over others, we treat others as "consenting wills" (WG 129). In this way, the rule of force that the powerful will do all that is in their power to do is suspended in another dimension of human experience.[29]

For inspiration, Weil turned not to the Ten Commandments but to the confession of the good soul before the goddess Maat in the Egyptian *Book of the Dead*.

I have made no one cry.
I have never raised my voice.
I have never made any one afraid.
I have never made myself deaf to words that are just and
  true. (AD 130, WG 144)

If Maat's just and charitable soul emulates divinity, it is not the
divinity of the jealous war God of the Old Testament. The just soul
does not exercise her power in controlling, punishing, or forgiving;
she *renounces* whatever power over others she might exercise. The
virtuous person refrains from commanding where she has the power
to command. She does not take the oppressed in hand, lecturing to
them, caring for them, organizing and providing for them; she turns
away from such manipulative involvement, recognizing others as centers of consciousness in their own right, seeing in them the humanity
they are in danger of losing. In the same spirit, she may even punish
them, as long as that punishment recognizes their autonomy and
responsibility (WG 155). Weil's devotion is more demanding than
an obedient tithing or a generalized feeling of benevolence for one's
neighbor; it involves a superhuman attitude.

A similar stance is required for appreciation of what Weil calls
the "beauty-of-the-world." Her source this time is Greek, Plato's "*to
kalos*,"[30] identified in the *Symposium* as the highest object of knowledge and inspiration. If Weil is no orthodox Christian, she is no orthodox Platonist either. Her differences with Plato come out clearly in
her critical discussion of his famous "Allegory of the Cave" in the
Republic (WG 211). She agrees with Plato that vanity and depravity
rule human affairs. She agrees that we must transcend these earthly
phenomena. She differs, however, on how that is to be done. The
Platonic philosopher encourages his followers to move away from the
physical and human world to contemplate the eternal world of ideal
forms. But, says Weil, this is impossible. It can only lead to delusion.
We cannot turn away from the material world because we are irrevocably physical creatures. To see true beauty, the inhabitants of the
cave do not turn away from the world but "remain immobile, without
ceasing to listen, and . . . wait for they know not what, deaf to solicita-
tions and to threats, unshakable shocks." They do not close their eyes
to physical and human reality, they are attentive to it. Then if they
are patient, beauty may reveal itself to them for an instant, after
which they must wait again, silent and attentive.

The nondelusive way to a supersensual divinity is through the
senses. Weil describes what such a passage might be like:

> Beauty is always a miracle. But there is a miracle of the
> second degree when a soul receives an impression of a beauty
> that is not sensible, as long as that impression involves not
> an abstraction but an impression real and direct like that
> which a chant causes the moment it makes itself heard. All
> this happens as if, by effect of a miraculous favor, it has
> become *manifest to the senses themselves* that the silence is
> not absence of sound, but a thing infinitely more real than
> sounds and the seat of a harmony more perfect than the most
> beautiful combination of sounds could produce. (WG 213)
> (my emphasis)

This is not the Platonism of the Christian ascetic, denouncing the
evils of the body and sensual experience in the name of abstract
Form. Weil's view is closer to the teaching of the Mantinean priestess
Diotima, whom Plato named in the *Symposium* as Socrates' mentor.

In Diotima's Erotica or religion of love, as it is described by Plato,
the initiate starts from individual beautiful things in which there is
a "divinity." From these physical loves, she progresses to a higher
love for virtue in persons and for the sciences and arts that bring
good things to households and societies. Finally, she may experience
the revelation of universal beauty. This highest most difficult revelation is not of "solidified abstractions" but is a "spiritual marriage
with the beautiful," with the generative source of the good in human
life (FLN 145).[31] Weil describes a similar divine beauty-of-the-world,
sensible and beyond sense at the same time. The means of approach
to such a divinity is not a turning away from the world but an attention
to the world so complete, so painstaking, that it transcends ordinary
perception. Weil drew on Greek mystery religion to describe such a
sensual passage to divinity. In the foundational myth of the mysteries
of Demeter at Eleusis, Persephone, Demeter's daughter, is picking
flowers in a high meadow when she is drawn down into the beauty
of the world.

> The perfume of the narcissus made the heavens smile, im-
> mense above, and the wide earth, and all the roaring of the
> sea. Hardly had the poor girl stretched out her hand than
> she was taken in the trap. She had fallen into the hands of
> the living God. When she left him, she had eaten the grain
> of the pomegranate which linked her with him forever. She
> was no longer a virgin, she was the wife of God. (AD 152–3,
> WG 163)[32]

Just as Weil's charity involves change in relation to others, Weil's vision of divine beauty involves a change in orientation in the physical world. As a child, each person sees the world from an imaginary self-center. Everything is arranged around the center of self, both in space and time, and in a hierarchy of values focused on the individual's own interests. Eventually, some manage to be charitable, give up solipsism, at least intermittently, and acknowledge others as independent and autonomous centers of consciousness. Even before that, and in preparation for it, if they are to successfully negotiate the physical world, they must have given up the false illusion of their own space and time. They have acknowledged that space and time are not arranged around them, but part of an order which is independent of them. This order beyond self-interest and self-concern is Weil's beauty-of-the-world, the mark of divinity. Grasping such an order, even if the grasp is always partial, causes a change at the very "roots of our sensibility" (AD 148, WG 159).

Weil's divinity can be approached through direct bodily contact with physical reality in the experience of both pain and physical work. In the utilitarian philosophy which has been in the modern West a dominant approach in ethics, pleasure is a universal good and pain a universal evil. From this philosophical perspective, Weil's treatment of pain is unintelligible. Far from accepting the avoidance of pain as a natural or moral fact, Weil identifies it with the psychological dynamics of cruelty and indifference. It is in the pursuit of pleasure that we refuse to hear the unfortunate. It is to try to rid ourselves of pain that we try to pass it on and vent it on others. Only when the impulse to avoid pain is suspended can charity be exercised. Then pain is absorbed back into the self, an inner equilibrium maintained, and balance in human affairs may be restored.[33]

Less controversial but just as unorthodox is Weil's contention that divinity is experienced in manual labor. In Christian myth, painful labor is a punishment God imposes on Adam for his disobedience. To the Greeks labor was degrading and to be done by women and slaves. In Marxist philosophy labor is valorized, but is still a necessary evil. Survival demands confrontation between man and nature, satisfaction as men comes from mastery in that confrontation, each man, to be fully human, must share in the project and have his chance to impose his image on the world, but in the end, he can look forward to a technological utopia where little labor is necessary. Weil's nature is not an inert substance to be manipulated and marked with an image of "Man"; it is the living environment in which action *can* make its way. That very "I can," for Weil, is the mark of divinity. Paradoxically, Marx, the champion of labor, looked forward to the possible elimination of work in mechanization. Not only is any such expectation unrealistic, Weil argued, but even if it were possible the elimination of work would mean the elimination of contact with a primary source of substantive ideals.

A Noncredulous Divinity

For Marxists, materialism has meant that the impetus for social change has to be found in material reality—if not in universal laws of historical process, then in the aspirations of an existent working class. But if, given Luxemburg's global economic analysis, the aspirations of the traditional Marxist "universal class," the industrial proletariat, are not necessarily progressive, then the goals of socialism must be pragmatically set. Any action can be defended, and socialism is adrift without a compass. Weil's problem was to conceive how, given that expediency and opportunism are inevitably driven by the dynamics of power and controlled by the relentless press of appetites and desires, the aspiration to justice can be understood. No group, party, class, sex's perspective is identical with such an aspiration. Its object has to be, in some sense, out of the world.

As a materialist, Weil rejected any resort to metaphysical absolutes or universals. Instead, she returned to the contradiction which Descartes's metaphysical dualism had reified: all that exists in natural life is governed by natural necessity, and yet subjective disinterestedness and justice are possible. Descartes's separation of mental substance from material substance had frozen this contradiction into metaphysical categories which became the stock in trade of philosophers: God/Nature, Spirit/Body, Ideal/Material, Reason/Passion. Separated from the natural world, God, mind, goodness become imaginary things; separated from divinity, the natural world, the body, and feeling become complexes of mechanical processes. Refusing to sidestep the contradiction in any dualistic ontology of spirits and bodies, Weil thought with it through to a conception of a divinity which is both a part of and is not a part of the natural world.

Natural life is ruled by force and necessity. But at times an order, regularity, balance of forces, is possible which is beyond the processes of physical causation but not other than them. The wave motion of the sea can be plotted and predicted, but in the glimmering regularity of its surface undulations there is also beauty. Labor is painful, but in skillful, methodical work, there is partnership with nature, "a point of equilibrium where necessity, by its conditional character, presents man at once with obstacles and with means in relation to partial ends" (IC 180). The very possibility of applied mathematics, of constructing series of actions, of imagining how practices might be altered to fill needs, and of projecting the series of steps which *must* proceed in a certain way, constitutes divinity in material life.

Necessity, for Weil, has two faces, one the crushing necessity of physical force and the other the divine necessity of ordered and balanced equilibrium. Pain, physical and spiritual, if it does not crush the spirit, can be used to tap that necessity deep in the human spirit. Resisting all attempts to escape pain, by drugs, diversions, or the venting of hostility against others, a sufferer, reduced to the very roots of desire, makes contact with material reality at the very level of ordered causality. In addition, some are able to suspend their striving for pleasure, power, and status, and attend to the world and other people as autonomous existents operating independently according to their own laws. Between such persons, a social equilibrium between opposing forces and impulses is possible which is not the same thing as either of their interests and is not other than them either.

Weil's divine equilibrium is not "super" or "above" the natural; it is not "non" or "not" the physical, "meta" or beyond the physical. Closer might be the etymological meaning of the Greek "metaphysics." The spiritual, for Weil is what is "meta" the physical, "among," "along with," the physical. Such a meta-physics is not in conflict with physical science; it shares the same impulse and goal. At the very origins of pure theoretical science with the Greeks, and especially in the fragmentary remains of Pythagorean philosophy, Weil found a revelation of divinity in the order, beauty, and necessity of the world.

> Could it be that this mysterious being, whose presence the faithful believe they feel in their ecstasies, to whom people have built churches and sung songs, is, at the same time, what, as reason, rules over the world of ideas? How is it that Plato, who did not allow anyone to enter his school if they were not geometers, was able to relate the most rigorous thought, and even geometry, to the same one that, many centuries later, St. Theresa evoked in her orisons? (O 290–1)

Scientific reason has often had to bow to sectarian religious sentiment, but if popular worship reflects proofs of divinity that are not in opposition to scientific reason but which are its very origin, then it is possible to conceive a "universal religion, a natural religion, founded not on a sentiment that happens to be common to all men, but on proofs that speak to everyone" (O 291).

In her studies of the origins of mathematics, Weil continued to repair the split between science and religion. The interest of Greek mathematicians was in ratio, proportion, function, the very elements that allow methodical work, facilitate harmonious relations between persons, and constitute beauty. When the purpose of mathematical science is only practical, as in ancient Egyptian mathematics, where the primary purpose was the marking of property lines on land and the assessment of taxes, accurate measurement is all that is required. In contrast, the Greek geometer's pursuit of necessary relations, which is the beginning of modern science, projected a beautiful intersection between material necessity and the good. "Beauty is necessity which, while remaining in conformity with its own law and with that alone, is obedient to the good" (GG 135). Without this divinity, lost in the modern schism between physical science and religion, religion is faith which can be fanned "white hot" in collective feelings that lead to zealous attacks on those of other faiths (IC 165). Without it, science is mindless instrumentality. Even in contemporary science, cut off from fanatical religion and split internally into formulaic representation and technological application, Weil saw a "pure theoretical core" which constitutes a true and universal religious knowledge. Natural necessity has two aspects; first the crushing operation of force grinding out evil and pain from which all goodness is absent, and second, just as a tangent intersects a circle at a minute point but does not penetrate it, the balance or order that is beauty, responsive social relations, methodical work.

The trace of divine presence that remains in the world as divinity absolutely withdraws is not only the fact of divinity's absence but also the moral quality of its withdrawal. Before the seventeenth century, the church's ethics was rationalized with the aid of Greek natural philosophy. God created the world according to eternal essences, either Platonic abstract Forms of goodness and beauty, or Aristotelian essences embodied in individuals. Rational argument, based on the intuition of abstract Platonic Forms or Aristotelian essences embedded in physical forms, resulted in definitions of goodness and virtue. When modern science made the Greek metaphysics of essence obsolete, the Christian church returned to its Hebraic inheritance. God's will is bound by no essence; man's virtue is to listen to God's commands through the authoritative transmission of revelation. The Christian's duty is to obey, not to think or ponder the nature of goodness. Protestant ethics refocused on the Ten Commandments, taken as the clearest and most unequivocal statement of God's will, with special attention to the first and most important of the commandments: "Worship no other God before me."

In many cases, commandment ethics was enforced as secular law subjecting anyone who transgresses the will of God, as interpreted by religious officials or religiously inspired jurists, to harsh punishment or death. Sexism and racism are written into law, archaic restrictions on sexual practice and family life are applied in radically different contexts, the patriarchy of the Greek aristocracy or Hebrew nomadic clans receives divine sanction. Even more important, emphasis on outward obedience to law can foster a inner depravity unenlightened by thought or sensitivity to others.

Given her noncredulous divinity, Weil conceived a radically different Christian ethics. To be good does not require that one read the Bible or listen to the priest. Weil's God is not a Master/Lord who commands and punishes his subjects. To be good is to refuse command. The world is God's; the only access to God's goodness is through the world; obedience to God can only be obedience to that necessity which is "God's will." But obedience to necessity is not blind obedience to the laws of nature or force, as one might obey a petty tyrant, giving oneself up to natural greed and corruption and imaginary rationalizations and illusions. The possibility of an equilibrium "along with" necessity constitutes another, moral, necessity. There is no absolute goodness in natural force, in "gravity" as Weil called it, but a substantive model for goodness can be found in the equilibrium and balance that is natural beauty. It can also be found in conscious, methodical work that fulfills human aspirations and in social relations in which obligations to others are met without conflict. In these cases, the cruel necessity that is God's absence becomes order and harmony.

Orthodox Christian believers acquaint themselves with God's will through the dictates of God's legitimate viceroys in the Church, which may result in evil or good. Weil understood Christian virtue in very different terms. Virtue is not in will but in the renunciation of will. Goodness is attained not through force, through a clenching of muscles or self-control, but in refusing to set anything aside, and in listening to what other people say out of the independent centers of consciousness that they are. From an understanding of each situation in its totality and complexity comes a binding sense of what *must* be done, what must be done to establish or reestablish the order and harmony that is the trace of divinity in natural life. If such a goodness has power, it is not the power of force or command, but the power of an attractive, compelling object of love and devotion.

The result is a justice which cannot be quoted from any authoritative texts, calculated, or rationally defined. Justice must be "read," and there are good and bad readings. Typically, people read according to "gravity," that is according to their appetites and desires, or according to the text of social conformity, what they want to hear, what it serves them to hear. These are inevitably distorted readings. A correct reading of justice, however, comes with painstaking and total attention to reality that includes in its understanding the social conventions and appetites that determine judgment. Then it is possible to penetrate to the necessity of each situation and a possible order independent of any individual's desire. The source of moral error, for Weil, is not willfulness or selfishness, but forgetfulness.

The setting aside of things has been a regular requirement of a commandment ethics which asks believers to set aside all else to obey the will of God (GG 122–24). In contrast, Weil's Maat is the wisdom of the wise leader, the ability to grasp a situation in its entirety and restore harmony to the Kingdom. Such a leader does not legislate willfully, but finds in reality a healthful balance which cannot be invented but is an objective measured quantity to be discovered. At the beginnings of Western philosophy, Plato contrasted the disembodied Forms of transcendent value accessible to an educated male elite with the sensual, diverse, self-interested disorder of Athenian democracy. That opposition, between the ideal and the material, between reason and passion, between masculine and feminine, between unity and diversity, generates the fundamental metaphysical categories of Western philosophy. Philosophy is a catalog of their possible combinations—there are no spirits, therefore mind and God are only deceptive words for natural phenomena; there is no physical world, only our ideal construction of it; there is both a spirit world and a physical world. Weil begins from the contradictory reality that is the origin of these beyond-the-physical alternatives: in natural and human events a pitiless necessity rules; at the same time, there are virtuous attitudes and actions in which women and men, not driven by desire, appetite, or self-interest, manage to institute a fragile equilibrium in human affairs that facilitates and supports acts of kindness and charity.

This naturalistic but still transcendent ideal opens feminist social activism to morality in a new way. Criticizing philosophical ethics as "masculine" in perspective, feminist ethicists have often seen no other recourse than to ground morality in the "feminine": in maternal care or nurturance, for example. For Weil, these instincts, as part of nature, are always mixed with good and evil. Maternal love can be stifling both for the giver and recipient. Maintaining relationships can be done at the cost of justice. Weil's ideal cannot be identified with any one aspect of physical life but permeates all of physical life.

Weil used the metaphors of Christ in his parables of the seed and the leaven (Matthew 13) to explain. The spiritual is not removed from the physical: it is the minute mustard seed that grows into the tree of life with birds singing in its leaves; it is the invisible leaven the woman puts in the meal to make bread rise. For Weil, the permeation of natural existence by divinity is so fine that the spiritual can never be separated from the physical. Whether a woman is alone in pain and despair, or struggling with others in oppressive work, attentive communication is the minute substance of divinity in her human experience that can foment social change. When a woman puts off escapist distractions and enters into physical contact with the body of the world in sensation and in productive engagement with physical necessity, the equilibrium that is achieved is the seed of a new sense of self and knowledge. As she joins with others, that goodness might come to permeate a society.[34]

4. Social Justice

Absolute Obligation

In the last years of the war, Weil was employed by the Free French to work with other intellectuals to draft a plan for the reconstruction of Europe. In an incredible last output in the months before she died, she worked to indicate the social ideals which would reflect the ethics and the metaphysics of her religious writings.[35] She was convinced that after the war there would have to be a general rethinking of the basis for political institutions, and that this rethinking would have to come from the various European peoples themselves. In *The Need for Roots* and in the papers collected in *Ecrits de Londres*, she outlined truths that any rethinking would have to take into account. Crucial, after Fascism, she thought, was the question of human rights ("Human Personality," SE). How and in what political system could it be made certain that the horrors of the concentrations camps would not be repeated? Is the legal protection of the human rights of persons sufficient protection? Weil's answer to this question was no.

Luxemburg rejected rights as metaphysical fictions attaching to an "essence of man," but she supported actual practices and institutions that guaranteed the vote, cultural expression, and free speech. Weil probed deeper to the metaphysics of the individual which is the basis for any rights-driven politics. With the mediation of Aristotelian essences and the church's interpretations of God's commandments no longer reliable, Descartes replaced the obedient medieval subject with a modern individual with free will to reject or accept any idea or any course of action. Moral ties between individuals were erased. Each would have the "right" to decide for himself or herself. The result was a society at war, with force and power deciding whose interests would be served. Weil's interactive "first philosophy" creates different alternatives: human beings can try to master nature, they can give in and allow it to master them, or they can find a point of equilibrium between natural force and human aspiration. These three kinds of relation, Weil argued, are also possible between human beings. In the first two, relations are between people unequal in power, but, as in the relation between human being and nature, there is a third possibility. In certain circumstances, when no person has more power than others and each person requires the consent of others, a balance can be maintained in human relationships. This "natural justice," even when legally mandated, is fragile and always vulnerable to the distortions of power and ambition. To guarantee its survival, Weil believed, there has to be something other than the fortuitous chance of a naturally occurring balance of power and something other than a rescindable or interpretable bill of rights: a source of goodness in "human relationships where, without there being an equality of force or need, there is a search for mutual consent."

In the philosophies of liberalism, justice is typically seen as adjustment of the rights of individuals. Each person owns and controls a private space that cannot be violated by other persons or by the state. At the very least, that private sphere includes his or her body and is typically extended to other areas of life considered to be private. The civil society in which rights are recognized is an association of free, self-interested agents who, in their competition with each other, respect certain rules and limits. In this view, argued Weil, rights are a fragile and compromised legal construction. Persons are put into opposition with other persons as claims to rights inevitably conflict. Even more serious, there is no substantive basis for rights but only a statutory guarantee which can be rescinded. The individual's protection is limited to whatever happens to be the current definition of what is private, and, as in the case of Fascism, that sphere of liberty can shrink to virtually nothing.

A right, Weil claimed, is a meaningless abstraction if it is not grounded in obligation. This is not to restate the trivial logical truth that every right necessarily implies a reciprocal obligation. For Weil, obligations in which rights can be grounded have a prior and substantive, "transcendental" identity independent of any convention or social formulation (NR 54). This does not mean that obligations belong in an otherworldly ideal realm of the spirit. Instead, drawing on her concept of divinity, Weil located obligation materially in the possibility of a certain kind of communicative relation between persons.

The mistake, as Weil saw it, of abstract conceptions of human rights is the belief that rights can attach to persons as unique personalities.

On this level, substantive obligation cannot take hold; the best we can do is be tolerant of differences in individuals because it is a natural fact that we like some individuals and not others (EL 29). In contrast, absolute obligation which cannot be suspended by personal antipathy or expediency is not to an individual, but attaches to what is the same in everyone and what is the same is an experiential core from which everyone speaks. In duress and affliction, everyone cries out "for good to be done to him" (EL 11–12), and to this universal "cry" for justice an absolute obligation is owed.

There is no one set of laws or institutions that can guarantee calls for justice are heard, but once they are heard, there is an obligation to respond. Weil distinguishes the call for justice from the yells of a mob, the statements of a collectivity, the demands of an ego or I, all of which can be heard and ignored. The cry for justice comes from a source deep in the person where all are the same; at the same time, it must be expressed personally as a unique experience. The call for justice comes out of a particular pain and despair, but it expresses a common claim. This is why, once heard, it has the power to elicit a response. Because justice is only possible on the basis of the substantive obligation that a call for justice from the abuse and oppressed elicits, a just society is not a society with the most efficient production, or even a society with the most individual rights. It is a society in which the cries of those who are in pain are heard and addressed.

Not only is the definition of rights in law no permanent guarantee, but rights may not touch the lives of those who are most in pain. The key to social justice, for Weil, is a reordering of social and political institutions so that nothing prevents from being heard the voice that cries out when a human being is harmed. This is by no means easy. The *malheureuse* are too broken in spirit to speak intelligibly; they have not the education that allows them to put their thoughts in logical order. Even more important, natural psychological law dictates that those who are more fortunate will try to avoid hearing them at all costs. The problem for postwar politics, as Weil saw it, was to generate social systems in which the "natural" failure of communication is minimized.

She laid down three necessary conditions for such a reordering: first, there must be mass education in effective and sincere expression; second, an atmosphere of silence and attention must be encouraged in all public institutions; and third, women and men of character must be recruited for public life who can hear and therefore respond to the cry of the oppressed. Neither capitalist democracy nor Marxist collectivism is likely to deliver such a society. Marxism rejects the idea of individual rights and obligations altogether. The result is that, in communist societies, the individual is not heard except as part of a collectivity; nothing she says is understood except in the context of that collectivity. The cries, for example, of peasants under forced collectivization are not heard but only interpreted as bourgeois or revisionist, consistent with collective ideology. In capitalist democracies, unique autonomous individuals are assumed whose private interests must be coordinated with other individuals' private interests. Public speech and political debate is for the purpose of regulating conflicts between these interests. Powerful interest groups strive for maximum advantage, while the disadvantaged in urban ghettoes and in rural poverty are mute.

Weil prescribed a basis for democratic solidarity among oppressed people, and even between oppressed people and their unwitting oppressors, that is neither a liberal association of self-interested individuals, nor a Marxist supraindividual collectivity, but a level of human communication where persons are the same and where they speak to each other of their individual needs in ways that result in understanding and obligation. When communication on that level is facilitated, justice results. People cry out in pain and no one cares or does anything, but the remedy is not to continue to be deaf and agree on a legal minimum each individual has a right to demand. Not only can legal guarantees always be revoked, but the real wrongs—poverty, loss of human dignity, human suffering—may be ignored. In her discussion of *malheur*, Weil described the many ways people make themselves oblivious to human suffering: geographical and educational segregation of the poor, public forums that intimidate rather than encourage communication, preoccupation with personal problems and concerns, obsession with gratification, ideologies that blame the poor for their misfortunes, or interpret their complaints as laziness. For Weil, only a particular kind of speech has the power to break through the force of these constraints. The problem is not that we hear the appeal of the oppressed well enough but consider we have no obligation to do anything about it, it is that society is so structured that the appeal of the afflicted is not heard. The very number and complexity of social devices that keep the unfortunate out of the way of the fortunate attests to the fact that, once heard, the appeal for justice imposes an absolute obligation.

Weil described an example of this failure to hear (EL 32–36). A vagrant has been accused of stealing some food. He comes before the judge, who is clever and articulate and cracks a few jokes while the man stands before him mumbling and stumbling. This, says Weil, is "truth" before "intelligence occupied with elegant opinion." The vagrant cannot tell the truth, cannot cry out, his thought is without order, confused and vague, his spirit imprisoned by his failure to make relations in thought. He does not know the jargon of the law. He cannot think coherently, cannot hold a thought in his mind long enough to frame another, and then hold both while he forms an idea about their relation. The judge dismisses him with a small sentence and moves on. For the vagrant to speak and to be heard there would have to be another atmosphere in the courtroom, a silence, an "attention that is intense, pure, without motion, gratuitous, generous" (EL 36). In the existing courtroom, no matter what the legal guarantees of fair trial, there is no hope for justice for the vagrant. Even if something did come from his lips that "pierced the soul" neither the judge nor spectators, protected by procedure and precedent, would hear it.

Certainly many women have shared the misery of Weil's vagrant, standing mute before obdurate authorities with ultimate power over their lives. The question raised by Weil is whether legally guaranteed rights can make their situation much better. In all the current controversy over abortion rights, for example, poor women who are teenage unwed mothers or beleaguered heads of poverty-stricken households are seldom heard. If they could be heard, a binding and not negotiable or rescindable obligation to pregnant women might be recognized that no rights of the fetus can cancel out. What that obligation entails would not be decided by the parceling out of private spaces, but by attention to the needs of women who are not married, employed in safe jobs, or housed in decent conditions. The obligation owed to these women might involve not only the right to abortion but also rights to better education, decent housing, childcare.

A Luxemburgian socialist standing with the oppressed can be based on intellectual decision. Weil's goodness, the ability to listen and to hear what people in trouble and pain say about their desires and needs, makes action obligatory. For Weil, the small grains of such a leaven are the vital source of actions that restore the moral base of politics, government, educational policy, and child rearing. Much of feminist political and social activism has remained within the conceptual framework of rights. Women have claimed the right to speak in public, to vote, to run for political office, to go to university, to compete for jobs. In the attempt to keep abortion legal, which takes so much contemporary feminist energy, a fetus's right to life is opposed to a woman's right to choose. Weil suggests another way of thinking about abortion and about social issues of concern to women, as questions not of rights but of obligation. Rejecting both the morality of the institutional Christian churches, which support the pro-life position, and the liberal philosophy of rights which supports the pro-choice position, a Weilian feminist might listen to women themselves as they attempt to make sense of their lives in order to come to a binding sense of what must be done to restore social balance and create a society in which obligations do not conflict.

What allows just and balanced human relations is that there is something at the core of each person which is the same, not a common nature or essence, not a common way of thinking or conceptual scheme, but something that speaks, not venting pain as an animal might, but calling out for needs to be met. What is the same in each person is the aspiration to Weil's divinity, to that illusive social balance and harmony in which no one is hurt, crushed in spirit, humiliated. That balance is only achievable, Weil thought, when there is a particular relation of communication between government and people.

Legitimacy

One of the problems assigned to Weil by the Free French was to develop a definition of legitimacy ("The Legitimacy of the Provisional Government," *Phil. Invest.* 53:1987). Given the breakdown of European territorial boundaries in the war, this was to be a major problem in the reconstruction of Europe. When peace was restored, Weil feared that utility and expediency would be the criteria for legitimacy, utility and expediency that would always be deflected to serve individual and group ambitions, creating national boundaries that are unstable and divisive. Like Luxemburg, Weil's concerns were prophetic of the ethnic conflict that would break out in Eastern Europe once the iron hand of Lenin's party rule was relaxed in the breakup of the Soviet empire. A different kind of legitimacy, Weil thought, is necessary to give continuity, permanence, and finality to social life and to protect institutions from greed and the abuse of power (GG 153).

Such a balance, as Weil saw it, is not in any particular kind of governmental structure. Like justice and goodness, legitimacy is an ideal, not a fact, and cannot be described as any particular set of institutions, whether they are democratic or collective. When legitimacy is defined as multiparty democracy or communist rule, legitimacy is made into an absolute to be forced on people. What passes for democracy in capitalist countries, where citizen participation is limited to an optional vote for preselected candidates, does not necessarily measure up to this ideal. Alternatively, an autocratic government might be responsive to needs in a way that does achieve legitimacy. Legitimate political institutions require a language similar to the language between lovers. The government must speak to the "heart," and be the free creation of a people that "pushes up like a plant" (EL 59). In order to insure this kind of communication between government and people, Weil insisted that after the war there would have to be extensive, local, nonpartisan discussions in France on a new constitution which would not be a plan submitted by parties and factions to the people for their approval, but would be generated by the people.

One of the most controversial aspects of Weil's politics is her refusal of the "party politics" which is the substance of both liberal democracy in a multiparty form and communism in a single-party form. Communication, she said, must not be confused with the electioneering of parties, which is only propaganda. There is no communication between government and people when politicians try to get others to vote with slogans that are manipulations of opinion. The party system is either sportive, like the British, or a heritage from the aristocratic clubs of the Jacobins, as in France. Two groups fight it out according to a set of rules. One group manages to impose their views on the people. There is no communication between people and officials, no thought about issues on the part of voters, only a choice between preformed alternatives. Even where there are multiple parties, what results is a kind of totalitarianism; one party rules for a period of time, exerting the same kind of restriction on its members' thought as in a one-party system. All parties are totalitarian, Weil argued; they want all the seats, all the offices. The alternative is a local and regional politics in which citizens who are known to each other and to their governors share a common living space and are in communication with each other.

Luxemburg noted the emptiness and lack of reference of a socialist rhetoric in which words had come to represent ideas detached from reality. Such ideas can be mechanically manipulated in schema which have no relevance to fact. Just before the outbreak of World War II, in her article "The Power of Words" (SE), Weil also discussed the way words had lost meaning. In Europe, empty rhetoric fanned a growing war fever.[36] It was not only that workers had made common cause with nationalist interests, but the very words in which national pride and patriotism were discussed had lost their communicative force. People were willing to fight for words, words that were only "symbols," signs to put on hats—"fascist," "democrat," "communist," "monarchist." Words, given fixed nominal definitions, became "abstract," names used to label a group or social system having only oppositional meaning—democracy is government that is noncommunist, Communism is what is not parliamentary democracy. To these false and dangerous uses of rhetoric, Luxemburg's answer was a materialist analysis of historical events which brought words and theories back to reality. For Weil, simple observation of fact and a matching of words still cannot capture the relation between language and reality. "Democracy" is not a name for a thing—so that "democracy" can mean "this way of life" or "our way of life" or "not their way of life"— it is a standard or measure by which to judge various systems. Only as marking ideals, Weil argued, do words like "democracy" and "justice" retain substantive meaning.

Naming Ideals

Words cannot be used meaningfully as absolutes indicating fixed sets of objects because of the very nature of human reality:

> Our lives are lived, in actual fact, among changing, varying realities, subject to the causal play of external necessities, and modifying themselves according to specific conditions within specific limits, and yet we act and strive and sacrifice ourselves and others by reference to fixed and isolated abstractions which cannot possibly be related either to one another or to any concrete facts. (SE 157)

Faced with the flux and relativity of experience, Plato had projected ideals as fixed, abstract objects. Such an imaginative transfer of objectivity to an otherworldly heaven of Forms only sidesteps the problem. The empiricist's phenomenalism is no better. If words cannot meaningfully refer to abstract objects with fixed identities, they cannot refer to the flux of sense perception either. This prevents any stable meaning at all, as language becomes the expression of an internal play of sensation and emotion in which there are no fixed points of reference.

Instead, for Weil, words relate to the only possible stability in human experience: limit, measure, relation, degree, comparison, contingency, interdependence, interrelation of means and ends (SE 156). These are not objects or perceptions, but moving relations between objects, forces and processes. If the meanings of words like "dictatorship" and "democracy" differ, it is not because there are different ideal forms of government in a Platonic supersensual reality, nor is it because people's experiences of government differ. The difference, Weil thought, is not between any "things-in-themselves," or between different private experiences, but between two different points of reference for weighing or measuring social phenomena (SE 160). On this view, there is no perfect democracy that "democracy" can name; no set of social structures that is equivalent to "democracy." "Democracy" does not "represent" a fact; it is a product of thought. As applied to the world, it must be continually reevaluated and replotted.

If words like "democracy" are given a truth—functional meaning, divorced from the human activities in which evaluation or weighing— how should I do this? what should I do? is this just?—is possible, reference disappears; words are "signs" or "symbols" oppositionally defined and tagged on to objects. Because the complex nature of reality makes any simple correspondence between stable facts and logically ordered representations impossible, eventually referential meaning must be artificially generated in a logical semantics or semiotics. In contrast, for Weil, truth is "the thoughts which surge up in the spirit of a creative thinking, uniquely, totally, only wanting the truth" (SE 139). Built into language, and an essential element in its capacity to refer, is human aspiration. When language becomes "objective," representation and aspiration are removed and language no longer serves its communicative function. But when someone speaks from the deep center of herself where she aspires to the good, as every human being aspires no matter how deluded or mistaken— when she speaks not manipulatively to get someone to do something, or expressively to vent emotion—then she speaks meaningfully and truthfully. Aspiration allows her to use words like "democracy" or "justice" not as names for absolutes, or abstractions from her own perceptions, but as yardsticks or measures constantly in communication with substantive possibilities for harmony and order in human affairs.

The problem of linguistic reference has been perennial in Western philosophy. Platonic essences, Descartes's clear and distinct ideas, sensory perceptions, empirical truth conditions are some of the various candidates philosophers have urged as stable referents for words. Weil's approach circumvents the dilemma in philosophy that frames these choices between private languages of sensation in which communication and reference are always problematic, and structuralist or logicist theories which define away reference in nominal definition. The direction she indicates for linguistic study might be contrasted with two currently popular versions of these alternatives: logical analysis in North America and Britain, and structuralist and poststructuralist linguistics on the Continent.

Both have their roots in an attempt to define a "science" or language that is value-free and objective. As with any science, paths in the world are plotted out: for logical semantics the goal of expunging from truth-telling language all meaning that is not generated according to the rules of mathematical logic; for structuralism ways to bypass the subjectivity of understanding in formal patterns of meaning that are independent of what speakers intend or believe. These are not projects it is likely that Weil would have found fruitful. She came to language not out of concern to defend Descartes's clear and distinct ideas, but out of concern for communication: how can citizens describe and name just institutions and practices; how can science be made accessible to students and working people? The reserving of truth and reference for a logical calculus of laboratory observations or for a system of signs only stands in the way of achieving these ideals.

For Weil, language must be rigorous and exact, but that precision cannot have reference to abstract symbolic patterns or to already existing groups of facts. It must refer to the fineness of the balance that can be achieved both between human beings and nature and between persons. Again Weil's approach was to rework core concepts. Language is not a neopositivist mirroring of facts, anchored or not anchored in references to sensory data; nor is it linguistic structures, in which meaning is generated as internal relations between signifiers. Neither view of language accommodates the weighing which, for Weil, is at the heart of linguistic meaning. Words do not refer to objects; they express human aspiration. Their meaning comes neither from empirical observation nor from internal semantic relations between words. They can be used as labels, but then their application is arbitrary because they are not related to human experience. They can be manipulated within an oppositional semantic system, but then they have no reference to reality. At the root of linguistic meaning is the human desire purged from language by both logicists and structuralists, desire understood not as impulse determined by appetite or drives, but as articulate movement at the core of human persons toward forms of life that are just and harmonious.

Several branches of current feminist theory have been inspired by recent linguistic philosophies. Grammatology, deconstruction, semiotics, all have been used to show that the very language in which politics, philosophy, theology is expressed has embedded in its semantics or grammar hierarchical gender oppositions. A new "textual" feminism has resulted. Avoiding any assertion of authoritarian truth on their own part, women disrupt and undermine claims to knowledge. Leaving rational discourses to men, they find a feminine voice in avant-garde poetry and expressive writing. Some have noted the irony of the fact that at the very moment in the late twentieth century when the claims of women and oppressed ethnic groups for justice have been expressed most articulately, the power of language to name reality and tell truths is called into question. Just as women and people of color have managed to name injustice; it turns out that the world is a text. Just as women and people of color found the voice to speak, it turns out that there is no speaking subject, only discursive or logical structures in which the subject is constituted.

A Weilian feminist philosophy of language might preserve for women the power and agency of naming. What women could name in Weil's language, and name in a way that communicates and carries authority, is not what things are in themselves, divorced from any human interest, but what people need and want them to be. If for many philosophers, evaluation has been a graft onto a logically ordered language whose core is representational and cognitive, for Weil, measuring is the substance of linguistic meaning to which the alienated representations of science and the symbolic structures of linguists are only supplements.

Human Needs

What Weil's truth-telling language might name are human needs and ways they can be met. Few societies are ordered so that the cries of despair and hope that come from human beings can be heard. Few, therefore, recognize an absolute obligation to meet human needs. In liberal democratic theory, needs are a function of the gratification of individual appetites. Whatever people crave or can be made to crave is what they need. People "need" processed food. They "need" chemical stimulants. Similarly empty is the Marxist formula: to each according to his or her needs, which, after Luxemburg's death, was interpreted in whatever way was congruent with Communist party policy or considered the "historical task" of socialism. Dissident intellectuals "needed" psychiatric treatment, peasants "needed" discipline on collective farms. For Weil, communicable human needs are facts of natural existence and neither a matter of personal choice nor a function of social or economic structure.

Again, the key for Weil is balance and equilibrium. Needs include not just the needs of the body but also the needs of the soul, which is as much a part of natural existence as the body. From the standpoint of Marxist materialism, the soul is a fiction. Persons are productive agents whose reality is the disembodied will that generates unique individual preferences; body and spirit are inseparable aspects of natural life. To be human is to be both a physical, sensing organism with self-protective instincts, and to be spiritually able to appeal to and respond to others. What distinguishes a human soul for Weil is not an autonomous will or a function as part of a collectivity—not that she is either an angel or an ant—but the nexus between sensation, appeal, and response that is the basis for the possibility of charity and friendship between persons.

Weil describes human needs from this understanding of a person. It is a presumption of life that bodily needs must be met; people must have food, shelter, medicine. These are material benefits that both capitalist and socialist production claim to provide. But equally important, according to Weil, are the needs of the spirit neglected in both Marxism and capitalist democracy. She describes these in "Study for a declaration of obligations towards the human being" (SE). The key to spiritual need, as it is to physical health, is equilibrium. Just as there must be a balance between waking and sleeping, working and resting, eating and fasting, for spiritual life there must be balance between equality and hierarchy, between liberty and obedience, between freedom and truth, between the private and the social. It is true that all persons need attention to their own desires, but there is also a need for hierarchy, for respect and obedience to superiors in which personal desires are subordinated. There is a need for liberty, but there is also a need for limits, a need to obey authority. That authority must be carefully constituted; people must be able to communicate with authorities and authorities must recognize the absolute obligation to fill human needs, but hierarchy, along with honor, obedience, and respect, is a natural part of human life. Similarly, people need the freedom to speak, but they also need to be constrained by the truth, and so censorship of hate language or pornography may be necessary.[37]

Each person needs privacy for the health of their spirit. Weil refused to accept the Marxist interdiction on private property. Each person should own a home, a garden, the tools of her trade. These for Weil are extensions of the body necessary if there is to be a sense of identity and continuity. At the same time there must be public spaces, schools, assemblies, courts, parks, libraries. Neither collective social life nor private individual life is an absolute good; no physical structure or state of affairs is absolutely good, instead what is good is a harmonious balance. Weil's just society is not a society in which individuals are subordinate to the collectivity, as in Communism, or a society in which the collectivity is the sum of individual's private projects, as in capitalism, but a social order in which conflicts between real and substantive obligations to persons have been minimized.

After Weil's death, her fears for Europe were realized. Boundaries were drawn on the basis of the convenience and security of the victors rather than on the territorial integrity of human communities, just as they had been in the colonial administration of Africa and India. Weil provided the arguments which might have made community preservation a priority and healed violent ethnic differences. A need recognized in neither capitalism nor Marxism is that a society must be "rooted." Weil argued in *The Need for Roots* that relations necessary if obligations are to be met can only be maintained in a community which has a history and a remembered tradition that is perpetuated in concrete ways. To achieve stable reciprocity in relationships, a community has to "preserve in living shape certain particular treasures of the past and certain particular expectations for the future" (NR 41). This includes not only the great monuments of culture, but also more humble ways of life, such as the traditions of "fishermen or miners" (NR 19). Weil shared Luxemburg's sense of the dangers of nationalism and isolationism. The nation cannot become an "idol." Not only must there be a guarantee of cultural expression, but there must also be the same respect for and acknowledgment of other cultures that support obligations to persons. Luxemburg's culturally diverse nation-state is a fragile and inevitably unstable abstraction if its only identity is as an economic unit. Nations should not serve as "idols," but they are more than productive units; for Weil, they are intermediaries, "*metaxu*," or mediums for realizing in embodied life the balance of opposing forces which for Weil is divinity in natural affairs (GG 133–4).

Colonialism was as passionately condemned by Weil, contemplating French policy in North Africa and Asia, as it had been by Luxemburg in Eastern Europe. A rooted culture must respect other cultures. A culture cannot shut itself off from outside influences; human environments are multiple and reciprocally related, and should be in invigorating relation to other localities allied in international federations. But influences from outside cannot be simply "added on" to uproot or supplant native traditions. They must be absorbed into existing cultures as something to be used by a culture for its own good. Non-Western cultures, forced into production that is exploited by colonial powers, might still implement industrial development in distinctive ways, so that traditional relationships and rhythms of work are not completely lost.

An absolute necessity for the rootedness of a human community is territory. There must be a physical place attached to a community with boundaries that protect and define it. Weil, like Luxemburg, is careful to make the distinction between nationalism understood as allegiance to a state, and nationalism as territorial integrity and rootedness. A state provides no roots. It is an abstract collective entity whose territory can be diminished or expanded by conquest or fiat. The soul cannot "stick" to a state (NR 152). The Roman "state," often cited by Weil as imposing the opposite of justice, governed a wide variety of peoples and territories; its effect was to destroy or supplant local traditions. With imperial conquest, geographical units lose their integrity; the family holding, the village, the county, the region cease to exist as functioning units. In the course of Western history, the leveling of capitalist development, wars of conquest in Europe, colonialization and imperialism, further confused and destroyed territorial boundaries, causing violent outbreaks of racism and tribalism.

Characteristic of twentieth-century life is the "uprooting" of human environments, in capitalist development where traditional patterns of social life are sacrificed for money and profits, in wars in which peoples and ways of life are destroyed, in humanities classes where young persons are taught the "great books" of Western culture or Marxist-Leninism ideology rather than local traditions, in technical education where mathematics is taught without the practical applications that give it meaning. Without these roots, there is no "honor." Weil did not mean the degraded honor of status, wealth, or even equality, but a sense of identity that comes from having a place and a tradition. Neither the liberal, civil rights branch of democratic social philosophy nor the versions of socialism with which many feminist social theorists have been aligned recognized the ideal of rootedness. More often, in both strains of social philosophy, traditional patterns of life stand in the way of progress, which is understood as industrial, urban, and nonlocal. The loss of human environments that such development brings was for Weil a "supreme tragedy." Some mentalities and some ideas, especially those of interest and importance to women, traditionally responsible for the day-to-day maintenance of civilized human life, may be possible only in particular settings and national environments; these "intermediaries" are fragile; when they are destroyed they can never be restored, any more than a plant pulled out by its roots can be replanted successfully.

In Weil's account, patterns of working, familial, communal life are not objects of a narrowly "feminine" interest, but are essential to human life. When they are destroyed, the only answer is centralization because the "living intercourse between diverse and mutually independent centers" is impossible. Something infinitely precious and frail is lost, "the living warmth of a human environment, a medium which bathes and fosters the thoughts and the virtues" (SE 79), the beauties of daily life: "home, country, traditions, culture" (GG 133), which nourish and warm the spirit. Weil did not take account of the ways in which traditionally feminine concerns have restricted women's lives in many cultures. What she did notice is that the jettisoning of traditional ways of life has grave dangers. Her defense of human needs might be of special interest to non-Western feminists who have been understandably suspicious of exploitative Western development and concerned for the survival of indigenous ways of life.

How can a traditional human environment be defended against military or economic aggression? Weil was deeply skeptical of the supposed benefits of violent conflict. In organizing for war, individuals are even more subject to central power; with the infrastructures that support reciprocal relations destroyed in war, autocracy may be the only possible order that can result.[38] Weil agonized. In some cases, passive resistance, she decided by the time she wrote *A Need for Roots*, could lead to many lives being lost, but defense of the glory of the state, which means conquest as well as defense, cannot be the purpose of a just war. In nationalistic militarism, the state becomes an absolute, demanding total loyalty, instead of a defendable territory that, like all earthly things, is both good and evil. But with national defense, instead of a standing professional army, people might defend a way of life and fight a war so that it does not destroy the life it claims to protect. Elements can be involved in the waging of war that retain the life-affirming values necessary for reconstruction. Weil used her cherished, perhaps impractical, plan for a corps of frontline nurses as an example. In the midst of killing, where all human values are lost, there could be the example of nurses' care and attention to the wounded to provide continuity with the ideals of peacetime and the basis for renewed human life.

To the Gaulists reconstructing France, Weil's papers on the reconstruction of Europe seemed unrealistic and even alarming. Her claim that monarchy was not necessarily oppressive was dismissed as reactionary. Her refusal to endorse the party system was interpreted as a support for authoritarianism. Her qualified approval of censorship was seen as disregard for human rights. Her plan for a corps of frontline nurses was seen as foolish romanticism. Beneath these controversies was perhaps her most disturbing claim: specific governmental or economic structures are not the determinant feature of a just society. The common dream of political theorists and social architects, that a correct model or blueprint for the just society can be drawn, is an illusion.

Goodness in Human Affairs

Weil did not survive the war to specify the forums in which the claims of women to justice might be heard. But with her analysis of power, she brought out deficiencies in much of the repertoire of social philosophical concepts available to feminist activists coming to terms with women's *malheur* and the obduracy of institutionalized power. The liberating force of Locke's property rights is the force of male entrepreneurs sacrificing the health of workers for profits. The force of Rousseau's liberalizing, democratizing "General Will" is the force of the corporate interests of the powerful men who manage elections. The force of the revolutionary socialist collectivity is the force of male leaders of the Communist party. Force is pitted against force; force transforms itself into more force. In opposition to these philosophic formulations of justice, feminist theorists have identified oppressive power with masculinity. Feminist practice has been conceived accordingly. Either women should make a claim to share in that masculine power; or they should valorize a different feminine power out of their opposing impotence. For Weil, the remedy for social injustice cannot be more power; it can only be goodness.

In philosophy after Descartes, the goodness of an individual has often seemed a suspect commodity. If goodness is in the soul, in the privacy of a thinking thing's mind, inevitably it imposes on others a subjective standard. Weil's goodness is not framed in the context of a philosophical dualism of private mind and public body, but in the reciprocal relation between individual and world. Goodness is not an idea, but a way of acting in that world: attentive, listening, capable of response to claims for justice. If, as feminist critics have pointed out, it is men who have exercised most of the destructive power that Weil describes and men who continue to seek that power in elections and commerce, it is women, for whatever the reason, who are more likely to have the communicative goodness Weil describes. If this is true, the recruitment of women for public office is not only redress of past discrimination, but a positive means to a more just society. For Weil, more important than the structure of institutions is the character of the persons who administer them. It is through good individuals that Weil's divine goodness, those infinitely small grains of the divine, permeate and leaven human affairs.

Weil used the history of Fascism in Luxemburg's Germany to show the stages by which goodness can be made to disappear from human affairs ("This War is a War of Religions" SE). In the period before the world wars, German culture had been characterized by an "indifference" to values; then came the uprooting of nationalities and economies caused by World War I, which accelerated the disintegration of European culture. Life was occupied with pleasure, diversion, escapism. Nihilism, however, is not possible for long and easily changes into "idolatry" in which some one social reality is adored as a divinity: the free enterprise system, the state, the universal church, or, in Germany, "the law of nature" that the Aryan race must be purified. Idolatry is also unstable. Rome, the church, colonial empires, the German Reich fall in a violent destruction of human life.

This natural movement from indifference to idolatry to holocaust, Weil believed, can be escaped only if there is access through individuals to a goodness that is not a thing, but a point of reference out of the world to which to aspire. When a society is infused with ideals through individuals capable of charity and attention, there is effective resistance to the evils of idolatry and indifference. If England was able to resist and defeat Fascism it was because imperialist England still had roots in a past "impregnated with mystic life" (SE 106), roots which allowed the British to wait and listen while Germany hysterically attacked Russia and wasted its strength. If the French had shown reprehensible weakness, it was because their ideals had been completely contaminated with colonialism and racism in North Africa. Weil's vision of a divinely inspired spiritual society is no theocracy, no rule of any church, Catholic or otherwise, but a society in which there is access to the divine. That access, unrelated to institutional allegiance, is achieved through people who share a sense of the beauty of the world, who have the ability to listen and respond to others, who are willing to move from value systems centered on private appetite to respect for the aspiration of others, and who appreciate the value of balance and equilibrium in human relations. When a people is infused with the divine in this sense, they are able to resist idolatry both from within and when it is imposed on them by force.

Political theory has traditionally been the study of force: evil force—the force of feudal privilege, capitalist exploitation, masculine domination—and the good force that is to oppose evil force—the force of corporate autonomy and multiparty rule, the force of a dictatorship of the proletariat, the force of feminist protest. Formulated as a particular political agenda, force becomes the moral absolute that guarantees justice. Weil would not have been surprised that the results have been disappointing. The world is ruled by force, which is natural, necessary and, in itself, neither good nor evil. Made into an absolute—what must be done—no matter its justification, force is inevitably evil; blind, mechanical, ruthless, it grinds out horror, just as capitalism produces the urban ghetto, or Marxism the Stalinist labor camp.

The source of social change for Weil is the individual woman or man, but her understanding of that individual is different from that in either reformist liberalism or socialism. A person is not the representative of a collectivity or class. Nor is she the autonomous, rational, self-interested, decision-maker of classical economics. As a physical being, she has no independence, physical or mental from natural processes; as an aspirant to the good, she does not form ideas in the privacy of her mind. In the place of a static dualism of mind and body is a movement of development: from the senseless churning of psychological impulse to a sense of herself in relation to the physical world, from a self-centered value system to the ability to hear and respond to others. Recognizing that the deepest core in each person is neither body nor mind but mutuality, a good person is in a position to grasp what must be done to move toward a social balance in which mutuality, and its circulation in appeal and response, are fostered and facilitated. She will understand that achievement of natural happiness requires the support of living networks of social relations that do not make it necessary for people to become deaf, heartless, and selfish. She will understand that sacred places of silence and retreat must be maintained. She will understand that the inspirational beauty of the natural world must be preserved, because, without access to beauty, human life would be ruled by mindless brutality. There is no law of force that says that such a balance in human affairs will be achieved. If the last *metaxu*, the last fragile living environments that support reciprocal personal relations rooted in the past, are destroyed, there may be little hope that such balance can ever be achieved.

Embodied Thought

Luxemburg's thought was concrete and theoretical at the same time. Departing from both Hegelian idealism—in which ideas frame material reality—and Marxist materialism—in which historical events determine thought processes, Luxemburg neither interpreted events in accordance with theory nor allowed events to dictate her thoughts. Her attention to particular phenomenon such as German militarism resulted in new theoretical models; thinking through theoretical constructs such as a supposed abstract right to national autonomy resulted in clearer descriptions of regressive policies. Weil's thought is in the same tradition. Beginning from painful experience in the natural and social world, Weil thinks and understands both religion and the most rigorous of mathematical theory not as a linear building but as a finding of pathways. Given the shifting nature of reality, paths turn and sometimes wander, even as mathematics and mathematical science help to project straight repeatable sequences. Rather than foundations, thought has experiential "roots," in alienation from a brother, in sympathy for unemployed and oppressed workers, in revulsion at the violence of war and the destruction of cultures. With no pretense to architectural integrity, Weil pursued threads of concern that there be an end to the pain, killing, maiming of souls that seem to be the natural consequence of human existence.

The elements of such a thought are related not by a deductive following of conclusion from premises, but by a sequential following of one footstep after another. The necessity of such a following is rooted in reality and not in any logical principle of identity. Because the goal of thought is not a definable absolute but an ideal or point of aspiration, thought does not need to validate itself as does the philosopher's foundations and the philosopher's logic. Because contradictions are not oppositions to be dissolved, but difficulties in the way of progress, problems can be absorbed back into thought, causing it to move off obliquely rather than to continue dogmatically in a straight line.

There are two important areas in which such thinking might be particularly useful to feminists: religion and science. Although many women now serve in religious office, they are seldom in top leadership; nor have they been able to expunge sexism from the religious language and doctrine of any of the Western religions: Christianity, Judaism, Islam. The response of many women has been to abandon religion altogether, as archaic and unredeemable. Given that atheistic Marxist materialism has failed to plot a just course for progressive social theory, this leaves a spiritual and moral vacuum in social theory. From where is the impulse to women's social activism to come? If it is generated from a woman's body—from maternal or sexual instincts, for example—feminism seems to be drawn back into biological determinism; if it is generated from an idea of femininity, feminism is vulnerable to charges of ethnocentricity and discrimination. What is needed, it would seem, are Weilian ideals to which all, women and men, those of different cultures and religions, might aspire.

In recent years, feminist spirituality has taken different forms. Women have remained within the Western institutional religions and attempted to revise sexist tenets and practices; they have rejected all existing institutional religions for the memory of a Goddess worship which predates the Aryan invasions of Europe. But feminist revision of language or liturgy has not touched the substance of belief in a omnipotent master deity which is the model for oppressive male power, and, although separatist rites of Goddess worship have given emotional gratification to women, they have not challenged the power of institutional religion to dictate conventional morality and proper practice. In contrast, Weil reframed Christian devotion in a transformation that goes to the very core of religious belief and practice.[39] Weil's noncredulous Christianity, released from the institutional control of male dominated churches, Islamic brotherhoods, and synagogues, draws on a living religious tradition. Religion is restored as a free and flexible devotion focused on revelations of divinity in natural life, a devotion which might permeate a culture, which imposes an obligation to act with and for others, and which is open to insights from other religious "languages."

Perhaps the most striking product of Weil's embodied thought was her utopian vision of the way we might practice, conceive and teach the science that now shapes our material lives. Women continue to suffer from a persistent science and math "anxiety" which keeps them from mastering the technical skills that are the prerequisite for scientific research. Like patriarchal religion, male-dominated science has been a frequent target for feminists. They have pointed out that science has been practiced almost exclusively by men. They have described how, at its very inception, science metaphorically characterizes itself as masculine against feminine-identified ways of knowing like alchemy or magic. They have documented science's implication in men's wars and men's economic strategies. They have uncovered the sexist background assumptions that frame much current scientific research. The remedies proposed have been various: preventing discrimination, affirmative action to recruit women into the sciences, a choice of research programs that support feminist policies and principles, the institution of feminine methods of research that involve empathy rather than manipulation. Weil raises the possibility of radical reformulation of virtually all of modern philosophy of knowledge, with its source in Descartes's reaction to the scientific revolution. Weil's science is not a different feminine science; it is the same rigorous, modern, mathematical science, conceived differently, not as representation whose truth is a function of logical coherence and experimental verification, but as the methodical working experience of women and men in contact with physical reality.

Much contemporary feminist epistemology has continued to understand science as representation, representation whose linguistic, psychological, and cultural symbolic structures are gender-laden. The remedial interpretations suggested have often seemed to make little headway against mainstream philosophical epistemology sanctioned by the technical resources of mathematical logic. In response, feminist philosophy of science has in some cases seemed to evoke a retrograde nostalgia for representations of prescientific ways of knowing no longer viable. Because Weil's modern science is not representation of any pre-existing reality, it must be judged effective on the basis of its contribution to human welfare, rather than on the basis of how well it serves the will of those in power. As such, it is a science expressly formed to be used by working women and men to inform their actions.

Such a science might engage the interest of women the way no representation, feminist or other, can. Especially useful to women might be a Weilian pedagogy in science. Although feminists have repeatedly pointed out the unfriendliness to women of the current climate of science and math education, the remedial measures proposed have dealt primarily with the removal of prejudice in the attitudes of teachers, and in the unbiased construction of mathematical and scientific problems. If math were not taught as representation from artificial examples and meaningless abstractions, but as Weil's "ways humans conceive paths in physical reality," women might come to science without coaching. A mathematics which is not a code for the delivery of weapon systems, but the study of the forms of actions in the world that make a path for human aspiration, a physics which is not the microstructural probability that facilitates nuclear reactions, but a repertoire of techniques to improve the lives of children and loved ones: this science might be, for women, the most popular of subjects.

Embodied thought from and about experience requires a language that is flexible, communicable, and expressive. Such a language has seldom been prescribed for science; instead, philosophers have constructed "ideal" languages specifically differentiated from the subjectivity of natural language. Plato proposed a rational text of abstract forms as the corrective to natural expressive language. Positivists theorized a calculus of facts based on scientific data and logical principles; structural linguists abstracted transformational grammars that reflect idealized "linguistic competence." Currently, much of the professional work of philosophers in English-speaking countries is taken up with the task of replacing the idioms of natural language with mathematical logic.

As with economics, few feminist theorists have been willing to take on linguistic and semantic theory, which is highly technical and at the center of contemporary establishment philosophy. Weil made only a small beginning toward conceiving concepts that might initiate a different study of language responsive to women's concerns. If words do not retain meaning when they are representations, what is the linguistic medium that insures Weil's cries of justice will be heard? If science is not privileged representation, what is the technically adequate language in which science might be discussed and evaluated by workers and citizens? These questions were not answered by Weil, but she provides an alternate starting point for their study: not the presumption of Descartes's privacy which makes any communication problematic in principle, but an original, interactive relation between self and physical world, a nondualist concept of a person, and the recognition of a communicative core in persons where they speak to each other from the heart.

The original impulse of Western philosophy was announced by Plato as escape from politics and the working body to a realm of thought uncontaminated by interest, appetite, or manual labor. In philosophy's subsequent history, alienation from natural life and its problems takes different forms: from Descartes's cordoning off of material substance from an autonomous scientific mind detached from its body, to empiricists' attention to private impressions and ideas rather than real objects of common perception, to contemporary logical and linguistic analysis which deflects attention away from politics and history to the disembodied traces of events in discourse. Separated from life in a heaven of metaphysical Forms, in the privacy of his own mind, or in the structures of logical form, the problem for a philosopher is to find a footing, a sure foundation on which to build up a truth that stands firm against ordinary opinion. The grand systems of philosophy are the result: at their base, intuition of Form—clear and distinct mathematics, incorrigible sense data, logical truth; in their scaffolding, principles of construction—formulas, rules of composition, logic.

A considerable body of feminist philosophy is critical of the disembodied rationality of this philosophical tradition, but that rationality is often contrasted with a feminine counterpart: the body, feeling, passion. To the "thought" of male philosophers denying the passions is opposed the expressive sexuality of a woman's body. Weil cuts across these oppositions. The body, as she understands it, is not primarily female, nor is it sexual; Weil sees sexuality not so much as a bodily function, as a spiritual impulse toward loving relationship. For Weil, the bodies of both women and men are working bodies, making ways in the world. These are the bodies that, for Weil, are the original thinkers, the thinkers to which all thinking, no matter how technical or theoretical, must return if it is to retain reference. The body is not the recipient of atomistic impressions and sensations impinging on its sense organs, as the British empiricist philosophers understood it, nor is it the medium for internally generated drives and impulses. It intelligently feels and thinks its way in a physical environment, recognizing and reacting to forms, patterns, relations. As such, it is the originator of concepts that are not empty abstractions but have reference in the world.

To the practical life of women and men, enmeshed in physical reality, looking only to the next practical problem, Plato opposed the philosopher's reason. Progressively losing sight of the concerns of ordinary women and men, the philosopher would concentrate on universal forms of goodness and virtue. Weil's lover of wisdom is described differently. She does not detach herself from physical experience. She does not ignore the multitude of particular opinions and ideas. She does not try to find a common denominator or induce consistency by setting aside what is inconsistent with established positions. She holds all particular views in mind, aware of the diversity of perspective and opinion, in all of which there may be grains of truth and human aspiration to the good. Without putting anything aside, she looks through and beyond particulars to a further way of thinking that presents an advance, a new inclusive course of action in the world.

Once the war began, Weil's passionate involvement in workers' movements and her pedagogical experiments in mathematics and science in the French lycées were no longer possible. Living environments, perhaps even physical life itself, were in question. The massive social transformation necessary for thoughtful labor and practical science as she had conceived it seemed all but impossible. Hannah Arendt survived the war to continue thinking. It was necessary to live on in a world in which the Holocaust had been possible, in which socialism was totalitarianism, and in which democratic politics had degenerated into media events. With continued technical development in computer programming, genetic research, nuclear reactions, worker's self-administration, the final remnant of nineteenth-century revolutionary hope now hung by the slender thread of Weilian superhuman grace. As Arendt continued to reflect on the role of necessity and force in human work, the thread snapped. Undertaking a comprehensive study of the active life in the past and present, Arendt concluded that work cannot be self-administering as socialists had dreamed. The grand utopian socialist project of the liberation of labor was ill-conceived. If work in modern economies is to be done efficiently, force will always be necessary; the workplace cannot be the place of liberation.

For Arendt, contemplating the remnants of Western culture which had survived the war, absolutes were not only dangerous but nonexistent. The very terms of human life had changed. Now the problem would be to make a hazardous way from one historical moment to another without ideals, without "banisters," as Arendt put it, with only the shattered remnants of Weil's *metaxu*, the living cultural matrixes which sustain human life. Weil's present and absent God, although it might give solace and energy, seemed of little use in the dispirited patching of what was left of the Enlightenment West. The embodied substance of Weil's ideal of social equilibrium is the core of mutuality in every person. That core is the source of Weilian social justice, as well as of a common aspirational language in which a visionary politics might be conducted. If a woman speaks from the heart, if she listens to others, progress can be made toward understanding the nature of democracy and freedom. Observing the rhetoric of postwar politics, Arendt questioned this involvement of passion in human affairs. Studying the history of revolution as an idea and an event, Arendt saw danger in Weil's absolute obligation to hear the cries of the oppressed. Absolute obligation to relieve the suffering of the poor had inspired the French Revolution; in the subsequent history of that revolution communicative relations had not been maintained. Absolute commitment to the working class had motivated Marxism: in the end violence and oppression were used in the name of the justice.

If Weil's thought was embodied, a component of the working and suffering body as it made its painful and joyful way through the world, Arendt temporarily withdrew from the press of events. Finding a foothold out of time, and yet posed at a perilous postwar intersection between past and present from which to reconsider the future, she reconsidered the human condition. That thoughtful moment of pause and reflection away from political activity, personal pain, and work, might be the only protection against evil, the only possibility for truth in politics, the only means to a new beginning in human affairs.

III

Hannah Arendt

"After her death, a sheet of paper was found in her typewriter, blank except for the following heading, *Judging*, and two epigraphs. Sometime between the Saturday of finishing *Willing* and the Thursday of her death, she must have sat down to confront the final section."

Mary McCarthy in her Preface to *Thinking*, Volume I of Arendt's unfinished trilogy, *The Life of The Mind*

3

Between Past and Future

The past and future Hannah Arendt found herself between did not inspire complacency. In the past was the nihilism of European culture and politics between the two world wars, the rise of Fascism, the failure of revolutionary Marxism, and finally, the Holocaust. The future looked equally grim, with the prospect of nuclear war, threatened destruction of the natural environment, and the numbing meaninglessness of life in industrialized, bureaucratized societies. In thought, Arendt never moved away from this painful present intersection between the horrors of the past and dangers of the future. In the late twentieth century, with no stable tradition or values intact, with the humanist ideals of the Enlightenment irrevocably compromised, she saw no nonillusory alternative. Her main business as a thinker, as she understood it, was to understand what has happened and what has been done, to learn to live with that knowledge, and to anticipate the future.

Arendt's relations with traditional philosophy were ambivalent: she deprecated herself as only a political theorist and not a philosopher, at the same time as she was critical of philosophy's pretensions to sovereign knowledge. She was a favored student of the famous Heidegger, but in a lengthy review of philosophical authorities in *The Life of the Mind*, she concluded that "professional" philosophical opinion on subjects like thinking and willing was unreliable. Nevertheless, in her attempt to understand past and future, Arendt asked fundamental questions about the nature of knowledge, truth, and reality. She did not come to these "philosophical" topics as a professional, but as someone who must attempt to make sense of the reality she experiences, and who, in the process, is forced to deeper and deeper levels of understanding. The result is that the ways she frames questions differ from traditional formulations. Because her questions and categories come out of problems in experience, she cuts across and through philosophers' categories and formulations at a level deeper than many have been willing to work.

Western metaphysics has been occupied with the question: what is there in the world in the most general sense? This is traditionally interpreted as a question about what *things* there are in the world: Are there minds, bodies, atoms, eternal forms, sense data . . . ? Arendt, as she tried to make sense of twentieth-century experience, did not think in terms of ontology but in terms of relations. The problem, as she understood it, is not to reconcile two different kinds of *things*, mind and body, as has been a major theme in modern philosophy, but to understand the reciprocal relations between a person's inner space and her appearances to others in public. Similarly in social theory, her concern was not the proper allocation of those "things" which are rights and duties, but the relation between private spaces in which thought is possible and the public world in which we appear to others.

Western philosophers from the classical Greeks to Heidegger have been preoccupied with the prospect of death and mortality. The inevitability of natural change and destruction prompted Parmenides to the original philosophic search for eternal homogenous Being. Even for twentieth-century positivists who claimed to reject metaphysics, contingency and change were the enemy of philosophers as they directed the search for Being to abstract logical structures grounded in the incorrigible "sense data" of science. The theme to which Arendt returned again and again was not mortality, contingency, and death, but "natality." The most striking thing about human life, she said, is not that we die but that we give birth, not only to children but also to new ways of acting, living, and thinking.

The history of Western philosophy has been intimately connected with the development of logic. Plato and Aristotle replaced ordinary human talk with "Logos," conceptually ordered discourse and inferences from premises to conclusion. A primary theme in philosophy has been progress in logic: from the syllogism to medieval consequential to modern mathematical logic. Arendt understood logic, as she did everything else, in the context of human life. She focused on logic's use, especially on its use in totalitarian ideology, where argument was more likely to represent lack of thought than understanding. Convinced that thoughtfulness is the only sure protection against evil, she argued not for training in logic or critical thinking, but for remembrance and stories, narrative forms of understanding which have had little standing in philosophy since Plato banished the poets from his ideal Republic.

Beginning from the standpoint of a rational, autonomous, thinking subject, Descartes mapped out necessary relations between mind and body and established the objectivity of knowledge. Realization of the fragility and disunity of Descartes's subject has driven postmodern critics to reify its counterpart: objective symbolic structures, constructed or deconstructed, which are prior to individual subjects and which provide the framework within which subjects find an alienated identity. The seemingly unsolvable postmodern dilemma—between the illusory autonomy and freedom of a unitary subject and alienated institutional and symbolic structures no one creates or can control—does not arise for Arendt. She does not start from an essential, autonomous self-consciousness that is a human essence. For Arendt, no aspect of the human condition is essential. Nor does she understand language as symbolic structure. Instead, a *relation* to the earth *conditions* a variety of forms of human activity. A *relation* to others *conditions* different kinds of linguistic behavior. With Arendt there is no "subject" to be exposed and discredited, no structures in which subjects are constituted to be deconstructed. She returns to Weil's questions: what is our relation to natural necessity? In making our primary end the mastering of that necessity, do we in fact institute in human life a necessity that should only be found in nature? What kind of spaces are necessary if harmonious human relations are to be maintained and are not to deteriorate into interested and selfish attempts by individuals and groups of individuals to gratify desires and cravings for power?

Philosophers have searched for the eternal, for truths that endure from generation to generation, truths that transcend the contingency of natural and human events. Universal philosophic truth has taken different forms: Plato's rational vision of the form of the Good, Aristotle's intuition of the essence in the particular, scholastic deductions from divine revelation, the forms of inductive reasoning in science, the dialectical process of the World spirit, the determinism of economic processes, functional laws that connect social phenomena, the necessity of grammatical structures grounded in the constitution of the human mind, even more recently the necessary ambiguity of any meaning that pretends to be based on a unitary presence. Arendt was never interested in giving such universal accounts of what reality or language must be, cannot help but be, has always been beneath whatever we thought it was. Her thinking begins from what actually happened, is happening, and might happen.

Spaces rather than forms, natality rather than mortality, narratives rather than logic, relations rather than the subject, the particular rather than the universal, understanding rather than refutation: these are the themes of Arendt's thought about history, society, language.

If no discipline has been completely willing to own Arendt—not philosophy, or political science, or sociology, or history—it may be because no "discipline" finds it easy to contain a thought which cuts so deeply into presuppositions that sustain its philosophical foundations. In another sense of philosophy, these anomalies—unacceptability in any of the accepted frames of knowledge, ability to give new answers to old questions and to reframe new questions relevant to human experience, personal questioning at the deepest levels of accepted modes of reasoning, concern for the threatened survival of human life—qualify as a love of wisdom.

1. Self and World

Real Appearances

Anyone who has tried to take effective action knows how illusory one's grasp on reality can be. Negotiation for pay raises can go on, while all the while, real power relations in a firm make it certain that a woman will not be promoted. A woman may extract a promise of childcare from her husband and find that his real identity depends upon a sense of himself as masculine that precludes housework. She may run for political office, but discover that the real policies of her party do not reflect her values. She deliberates on difficult questions even as the situation that confronts her shifts and changes: what people say is not what they think, what they think is not what they are, what is true one day is no longer true the next. The philosophers's question: what is really and truly real?—is not an academic question for women trying to find footing from which to initiate lasting significant change.

The primal impulse in Western philosophy has been the search for a reality that neither dies nor is born. Especially this has been true in times of crisis, in times, as Arendt put it, of the great philosophical impulses—the clash between Hellenic invaders and indigenous Mediterranean culture, the expansion of the Hellenic empire, the wars of religion and conquest of the sixteenth and seventeenth centuries, the mass destructions of the world wars. In reaction to these events, Plato, the Stoics, Descartes, logical positivists, phenomenologists pursued a "Being," not subject to natality or mortality, which might replace unstable objects of mortal opinion, shifting mores of particular cultures, deceptive sensory impressions, subjective ideals. Because everything in the natural world, including the most permanent structures, is subject to change and mortality, philosophers looked for another hyperreality in opposition to the phenomenal world, a reality that could be relied upon and that could be the basis for infallible judgments. Appearance and reality have been understood in philosophy accordingly, as opposites which take their meanings from each other: appearing is the lack of Being which is true reality; true Being is the lack of illusory appearance.

In contrast, for Arendt, appearances *are* primary reality and cannot be understood as a negation of anything. If appearances shift and change, it is not because they are unstable reflections *of* a higher order of Being, but because they are a positive appearing *to* something or someone. The shifting and changing of appearance is a real "response" to others, directed toward an audience. Living things, perhaps even nonliving things, "appear"; they display themselves: "whatever can see wants to be seen, whatever can hear calls out to be heard, whatever can touch presents itself to be touched" (T 29). Any attempt to reduce the richness and variety of appearances to permanent underlying structures, Arendt argued, distorts substantive reality. Reality *is* the appearances of life in their confusion and diversity. If philosophy begins with Parmenides' attempt to escape from "mortal opinion," from the shifting, changing, "it seems to me" of human affairs, Arendt stays with the phenomenal world as it is, constituted by *relations* between beings who present themselves to others and the other beings who see them and respond to them. Solitary Being is impossible; all existence is dependent on plurality, on the others who see it, think about it, understand it, judge it, will it to be different. The philosopher's unreliable "it seems to me" is the very substance of reality (T 21).

In much modern philosophy, it has been assumed that ultimate reality is represented in science. Descartes, beginning from the shock of realizing that sensory illusion was the basis for earth-centered medieval cosmologies, announced the new mathematical science that would discover and represent real and permanent structures beneath the shifting perceptions of physical things. His conciliatory dualism of separate mental and physical substances was soon replaced by a homogeneous material world of atomic bodies and forces whose objective reality is represented in physics. In the twentieth century in the face of surrealism, nihilism, Nazi rhetoric, non-Newtonian physics and non-Euclidean geometries, the philosopher's dream of eternal Being took linguistic form in the positivist's ideal of a perfected logical language of science, self-consistent and anchored in incorrigible protocol sentences.

But to project techniques of science as the one reality that underlies all physical appearances, Arendt argued, is to lose touch with phenomenal reality and see only ourselves and what we can do. In the philosopher's "science as truth" the real world of appearances has disappeared. A strip miner plots the lines of her excavation, but misses the damage to landscape and wildlife; a manufacturer of diet aids calculates the calories in his packaged milk shake, but misses the cycles of fast and feast that put on weight; an engineer measures the force of the water behind her dam but misses the fact that the fertility of the land below has been lost. In each case the mathematical formulas of science are taken as reality; the real world of experiences and appearances is ignored.

Arendt traced the history of modern science's eclipse of a common phenomenal world accessible to the senses from its beginnings in the seventeenth century. The "shock" of the revelations of the telescope, which seemed to indicate that what we see with our eyes cannot be trusted, resulted in the strange view that seeing, hearing, touching, are sensations like pain.

> Only an irresistible distrust of the capacity of the human senses for adequate experience of the world—and this distrust is the origin of all specifically modern philosophy—can explain the strange and even absurd choice that uses a phenomenon which, like pain or tickling, obviously prevents our senses from functioning normally, as examples of all sense experience. (HC 114–5)

Empiricist philosophers used the analogy of pain—the pain of a cut does not tell us about the nature of the sword that inflicts the wound—to argue that the senses cannot tell us about the external world but, at best, are only evidence for a nonexperiential reality. To see was to have a "visual sensation" similar to a bodily sensation like an itch or tickle. Perception turned inward, imprisoned in a body only able to sense the throbs and ticks of its own physical processes (HC 114–5). When the empiricist's ideas lose all phenomenal reality and become the nonpsychological logical and linguistic structures of cognitive science, all external reference is gone. We know only the imagined working of our own brains.[1]

Like Weil, Arendt's concern was not to refute modern empiricist philosophy but to understand what it is about. She reads in philosophers' own accounts of knowledge the experiences their philosophy reflects. Empiricist philosophers describe a life in which the communicative relations which allow a common world and a grasp on reality have disappeared. This, Arendt pointed out, is increasingly the modern condition. Without a public life, we have, in fact, come to live in a world where perceptions—sight, sound, touch—are dulled and experience is degraded to inner sensations which are experienced only as pleasurable, painful, interesting, relaxing. In the place of perception, managers and scientists devise ways to reduce or dull the painful sensations and multiply the pleasurable. With the techniques of advertising, women and men lose touch with even their bodily sensations, and come to live in a semiotic world of manipulated symbols.

The epistemological problems that have exercised philosophers in the modern period reflect this experience: how can private sensations support public truths? Does the external world exist? How can private sensations be named and communicated to others? Do other minds exist? Inevitably, Descartes's nightmare of an evil demon who maliciously deforms thought comes true. The usefulness of non-Euclidean geometries is taken to show that any conceptual scheme might be true—we cannot rely on the structure of our own mind, which God might have made systematically defective (HC 70). The possibility of alternative theories equally supported by evidence suggests that science may be an imaginary projection—an evil demon might be playing with our minds. Either an anarchy of possible scientific worldviews is accepted or a conventionalism that takes as true whatever the scientific establishment at any time takes as true.

A further change in science makes the situation even more dangerous. Weil envisioned a science that acknowledges that it is paths in the natural world, forms of methodical interaction between humans and physical reality. But with contemporary developments in science, this may no longer be possible. Early industrial development was powered by steam, a natural force that was used, molded, and interrupted by workers as Weil describes. But with the invention of electricity and nuclear power, nature itself is changed. From the outside-the-earth vantage point of Descartes's science, "unearthly" natural processes are invented which have their own dynamics, which cannot be controlled or molded, whose unnatural course is not predictable or related to working methods, and which may turn out to be demonic rather than divine.

If Descartes's mathematical physics cannot give us the truth about reality, biology, argued Arendt, is not much better. In biology the dominant approach has been functional. Biological structures are understood with reference to their contribution to the survival of organisms, with the understanding that the natural urge to survival itself may be ultimately reducible to genetic or chemical structures. What a functional biology misses, however, is that skin, feathers, fur, behavior may not contribute to survival at all, but express a universal impulse to display and to reach out to others for response, whether sexual, amicable, bellicose, cooperative, defensive, or sociable. The rich profusion of living forms cannot be explained by a unitary and universal urge to physical survival, any more than they can be reduced to underlying mathematical structure.[2]

Nor can a social science which borrowed its methods from the physical sciences be relied upon for the truth about social matters. The claim of social science to discover a functional reality beneath social phenomena and experience also neglects the reality of appearances and experiences. If there are such things as alienation, powerlessness, or poverty, reference to them cannot be a matter of definition. These are phenomena that exist in the world, not underlying determining structures of behavior or functional regularities. What they are in reality cannot be defined by one researcher studying data or even by a group of researchers, but only in public discussion in which diverse people present themselves and their stories for others. Words cannot be meaningfully used in ways that do not take into account the experiences they name. Social scientists, for example, can define religion as what "functions" as a religion. Under this definition anything can be a religion, just as the heel of my shoe with which I pound in a tack can be a hammer. Marxism "functions" as a religion for Marxists, therefore Marxism is a religion. Television functions as an authority, therefore it is an authority. Once we look at the original experiences that words mark, however, reference is restored and it becomes possible to make a distinction and a judgment, to say: now there is no religion, there is no authority, it is no longer possible to have that experience (BPF 102ff.).

If reality is not metaphysical Being or the mathematical formulas of science, or biological functions, or functional relations between social variables, what is it? It is, Arendt says, simply what stays still long enough to be named and examined (T 44). From the standpoint of the philosopher's Being, this account of reality is unacceptable. It implies that certain knowledge is impossible; it implies there is no truth. But this is only the case if truth is understood as a set of propositions, existing in a timeless present, discoverable by one person or by no one at all. Factual truth understood in Arendtian terms is not ready-made or already there but a function of a multiperspectival reality of appearances. When science is understood not as a privileged representation of a reality behind those appearances but as a projection of useful techniques, it cannot replace a determination of the factual truth of appearances or phenomena which has its source in sense experience of the world. The question to be asked about phenomenal reality are not the philosopher's questions, but questions directly relevant to experience in and engagement with the world: does one account of what happened have more authority than another? Are there privileged perspectives such as Luxemburg's working-class standpoint or feminist standpoints? How is it possible to detect lying and deceit? By what process can we extract from particular events general concepts that link events to other events? Is there a "logic" of narrative discourse? The assumption behind these questions is not that there is a primal reality opposed to appearances, but that there is no truth, whether of science or of metaphysics, that does not have to be discussed and submitted to shared experience for verification and revision, no truth immune to a fresh view of matters of interest. To the "most important question of our time"—will science bring me freedom or chains?—Weil answered with the utopian possibility of a science integrated with working practice and education. Arendt gives another answer: it will bring freedom if there is public discussion of and principled action on the objects of science.

Physical reality is made up of "objects," but the very objectivity of objects, for Arendt, is relational and interpersonal. More primitive for Arendt than any objects, which may only be the adumbrations of concepts abstracted from their reference in experience, are the real relations in which objects come into being: relations between inner sensations and emotions and outer appearances in action and words; relations between the private spaces of homes and public spaces where there can be discussion and interaction; relations between persons which create objects of "inter-est" to them, concrete relations out of which objects in the sense of stable appearances are generated. The commonality that allows relations between people requires that they have interests in common; that they have interests allows new relations to be formed. Traditional metaphysics takes one end product of this complex social reality, objects, as given. All is objectified, the spaces, the relations, the emotions, the actions. From the point of view of Arendt's metaphysics, none of these are objects; to make them into objects is to construct an alternative reality in which objects stand independent of persons, their relationships, their feelings, and the spaces in which they exist. Everywhere life hardens into things: neurons, atoms, distances, sizes, social determinants, psychological complexes, productive relations that determine how we must live and act.

What gives an object its objectivity and allows it to be named, for Arendt, is that it is "between" people. Not even the objects of physical science—atoms, force fields, quanta—are determinable independent of human interests. It is always possible to ask: why are we interested in atoms? What is "between" us when we talk about them? For Arendt, these are questions about what an atom *is* and they cannot be answered by science. Science tells us how to do things with atoms, but the singling out of the atom as an object, rather than organic structures for example, is a subject of interpersonal interest. Because the very nature and identity of the objects of theoretical science are linked to human interests, a discussion of what atoms *are* properly includes a discussion of the use of nuclear energy, the project of military domination, as well as the larger issue of any proposed abandonment of habitat earth. Judgment on these questions, which are often dismissed by philosophers as secondary questions about the *use* of a science whose truth is independent of values and interests, are also questions about the objects of science.[3]

> Since the disclosure of the subject is an integral part of all, even the most "objective" intercourse, the physical, worldly in-between along with its interests is overlaid and, as it were, overgrown with an altogether different in-between which consists of deeds and words and owes its origin exclusively to men's acting and speaking directly *to* one another. (HC 182–3)

Much recent feminist philosophy has been critical of mainstream philosophical epistemologies in which an objective science is taken as the model of truth. Their well-supported claim has been that the supposed value-free objects and categories of science reflect the masculine interests and beliefs of the men who have defined science. Less clear in feminist philosophy has been what a feminist science not dominated by men might be like. Would it reflect feminine rather than masculine interests? Would it return to Descartes's paradigm of sovereign truth and attempt to institute an empiricism without bias? Arendt suggests another possibility. Science works its truth functions, but the real objects of science must be determined, like any other objects, by people, women and men, remembering together their experiences and thinking about their meaning. At stake, for Arendt, is not only the participation of women in the discussion, which she certainly would have approved, but reality and truth. If science is to be about real objects, those objects must be part of a common world between persons.

Much contemporary critical theory, including feminist theory, has been focused on refuting the claim of science to inviolable truth. Neither of the two poles in this dispute—science is truth or there is no truth—are likely to be of much use to women struggling to better their condition. Arendt's science of objects of common interest identified in free political speech and action between diverse individuals might, however, lead to scientific knowledge of the reality that women experience. Arendt, following Luxemburg and Weil, continues to knit back together philosophy of science and political and ethical philosophy. A feminist politician's business is with the objects of science, with the weapons that military science invents, with the work methods that engineering projects, with the organisms that determine the style of medical treatment. The real objects of medical science, nuclear armaments, engineering, objects about which people want and need to know cannot be determined by scientific fiat but only with reference to publicly understood, remembered, compared experience.

Self as Presentation

If the objectivity of a male-defined "Being" has been a major topic in recent feminist philosophy, even more controversial has been the nature of the female self. Again philosophy has marked out the perimeters of the problem. Either the self is as Descartes conceived it: an autonomous genderless consciousness set off from the sexed body and the natural world and capable of denying received ideas about femininity. Or the self, as is understood in recent continental philosophy, is constituted in cultural and linguistic structures that no one controls. In the first case women should claim the right to assert themselves as men do. In the second, women can make an oblique textual attack on the languages and discourses in which female identity is inscribed. Difficulties with both these approaches have been a frequent source of discussion in feminist philosophy. Can asserting oneself as a masculine consciousness be the means to an authentic feminine self? Alternately, if sexist reality is constituted in language, a woman who rebelliously confounds established categories courts unintelligibility and impotence and risks having no self at all.

For some feminist theorists, an alternative to the alienated rationality of the post-Cartesian masculine subject—whether self-constituting or constituted in linguistic or discursive structures—has been the female body. Women, like modernist poets of the turn of the century rebelling against bourgeois culture, should turn to their neglected bodies' urges, drives, desires, pleasures and reclaim an original female identity. But even in this more radical strategy, women continue to respect philosophical tradition: since Plato, the rational soul has been defined against the physicality and emotionality of women, and in contrast to women's dependence on bodily processes and immersion in practical affairs. Arendt undercuts the philosopher's assumption of an opposition between two things, mind and body, at a deeper level, before the identification of mind with masculinity or body with femininity. She does not understand soul and body as any kind of objects or pseudo-objects. Nor are they spaces in which objects can be placed. There is no inner mental space analogous to physical space accessible to introspection. Body and soul cannot be understood as opposing spaces because there can be no common boundary between them, as there is between the real private spaces of homes and the public spaces of politics.[4] In the place of a contrast between two things, mind and body, is a contrast and a relation between two aspects of human life: inner, showable sensation and outer appearances to others.

There are no mental objects such as bodily sensations or drives to constitute a female identity because the inner life cannot be an object of inter-est between people. The self, as experienced by living things, refers to the fact that, although a person shows herself to others, there is a part of her which remains private, unshowable, and nonobjective. The soul, anchored in the body, is inside, but not inside in the sense of another space or object which might be revealed. Again, Arendt refused the opposition of appearance and reality. It is not that there is a real mental place or thing which the "appearance" of behavior reveals or hides. It is not that the soul is an epiphenomenon of behavior or a "function" of physical mechanisms. There are ways we appear to others, and *in addition* and in relation there is an inner life of emotions and sensations which can never appear and which has no "objective" existence. Inner and outer life are related experiential realities.

The identity of mental "objects," such as emotions and sensations, has been a perennial source of philosophical perplexity. Are they cognitive states or sensations like pain? Are they physical bodily processes? Are they reducible to behavior or dispositions to behavior? All these questions, from Arendt's point of view, rest on the mistake of understanding inner life as made up of objects. Emotional life is not life in the world. It is not *objective* in the same way. Feeling is ambiguous, shifting, and conflictual. There is a constant fomenting and tossing of emotional strands. Even if psychoanalysts claim to locate a "logic" or pattern to these processes unlike physical processes, inevitably there is distortion, as what is inner and unshowable is made to appear, and the richness of human behavior is reduced to a few primal urges (T 35). We may decide to tell others about our experiences of anger or pain but in this telling we have already passed judgment on our feelings, chosen how we are to appear to others (T 34).

A woman, by herself, can never know what her sensations, emotions, and motives are with any certainty. Arendt defuses the intractable philosophical problem of mental privacy. Once a mental substance or an inner mental space is thought to be introspectable, a class of objects is created that are only observable by one person. Commonality then has to be found outside beliefs and experiences in structures of meaning independent of individual speakers. In Arendt's view, no one can tell a woman what her sensation or emotion is, but she can't know either. There is no privileged access to an inner private world of pseudo-events and objects. One's sense of an object "is so bound up with the presence of others that we can never be sure of anything that only we ourselves know and no one else" (OR 92).

The result is that we are often suspicious of ourselves. Unless the inner life has died as a result of *malheur* and a woman has lost the capacity to feel or hope, she questions her motives. This self-questioning is not lack of identity or the sign of a primal feminine plurality of consciousness, but the impulse to thought, to the kind of critical reassessment that Luxemburg made of economics and Weil of philosophy of science. When it becomes a false demand for sincerity in the form of a politically correct, substantive, inner self, it can lead to an unmasking zeal which often infects and ruins revolutionary movements. Is she in her heart a real Communist? Is her sexual pleasure truely feminine? Is her imaginary phallomorphic? The destructive purges, divisions, violence of revolutionary movements can result, as suspicion and internal dispute tear apart solidarity.

We have a real inner life. In extremity or in Weil's *malheur*, it is kept alive with great struggle. But this struggle needs darkness to survive (T 31–2). If a woman determines to confess, bear her heart, and show all that she feels, the reality of her inner life is gone. Such an exposure is ugly and distorting, just as exposing the inner organs of the body exposes blood and guts and destroys the living organs in the process. Emotions, like bones and stomach, are not meant to be exposed. Just as the inner life of organs is necessary for the survival of the body, so an inner life is vitally necessary to nourish and support human activity. When a person is maimed in the soul by Weil's *malheur*, action may be impossible. Emotions are the depth out of which a woman speaks and acts; without them, her words and actions are empty. But emotional depths do not and cannot "appear" in words or actions. They are expressed, if at all, in gesture, instinctive movements, and inarticulate expression appropriate in private. Emotions, bodily drives, sexual instincts do not make an authentic self. More important than any emotional expression or introspective examination of motives for a stable, authentic self-identity, for Arendt, is that a woman be able to "choose" how to present herself to others. For Arendt, there is no self that is not a public self. The presentation of self is the primary reality and characteristic of self. A woman's real self cannot come from bodily sensations, emotions, inner feelings, all of which are unshowable, but only from how she appears to others. Acting is not possibly deceptive, lying, or inauthentic appearance in contrast to a real inner life; it is the self; it is what we are.

From the vantage point of philosophical distinctions between a real inner self and its possibly deceptive outer appearances, Arendt's self seems no self at all. If emotions are unshowable without distortion and all appearances are presentations to others, then nothing mirrors a real self, male or female. Then do "hypocrisy" and "sincerity" mark no real difference? As always for Arendt, words and disputes over words mark distinctions, although those distinctions may not be the differences philosophers think they are.[5] The hypocrite, unlike the liar, convinces herself that she is what she is not; she no longer thinks, she no longer engages in the inner self-questioning which Arendt identifies with thought. To be "true to oneself" is not to appear to be someone identical with a real inner self. It is to think, to engage in a constant questioning of words and actions that results in a degree of consistency in words and actions. The real distinction marked by the word "sincerity," Arendt argued, is that some appear to others consistently and others do not. The evangelist who harangues from the pulpit against the sin of adultery, but who visits prostitutes, is a hypocrite. The politician who campaigns against corruption and who takes bribes when he gets into office is a hypocrite. The feminist who confesses sympathy for African women, but who supports exploitative trade practices, is a hypocrite. The professor who proclaims her freedom from homophobia, but who never mentions lesbianism in her classes, is a hypocrite. To be sincere is not to authentically reveal an inner self, but to be a real self in the world by keeping implied promises to others to act consistently (T 36–7). In Arendt's view of hypocrisy, someone who insists on constantly expressing her changing emotions and sensations in actions and words may be the worst hypocrite of all, as what she says and does waver in response to the play of her drives, sentiments, enthusiasms and sympathies.

Nor can a self be founded in reason. Out of a reservoir of feeling, sensation, and sentiment, we return to public life to present ourselves to others in actions and words; what we are in these presentations is stabilized not by philosophical logic, which can always be manipulated, but by the explicit and implicit promising of consistency which is both a necessary accompaniment to human action and the driving impulse to further reflective thought. Weil's self in reciprocal relation with the physical world makes her path in the world alone. Others are forces she must negotiate or souls to which she responds. Arendt's self is not alone. She is not the rational and autonomous Cartesian subject, nor is she constituted in preexisting social or symbolic structures, which might be subverted or resisted.[6] Her self-identity is established in others' acceptance and response. Arendt's self is not the result of a postmodern turning-operation in which the Cartesian master of rational structures turns out to be constituted only within those structures. Self-presentations, actions, and words, do fall into and are interpreted in preexisting webs of relationships, generated in actions and maintained by tradition. But each self-presentation is also the beginning of something new, an appearance in the world with the potentiality of remaking relationships and selves.

Arendt used the birth of a child to explain. The birth of a child is a miraculous new appearance. Parents may have some fixed, or not so fixed, idea of what their child will be; if they are realistic, they are willing to be surprised. If they try to impose on their child a life like their own or a life they wished they had, they are never successful; the child reacts to their pressure in ways they cannot predict and will not necessarily approve. An adult self continues to be the result of similar "births." Again and again, given the opportunity, people present themselves with hope and expectation, and the substantive reality of what results is not predictable or determinable by private or social meanings. It depends on how they are taken and understood by others. This radical dependence on others cannot be avoided except at the cost of lack of being. Free speaking and free acting, unwelcome, misunderstood, dangerous as they often can be, are the bedrock of a woman's self-identity as well as her grasp on reality.

2. Historical Understanding

Conditions and not Causes

Reality is appearances. Persons are how they present themselves to others. If this is true, knowledge of fact must be knowledge of temporal phenomena. There is no way to go beyond or beneath history to find universal economic laws, or universal social functions, or universal cognitive structures or semantic constants. Understanding of reality and persons must be historical. But history can be read in different ways. Stories of exceptional women can show that individual women, if they would only exert themselves, can succeed in a man's world. Stories of male dominance can show that sexism is a permanent structure in human life. The choice between voluntarism and determinism has been a repeated theme in philosophy of history: can a woman think freely and conceive original actions in the world, or is history determined by processes or structures out of any individual's control?

For women trapped in interlocking and overlapping systems of discrimination the question is pressing. Will feminist critique of philosophy as it has been practiced by men result in the freedom to conceive new courses of action, or can women only hope to find in existing currents—Heideggerian, Marxism, phenomenological, postmodern—ideas and arguments which they can use to their advantage? Are male perpetrators of violence or discrimination willful aggressors who can be taught or forced to change their ways, or is male violence a function of permanent structures that will reinstate themselves no matter what reprisals or persuasions are directed at men? Arendt's study of historical "conditions" is groundwork that might help to resolve some of these dilemmas.

Like Weil and Luxemburg, Arendt took as her subject matter in her first published book, *The Origins of Totalitarianism,* catastrophic historical experience, this time Fascism, in which she as a German and a Jew was personally involved. For Arendt, after the revelation of the death camps, the Holocaust had to be a major concern of any serious thinker. Fascism cannot simply be put in the past and forgotten; not when it represents the final, and perhaps irrevocable, dissolution of the West's pretension to universal humanitarian values. Arendt placed the collapse of Germany into fascist brutality, along with the failure of revolutionary socialism and the two world wars, in the context of the failure of the modernity that was to have guaranteed to Western culture its superiority and to the rest of the world prosperity under Western leadership.

As a philosophy student between the wars in Germany, Arendt noted the postmodern mood of despair: we catch onto any fad in ideas, which shows that we have no concepts of our own, rooted in shared experience (OR 222). We have lost touch with the classical traditions which founded our culture (T 211—2). Our experience is so impoverished that we are incapable of contemplation or wonder. Our thought is only calculation and is replaceable by computers (HC 310). Arendt did not construct a theory that would account for the failure of modernity and the rise of Fascism, a theory from which correct remedial measures could be dictated. She agreed with Weil that nonoppressive institutions and relations can only be generated by people themselves in their practical affairs (HC 5). Rather than theory, she offered thought, a reflective historical understanding which does not fit events into satisfying causal patterns, but which attempts to locate specific conditions of painful human experience.

For Arendt, a historical "condition" is not an absolute determinant.

She was critical, as were Luxemburg and Weil, of determinism both in its idealist and materialist versions. Hegelian and Marxist accounts of history make history a "process" subject to necessity, whether it is the necessity of the eventual self-realization of a World Spirit or of the progressive development of means of production. Arendt applauded Luxemburg for being one of the few Marxists who had avoided this Marxist mistake ("Rosa Luxemburg," MDT).[7] Arendt also rejected functionalist accounts of history that locate patterns and determine the "causes" of historical events (BPF 89). In such accounts, ideas and phenomena are separated from their basis in experience, and relations are established arbitrarily. At functionalism's extreme, the historian's world is purely subjective: he is "forever playing with his own images, unaffected by experience and with no relation to the world" (BPF 69). Functional "theories" are "hypnotic," they "put to sleep our common sense" (OV 8).

Even traditional historical accounts which attempt to isolate causal sequences of events like the Holocaust are false histories, because they fail to grasp the relation between such events and their conditions. Even more important, Arendt believed, causal accounts threaten to take away responsibility for historical events. If there are causes and functions at work, people caught up in anti-Semitism, violent racism, or witch-burning may not be held accountable. Crimes are seen as anonymous effects of social causes and not as specific actions for which actors are responsible. To take as the *cause* of Fascism a defect in the German character, for example, is to construct a artificial "collective responsibility," and to fail to make distinctions that are the basis for impartial judgments of guilt.[8]

On causality, Arendt took her inspiration from Duns Scotus rather than from Kant. To Kant, and to modern philosophers in general, it has seemed that scientific knowledge requires events to be determined in necessary causal sequences. The problem, then, for Kant and other philosophers is how to reconcile human freedom with determinism. Even if freedom is transferred inward to the will, it seems that the will, like any other phenomenon, must be determined and have a cause. Philosophers, influenced by science's claim to represent reality, took causality to be a prior reality that operates behind and determines appearances. This, argued Arendt, as she read Duns Scotus, is a mistaken understanding of causation. There is no one, essential, causal sequence that determines an event, but a plurality of causes and conditions. An event is the coincidence of a number of partial and independent causes that are part of a "texture of reality" (T 137).

Historical causality, far from indicating determinancy, involves contingency; the realization that another cause could have intervened and changed what happened. The idea of causality is based not on the intuition of a transcendental Kantian necessity but on experience after an event: the sense we have that what happened had to happen. This, for Arendt, is not the discovery of another deeper level of reality, but a function of human understanding temporally located between past and future. To understand what happened, we tell stories, stories with plots in which inessential elements are omitted, and in which one event leads to another in a coherent sequence of events. Interpersonal human narration, and not any superhuman metanarrative of events, is the source of the idea of causality.

If Arendt was no historical determinist, she was not a voluntarist either. It is not individuals' aims, any more than it is the aims of history, that are the subject matter of history. The war criminal Eichmann's "intentions" are irrelevant to what he did. What he, or any other man, thinks he is doing does not determine the meaning of his actions. The meaning of what someone does is determined by its effect on others, who continue to react and act in ways which cannot be controlled or predicted. Like so much else in modern philosophy, the choice between determinism and voluntarism is conditioned by Descartes's dualism. Once Descartes's individual autonomous "subject" with private intentions confronted an alien physical world it was inevitable that one side or the other in the opposition would have to be suppressed. Either the subject would have to be absorbed back into a determinable chain of events or reality would turn out to be a creation of will and intention.

For Arendt, action is not opposed to material reality. It is on earth and *with* other people. Neither a manifestation of an ideal world of the spirit nor an element in a physical process, it is part of a web of human relations. If the private mental world of intentions cannot give meaning to action, neither can the objective structures of history. Both are illusory; what is real are past events grasped in memory and in the telling and retelling of what happened, and what was done and said. This concrete and interpersonal understanding of what happened and what it means cannot be gotten through any intellectual schema, but only through access to events and experiences as they occurred and are recorded in diaries, letters, memoirs, political writings, and philosophy tracts. The conditions, unlike the causes, of racism, sexism, violence, are plural; they do not necessitate a given effect, but "crystallize" into historical events which must be described in their specificity.[9]

From conditions it is impossible to extract any strategy for manipulation. Although the substance of history is free human action, that freedom is never freedom to impose one's own will on reality. Lenin's Bolsheviks designing and "making" the new society were bound to fail. But Arendt did not understand this frailty and ambiguity of human action against a "law of history" which overrules human agency. If Communism became Stalinism, this was not because the invisible hand of the market always rules, or because history dictates that Socialism comes after capitalism. It is because the worldly nature of human action is to be always for and with others, which means that consequences of action are never determinable, no matter how efficiently an action is planned or how much force accompanies it. A Women's Studies program may result not in new dignity for women professors but in marginality for women's scholarship. The establishment of a Jewish homeland can lead not to a nondiscriminatory society but to a racially exclusive enclave.

The source of this indeterminacy, for Arendt, is not the philosopher's mortality—the necessary deterioration, decay, imperfection of all mortal things—but "natality"—the coming into the world of "strangers" (HC 9), capable of doing new things, capable of acts of foundation and beginning again. Natality, like giving birth, is not omnipotence. One person cannot, by an act of will and with sovereign power, construct a new reality, anymore than a child born into the world will fit parents' preconceived images of who that child should be. Action, like a child, is born into a world of human relationships in which it must find its own place. Nothing can dictate what that place must be.

It is with these concepts—natality, remembrance, narrative—anomalous in philosophy—that Arendt understood both the particular meaning of the Holocaust and the larger failure of modernity and Western culture that it signaled. Thought is historical for Arendt not only in the sense that the subject matter of her concerns is drawn from her own particular situation—German, Jew, woman, emigrant; in this case thought might still proceed rationally to produce objective truth. Her thought, itself, is historical, situated "nowhere," in a suspension of time between past and future, at a precarious intersection through which weave thought "trains" of remembrance and anticipation. The very motive force of thought, its dynamic, comes from temporal positioning in the present and a resulting struggle with the future against the past and with the past against the future. If a woman does not lose her nerve and escape into idealism, cynicism, or despair, if she does not succumb to the temptation to stop thinking, she can, when she thinks, manage to walk a diagonal between past and future, forward and then back again, precariously and painfully.

The Racist Past

As a Jew and as a woman, prejudice was of particular concern to Arendt. Her understanding of racism was neither rational—based on a theory of universal human rights—nor subjective—a study of the psychology of racism—but historical—an understanding of racism's actual conditions and effects. Arendt approached this crucial history in a number of different ways. One of the earliest was a detailed study of the life of a Jewish woman, Rahel Varnhagen, briefly a celebrity in salon society at the turn of the eighteenth to nineteenth century.[10] In the preface to her biography of Varnhagen, Arendt explains her aim: she will not give an account of Varnhagen's life as an observer from outside, from the vantage point of a theory, or of current social scientific understanding of the Jewish question or the "woman's question."[11] Drawing on Varnhagen's voluminous correspondence, she will tell the story of Varnhagen's life as Varnhagen herself experienced it.

Of primary importance in that story, for Arendt, are Varnhagen's attempts at assimilation into gentile society and her consequent failure to own her history as a Jew and as a woman. Arendt's emphasis on Varnhagen's Jewishness was controversial. Her old teacher Jaspers, clinging to the remnants of German high culture, which he believed would survive even the Nazis, complained that she had not done justice to Varnhagen's "humanity," her greatness as a human being: she had not allowed Varnhagen to speak from her human center, in comparison to which her Jewishness was only a contingent misfortune.[12] But Arendt did not read Varnhagen's diaries and letters as documenting the humanitarian and rational ideals of the Enlightenment—ideals which for her had been irrevocably compromised—she read them as an account of a story which might have been her's, Arendt's, and other Jewish women's own story.

As a Jew and a woman, without a profession, a place in society, or secure family ties, without any "position in the world of men which guaranteed her permanence" (RV 89), Varnhagen had only her present existence with which to make a life. That this was possible, even preferable, to an identity rooted in the past was assumed by the influential philosophies of her day. Both rationalism and its rival, romanticism, professed to liberate the individual from tradition and history to a present in which there would be no more prejudice by race or sex and no more conformity to societal norms. Recounting Varnhagen's life as she lived it, Arendt concluded that neither romantic feeling nor rationalist reason had been sufficient to establish a self or make a life. With only her inner nature and the sentiments of love and loss extolled by romantics like Rousseau, Varnhagen was infinitely vulnerable. With no resource against misfortune, she was crushed by events. Her emotions were fragmentary and unpredictable. Her love affairs, whether based on a distanced aesthetic appreciation of masculine beauty, an ideal merger of souls, or opportunism, were transitory, unsettling, and failed to provide the mutual recognition that depends on difference and a self for others.

Enlightenment reason, which established the natural rights of man as rationally self-evident, was equally useless. Intelligent and progressive though Varnhagen's ideas may have been, they had little force against the real world of nineteenth-century German prejudice against and exploitation of Jews. When those to whom she appealed refused to listen to reason, as many did, there was left only "the eternal differentness and incomprehensible otherness of inorganic substances" (RV 124). Retreat to an inner life of the mind provided no stable refuge from these painful and inevitable encounters. "Without reality shared with other human beings, truth loses all meaning. Introspection and its hybrids engender *mendacity*" (RV 8). And so Varnhagen lied, attempted to pass, married a non-Jew, changed her name, all the time crippled by vulnerability and the volatility of her emotions.[13]

In question, for Arendt, was not only one woman's failed life—a life that might be, might have been, Arendt's own life—but the texture of German Jewish experience in the nineteenth century, experience which conditioned twentieth century anti-Semitism. Already in this work, begun before the full evil of Fascism was evident, and long before Arendt's controversial treatment of Jewish collaboration in *Eichmann in Jerusalem*,[14] Arendt understood the Jewish experience in ways which would anger much of the Jewish community. Varnhagen's story, as told by Arendt, is not that of an "innocent" struggling against demonic anti-Semitism, it is not the story of a scapegoat chosen at random as the butt of gentile frustration, but the story of a Jewish woman who failed to live a fully human life and who made the "mistake" of denying her history by attempting to assimilate.

Varnhagen failed to live, a failure whose conditions are complex, but in memory that failure could be "desensed." Remembrance, for Arendt, always involves thinking how it could have been different, how another's story might have come out differently, how one's own story as a Jew and as a woman might come out differently. "Desensing" Varnhagen's story in this way, Arendt concluded that the effects of oppression are not only that people excluded from power cannot press their interests and so are exploited and mistreated. The damage goes deeper. Denied the opportunity to appear to others, the oppressed either retreat into themselves to find a positive but private identity, or they suppress their difference and attempt to pass. Not only does neither alternative produce a stable self or a liveable life, both contribute to a political unworldliness which takes away the ability to resist. As a woman, as well as a Jew, Varnhagen or Arendt might use Jaspers's humanity to pass as a generic "man," or try to find in her own feelings and emotions a essential femininity or Jewishness. As a woman as well as a Jew, she would find herself without the sense of self or the political skills to combat a renewed campaign to reduce women or Jews to subjection. The past must be owned, learned, lived, understood, assumed. This, for Arendt was the lesson of Varnhagen's life. Coming to terms with the past does not mean preserving archaic religious practices, or projecting an essentialist identity as a people set apart by God, but speaking and acting out of one's history as a member of an oppressed group. The tragedy of the German Jews, and specifically of Varnhagen, was to have thought that this could be done apart from a public life in which a woman could tell her story to others to whom she appeared as different.

Varnhagen's was no simple personal failure; it was a failure of philosophy. Her rejection of the past was supported by the leading philosophies of the nineteenth century. Romanticism and rationalism both held out the false hope that there could be a fresh start, either from the individual's natural healthy feeling, or from innate rational truths that would erase the errors of the past. But what was lacking in Varnhagen's life was not reason or sentiment; it was the worldly spaces in which diverse persons—women, men, Jews, Gentiles, Poles, Slavs, Germans—could have appeared to each other and established new identities for each other and new relations. The hope of rationalists and romantics that persons can shed their pasts and their social status and begin again from only their own reason or natural sentiments is not only vain; in its suppression of diversity and interpersonal identity, it drew attention away from the historical fact of the disappearance of public spaces in Europe in which mutual understanding between Gentiles and Jews might have been established.

Although Arendt did not generalize and allowed Varnhagen's story to speak for itself, the lesson might be applied to any oppressed group. Faced with a dominant culture, those inferiorized because of sex, race, religion can attempt to be accepted as equals in the dominant culture, supressing their difference, or they can separate, embracing their pariah status. Neither allows the development of a stable identity which requires, not heroic individual actions of refusal or accommodation, but participation in institutions in which exchanges between different persons are possible.

Arendt continued her reflection on the failure of the Jews to become politically "worldly" in her study of totalitarianism (OT 56–67). A Jew in Europe was forced to be either a "parvenu" or a "pariah."[15] Either Jews lived a separatist existence on the fringes of society, performing some specified function for government or business, or they attempted to assimilate, an achievement which often required them to manage to appear exotically Jewish and not like a Jew at the same time. The result was Varnhagen's virtuosity, the virtuosity of an actor cultivated for her liveliness and expressiveness but expendable when fashions changed. Unable to establish a public identity and a place in a publicized web of relationships, Jews were "worldless." Whether they were parvenus forced to invent a fictitious and guilty non-Jewish persona, or pariahs with only "an empty sense of difference" (RV 67), they were condemned to solitude. They could pretend to be like gentiles and so nullify the difference necessary if one person is to relate to others. Or they could resign themselves to being outsiders whose only identity is a negative "not gentile." With no chance to develop the skills of public life, they remained politically naive. Content with a protected status outside of politics, or alternatively struggling to dissolve their Jewish identity in assimilation to gentile society, when the time came to understand what was happening in Nazi Germany, they made the fatal mistake of collaboration.

A final condition for the tragedy of the Holocaust was the development of "racial ideologies." Here, Arendt noted the coincidence of the lack of public forums in which Jews or women could participate, and the eclipse of the nation-state by Luxemburg's expansionist imperialism. In the place of citizenship in a nation-state with established boundaries—a concept already compromised by ethnic nationalism but retaining some of its classical meaning of civil equality—a supernational white racial identity supported the "scramble for colonies in Africa." Similarly, the pan-German movement and the pan-Slav movements in Europe replaced citizenship with a mythical "tribal identity." Neither required any political forum for the presenting of oneself to diverse others which for Arendt is the only means to stable identity. If, in a world in which no public appearance was available to her, Varnhagen looked to her inner life or to universal reason, racists and pan-Germanists looked to even more dangerous fantasies of divine origins and of divine missions to exterminate unclean races. Dispossessed of land and homes in capitalist Europe, a mob of desperate and impoverished men without jobs or family was available for the violent conquest of foreign peoples and lands. In Africa and elsewhere, confronted with other cultures and with the promise of great gain, their sense of racial superiority and their obsessive hatred of those who are different were reinforced. Coming back home, colonists looked at Jews with renewed animosity. In central Europe, where civil space and the unity of the nation state had been retarded, artificial unities of blood were formed against other ethnic groupings. Racism, the "ideology of imperialistic politics" (OT 158) was neither a symbolic system or mistaken science. It had an experiential source in the rootlessness and homelessness of impoverished mobs, emigrating to European cities as land was appropriated for capitalist production, and nation-states failed to provide within stable boundaries the spaces for a public life among diverse citizens.[16] This insight was the basis for one of Arendt's most controversial claims: there is an affinity between Zionism and racism. In both cases, the political identity of citizenship had been rejected for superpolitical status as a divinely chosen people set apart from human affairs.[17]

Arendt's study of the historical conditions of racism and sexism, unlike a study of historical determinants which may lead only to resignation, or a study of individual initiatives which may lead only to personal ambition, suggested a further question. How might it have been different? Even when European politics had been infected with racism and colonialism, even when women like Varnhagen had been excluded from public life, what might have prevented the German people from participating in the Holocaust? What might have allowed Jews to better defend themselves? Observing the Nazi war criminal Eichmann through his long trial, Arendt was struck by his thoughtlessness, his failure to grasp what was happening around him and what he was doing. Might something as ordinary as thought have helped Germans to resist Fascism? Might thought similarly protect against racist ideologies in the future? For an answer to this question Arendt turned to the "professionals," philosophers, who, throughout the history of the West, claimed thought as their special expertise.

A History of Professional Thought

In her last work, *The Life of the Mind,* Arendt reviewed the history of philosophy with reference to the topic—the life of the mind—on which philosophers claim to be experts. Her aim, like Weil's, was not to find how far or how close a philosopher came to some standard of truth. She rejected counterexamples and logical critiques as exercizes which exhibit the ingenuity of the analyst rather than reveal any substantive reality. Her trenchant comment on "Analytic" philosophy:

> It is characteristic of the Oxford school of criticism to understand these fallacies as logical non-sequiturs—as though philosophers throughout the centuries had been, for reasons un-

known, just a bit too stupid to discover the elementary flaws
in their arguments. The truth of the matter is that elementary
logical mistakes are quite rare in the history of philosophy:
what appear to be errors in logic to minds disencumbered
of questions that have been uncritically dismissed as "meaningless" are usually caused by semblances, unavoidable for
beings whose whole existence is determined by appearance.
(T 45)

The question, then, is not the facile: "is the argument valid"; but
whether the semblances on which a theory is based are "authentic"—
"inherent in the paradoxical condition of a living being" or "inauthentic"—caused by dogmatic beliefs and arbitrary assumptions" (ibid.).
She describes her aim:

> In my discussion of *Thinking*, I used the term "metaphysical
> fallacies," but without trying to refute them as though they
> were the simple result of logical or scientific error. Instead
> I sought to demonstrate their authenticity by deriving their
> form from the actual thinking ego in its conflict with the
> world of appearances. (W 55)

The philosopher's view of the world was often fallacious, but his
fallacies have elucidating histories whose story can be told.

Arendt's treatment of the history of philosophy in *The Life of the
Mind* caused some perplexity. Did she see Socrates as the paradigm
of the thinker, or Kant? Did she agree with St. Paul on the will, or
Heidegger? Would she have revised the book for greater consistency
if she had lived longer? What is not understood is the historical nature
of Arendt's thought about thought. Most philosophers read the history
of their subject from a particular theoretical investment, but Arendt
came to the subject of *Thinking* out of a pressing present concern to
define what it is that might protect against the thoughtlessless that
had allowed Eichmann and others to commit atrocities. She turned
to philosophers not for true or false approximations of timeless truth
about thought, but for the various forms and past conditions of thinking. The point was not to categorize, review, or criticize theories and
definitions, but to understand what thinking has, in fact, been. To
reach that understanding, Arendt thought about thinking not against,
but with and through Socrates, Plato, Descartes, Kant, identifying
the conflictual "historical appearances" each confronted, and following the strains of their thinking about thinking, to coax out implicit
meanings and identify blockages. Following Luxemburg and Weil,

Arendt read philosophy not as representations that more or less approximate an independently existing truth about thought, but as self-revelatory communication with reference to thinking experience.

In a description that could have been of her own work, Arendt noted the way in which readers were "led astray" by Duns Scotus:

> It is his close attention to opinions to which he remained uncommitted, but whose examination and interpretation make up the body of his work, that is likely to lead the reader astray . . . he had a critical turn of mind, something that is, and always has been, very rare. From this perspective, large portions of his writings read like a relentless attempt to *prove* by sheer argumentation what he suspected could not be proved; how could he be sure of being right against almost everybody else unless he followed all the arguments and subjected them to what Petrus Johannis Olivi had called an "*experimentum suitatis*" an experiment of the mind with itself? That is why he found it necessary to "reinforce" the old arguments or "touch them up" a bit. He knew very well what he was doing. As he said: "I wish to give the most reasonable interpretation to [other thinkers'] words that I possibly can." Only in this essentially non-polemical way could the inherent weakness of the argumentation be demonstrated. (W 127–8)

By painstakingly following trains of philosophical thought in long, critical, and sometimes revisionary exegeses, Arendt, like Duns Scotus, came to novel insights, based on "*experientia interna*" or internal evidence, that result not in simple conceptual reversals but "genuine new insights" (W 145). The theories of philosophers, no matter how fallacious, obscurantist, artificial, are reactions and responses to events, and only in this way can they be understood.

As a response to traumatic events, Arendt found most philosophy, from its beginnings in Greece to Heidegger, disappointing. Philosophers' thought was typically blocked, traumatized, diverted to a quest for an illusory superhistorical Being, and set rigidly in abstract categories with no reference to experienced reality. Philosophers had not been innovators in thought, they had not founded new beginnings. Instead, they registered shock, shock that often took the form of escape into alienated forms of reasoning or systems of ideal metaphysics. Descartes, for example, "reacted" to the invention of the telescope, and to the disorienting fear that we cannot trust the senses that give us a world in common with others, by articulating two of the most extreme versions of this fear: everything we see and think may be a dream, and God may be an evil demon who only wishes to deceive us (HC 272–274).

Modern philosophy continued to register shock. The empiricist tradition, one of the most fertile of its strands, and the basis for most contemporary philosophical research in English-speaking countries, obscured rather than enlightened the modern condition. Attention turned inward: sensation was now private "data," and not perception of a common world. This turning of philosophic attention inward to sensations of the body ratified and radicalized but did nothing to meet the crisis of finding that the familiar universe of Christian or Aristotelian metaphysics is an illusion. Positivism and neopositivism continued in the same vein, struggling with resultant problems of skepticism and privacy. How can we know that other minds exist? How can any objective reality be based on private "sense data?" How is the working of the human mind different from that of a computer? Empiricist philosophy "reflected" but did not address the nihilism of a scientism in which we see only ourselves, only the sterile workings of the structures of our brains. Empiricism failed to illuminate what it registered: the meaninglessness of late modern experience, in which there is no longer any history, nature, common world, only alienated individuals either alone in their privacy or in a homogenous mass, administered by bureaucracies and driven by a biological urge to physical survival (BPF 89).

If the promise of enlightened philosophy based on empirical science had begun to falter by the nineteenth century, the great iconoclasts of the century who broke with tradition were no more helpful. Hegel managed to detach himself from Western history and human experience sufficiently to pretend to see as a whole the course of human history. Marx "overturned" the categories in which this vision is described, just as Nietzsche in his *Genealogy of Morals* overturned the Christian value system of the West. What this means, said Arendt, is that the traditions of Western thought no longer had a basis in living experience; they had become "guideposts to a past which has lost its authority" (BPF 28). The philosophic rebels looked at modern culture with fresh eyes, but, in the end, could only reverse traditional categories. Kierkegaard leaps from doubt rather than reason, but back to faith. Marx translates the consciousness of Hegel's World Spirit back into the utilitarian economic realities of industrial production. Nietzsche inverts Platonism with his return to the sensuousness of life (BPF 29). The outcome is only negative: an empty radicalism characterized by silence and anxiety, with none of the new beginning or fresh reconsideration of the past that is the only possibility that can redeem human affairs (BPF 28). After Kierkegaard, it is clear that religious faith must always be permeated with doubt; after Marx, it is clear that action must be relativized to ideology and history is meaningless; after Nietzsche, it is clear that nihilism follows from the realization that there are no transcendent values, but only a biologically based will to power (BPF 30).

In Arendt's judgment, the continental tradition was no better. In "What is Existenz Philosophy," she reviewed recent continental philosophy—Husserl, Heidegger, Jaspers—as various regressions from and avoidances of the implications of Kant's critique of metaphysics. Kant had realized the implications of the new scientific understanding of the world; but he had not been willing to give up a noumenal Being behind the appearances of the physical world. Afterwards, continental philosophers continued to sacrifice human freedom in order to reinstate some form of permanent metaphysical Being. At the end, in full retreat from the interpersonal world of human affairs, Heidegger, with his "Being as nothingness," posited a dangerous solipsism that can only be reconciled with others in a totalitarian Overself.

Arendt's discussion of these pivotal figures, often claimed as feminist allies, is particularly interesting (BPF 31–5). For her, their reversals reflect experiences that irrevocably compromise rationalism: for Kierkegaard, doubt of the senses and of any revealed truth inherited from the seventeenth century; for Marx, the necessity of a mass labor force for industrial production against the classical view of labor as degrading; for Nietzsche the collapse in modern society of traditional values. But their response to these experiences was only to turn concepts around. Instead of reason taking precedence over faith, faith would take precedence over reason. Instead of thought taking precedence over practice, practice would take precedence over thought. Instead of ideas taking precedence over sensuous experience, sensuous experience would take precedence over ideas. Each tried to reassert a positive presence: faith, labor, sensuous experience; but only succeeded in reversing an opposition in which one term is defined in terms of the other.

> The very assertion of one side of the opposites—*fides* against *intellectus*, practice against theory, sensuous, perishable life against permanent, unchanging suprasensuous truth—necessarily brings to light the repudiated opposite and shows that both have meaning and significance only in this opposition. (BPF 35–6)

But Arendt did not stop with this insight, which might have made her a protodeconstructionist. With structuralism the thought essences of idealism became their opposite—symbolic structures inherent in any language; in deconstruction, symbolic structures oriented around an axis of opposition become their opposite—decentered tracings of deconstructed meaning. In Arendt's remembering of the past of philosophy, the very technique of conceptual reversal has a history and a meaning.

> The turning operations with which the tradition ends bring the beginning to light in a twofold sense . . . to think in terms of such opposites is not a matter of course, but is grounded in a first great turning operation on which all others ultimately are based because it established the opposites in whose tension the traditional moves. (BPF 36)

To recover that meaning, Arendt, like Weil, returned to the archetypal philosophical myth, Plato's Allegory of the Cave. In Plato's story, the philosopher, "chained" to involvement in human affairs, "turns" from the shared world of the senses to the unitary source of perceptual images and then to the heavenly source of all things, the Good. Behind these metaphorical "turnings-around," Arendt saw a historically specific reversal of the prephilosophic world of Homer. In his Allegory of the Cave, Plato stands this Homeric world "on its head." Ordinary experience becomes deceptive, shadowy appearances, in contrast to a brilliant, otherworldly heaven, lit by the form of the Good; the disembodied soul, the shadow of the body, becomes the reality for which the living, acting body is only an insubstantial covering. The primal philosophical reversal, rooted in Plato's painful experience as Socrates' pupil and motivated by Plato's conservative politics, was meant to show that the contemplative life of a philosopher is superior to the active life of the politicians who condemned Socrates to death. The original Platonic turning was not a simple reversal of categories; it created the world of Forms or concepts defined oppositionally which "established the framework" in which the turning operations of later philosophers were carried out (BPF 37).

> This original reversal determined to a large extent the thought patterns into which Western philosophy almost automatically fell whenever it was not animated by a great and original philosophical impetus. Academic philosophy, as a matter of fact, has ever since been dominated by the never-ending reversals of idealism and materialism, of transcendentalism and immanentism, of realism and nominalism, of hedonism and asceticism, and so on. (HC 292)

One of the discoveries of recent feminist philosophy has been that in this play of hierarchical, reversible, oppositional meaning, sexual difference has been a ruling contrast. Arendt suggests another way of understanding that fact. For Arendt, the oppositional structure of conceptual reversal is not symbolic articulation of any primal opposition between male and female, nor is it inherent in the constitution of meaning or in the origins of human culture, as some versions of continental postidealism have made it. Conceptual reversal itself, as well as specific reversals, has a history, a history which many Western philosophers, traditional and feminist, have forgotten. They no longer remember the "birth" of philosophy in fifth-century Athens, but continue to turn, return, struggle in Plato's closed universe of structures and destructurings, in which links to living experience have all but disappeared. Once the experiential meaning of concepts is forgotten, reversal becomes an end in itself, and philosophy becomes a string of textual studies. Just as Luxemburg restored narration to economics, Arendt restored narration to the history of philosophy. Words, even the words of philosophers, bear traces of the lives of the men or women who have spoken them. The meaning of theoretical concepts, even of opposition itself which rationally orders meanings in Western thought, can be recovered in a history which traces the problems and uncertainties which theory is about. An Arendtian history of philosophy illuminates those moments when events occur which "animate an original philosophical impetus:" the overturning of the world of Homer by the Greeks, the crisis of faith in the Middle Ages, the discovery of the telescope in the seventeenth century, the breakdown of traditional values in the nineteenth century.

The relation between feminist philosophers and traditional philosophers in the past few decades has been confrontational. Feminists have claimed that philosophy reflects exclusively male experiences, others have gone further to find in the rational categories of philosophy a matricidal attack on women as feminine-identified nature, body, and passion are inferiorized in contrast to masculine-identified culture, mind, and reason. Arendt approaches the history of philosophy with a different question. Can the great philosophers of the tradition, men as they happen to be, show the way to a thought that is remedial and progressive? Convinced that the answer to that question is no, Arendt continued on. For Weil, work and labor are the center of a woman's life, the place where she comes to have a stable identity and sense of herself in the world. Similarly, Arendt began her rethinking of the human condition with the active life.

Philosophers had defined action as all the same, as not thought. Turning the opposition around, Marx elevated laborers to the dictatorship traditionally exercised by Plato's philosopher kings, redefining human "species-being" as active production rather than the philosophers' rationality, and claiming that theory is the reflection of practice rather than practice the reflection of theory. Arendt's rethinking was not to be a philosopher's "turning operation" in which a hierarchy is reversed but the categories stay the same. Leaving aside philosophical definitions of theory/practice, contemplation/action, thought/bodily movement, she would try to understand human activity as it actually has been experienced by women and men in various forms.

3. Labor and Work

Making Distinctions

Arendt agreed with Weil that there is no "species-being," or essential form of human life. But forms of human life and activity are not arbitrary or random either; they are "conditioned" by *relations* to a human "habitat," the earth. Because of that habitat, humans are subject to natural necessity and must provide for biological needs in ways dictated by laws of nature. This insight, and not the philosopher's quest for eternal being, was the starting point of Arendt's *The Human Condition*. Even this "universal" subjection to nature she took, not as a fixed "nature," but as a contingent "relation" that humans might choose to abandon. Descartes's universal science, taking a vantage point outside the earth, had begun a process of "earth-alienation." Since the seventeenth century, we in the West want, or think we want, to replace the earth, which comes to us as "a free gift from nowhere," with a man-made world (HC 2–3). In the fantasies of science fiction, life is contemplated in a technological future in which the earth may not be necessary as a home. If this comes about, our condition, and with it the forms of work and labor, will change (HC 9).

For Arendt, as for Weil, the inaccessibility of Cartesian science poses one of the most pressing problems of modernity: because knowledge of the earth comes from a science inaccessible to ordinary understanding, there is no forum in which such a radical choice can be discussed or judged. Like Weil, Arendt saw the danger in a science which has broken all ties with spoken language and therefore with thinking and discussion. Thoughtless creatures at the mercy of every gadget technologically possible, no matter how murderous or dangerous, we trust with our lives scientists who "live in a world in which speech has lost its power" and therefore its human meaning (HC 3).

It would be difficult to find anywhere in mainstream contemporary Western philosophy, split between the heirs of Anglo-American positivism and idealist continental phenomenology and structuralism, discussion of the earth as a threatened habitat or living environment to which humans have differing relations. From the perspective of the empiricist tradition, it has been clear since the seventeenth century that the earth is a material substance properly understood by physical science. Alternately, continental phenomenology and structuralism focus on symbolic and ideal meanings which have none of the materiality of an earthly home. Arendt, in contrast, distinguished three primary kinds of human activity by their differing relationship to habitat earth.

A laborer works in subjection to the earth. She plows, cleans, cooks, gathers food in ways dictated by natural cycles and rhythms. She produces no durable product; her labor is never finished; food is eaten, fields are replanted, clothes get dirty; the cycle of effort and consumption is endlessly renewed. The aim of labor is subsistence, the maintenance of physical life. In traditional Greek society, Arendt pointed out, labor goes on in the home where tasks are dictated by natural necessity; force and tyranny rule as a male head of the household directs women and servants or slaves in their tasks (HC 30).[18] Women and servants discharge humiliating bodily functions in private: clothes are laundered, dishes washed, bodies bathed, the dying nursed. Women also labor in the household in a way even more subject to natural necessity: they "with their bodies guarantee the physical survival of the species" in pregnancy and birth (HC 72).

Arendt distinguished labor directly subject to natural necessity from work. Workers make a durable object for use. Their making is ruled by the nature of materials, but they also impose on nature a model or design to make an enduring object with use value. Workers' activity is instrumental; they use various tools and procedures as the means to an end they have in mind. The difference, for Arendt, is relational. The laborer, as she plows a field, is subject to nature. The blacksmith who forges a tool is also bound by natural law, but his relation to nature is adversarial as he wrestles, grasps, tears from nature a human artifact which has permanence. Unlike an agricultural laborer, he partially escapes natural law. There is subjection to but also violence against nature in what he does, as he burns, chops, cuts, chisels, carves an object to conform to an idea or form. The objects produced in work make it possible for humans to have a "home" in habitat earth. A "world" of durable objects is made—buildings, houses, furnishings, tools. Use-objects are eventually subject to decay, like any material substance, and have to be repaired or replaced, and so the distinction between consumption goods produced by labor and use-objects produced by work blurs. But artifacts last long enough to create "worlds" of familiar objects, both useful and meaningful, that are Weil's *metaxu*, spaces of human culture which outlast individuals.

Arendt contrasted both labor and work with a third activity she called politics, the beginnings of which she found in classical Greece. There, as she tells it, a few men gathered together not for a common physical task but for discussion and deliberation in which each appeared to the other as free agents. Public spaces for Greek politics were set aside from the private spaces of households. The labor of women and slaves and the craft of working women and men were the conditions for the freedom of a few propertied men to engage in the speaking and acting that makes up the story of Greek history and culture.

Arendt rejected the dialectic of domination with which Hegel, and Marx after him, explained the master/slave relation. Masters did not keep slaves as captive "others" in whose recognition they established a reciprocal identity. According to contemporary accounts of Greek philosophers, slavery, so normal in the ancient world, reflected the earthly condition of human life: survival requires labor servile to nature in which there is a degrading futility—food must continue to be cooked, fields plowed, clothes washed. Some escape that futility by enslaving others. Women, it was argued, are better suited to enslavement or domestic labor because of their natural subjection to bodily processes in reproduction. Labor was degraded in classical Greece, Arendt pointed out, not because slaves and women did it; women and slaves had to do it because labor is degraded and unfree.

If idealist accounts of oppression and domination fail to come to grips with the terms of life in habitat earth with the result that they can promise an illusory reconciliation of consciousnesses, so do their materialist reversals. What makes the difference between labor that is drudgery and toil, and labor which is an expression of species-being, for Marx, is not labor's necessary relation to nature but relations between capitalist owners and laborers. Plowing a field is slave labor, not because it is subject to natural necessity, but because it is done under the direction of an oppressive landowner who says how it will be done, and who takes the surplus value of labor for himself. Eliding the earthly condition of labor and the worldly "home" made in work, and invoking the magic of technology, Marx held out the false hope that when owners are eliminated so will be the subjection of laborers. In both Fascism and Stalinism, a false rhetoric of national reconciliation covers over the fact of political oppression.

Arendt found vestiges of the real and experienced distinction between labor and work in various modern political philosophies—in Locke's "the labor of our body and the work of our hands," in the economist's productive and nonproductive labor. But as work and labor in modern economies is relocated from the private spaces of the household and family-owned workshop or business to the public factory, the distinction blurs. In classical Athens and other traditional societies, labor is marked off from work in the separation between households and workshops. In turn, private spaces for labor and work are distinguished from spaces for politics, in the separation of households and workshops from assemblies, councils, law courts. But in nineteenth-century political economy, both bourgeois and Marxist, an anonymous labor force appears. In the place of labor and work conditioned by differing relations to habitat earth, labor power produces goods immediately sold and absorbed back into production. In the place of households, workplaces, and political forums is a homogeneous administered society or a more-or-less regulated free market. Work in which a person achieves a balance with nature has disappeared, as has labor with its direct engagement with physical reality. In their place is production administered by the state or by corporate managers.

The result, as Arendt saw it, is that the texture of human life is threatened. Work, with its lesser degree of subjection to nature, can be done with dignity and status. Workers created the city of Athens, its public buildings, its residences, the furnishings of its great houses, its temples and statues. Even labor, Arendt agreed with Weil, has a distinctive "blessing and joy." In Weilian contact with physical reality, the laborer achieves a "natural happiness"; she experiences the "sheer bliss of being alive." Labor may be painful, but the fertility of labor is an earthly fact, making labor "naturally redundant" in that it is possible to produce more than is necessary for bare survival. Outside times of famine or drought, the laborer rests in a cyclical relation to a nature which provides and often richly. When that cycle is lost, and poverty makes regenerative rest impossible, or when wealth makes consumption the only contact with reality, the material substratum and the natural happiness of human life disappears (HC 108).

The Socialization of Labor

Much modern political philosophy has focused on the injustice of condemning one or another group of persons to more than their share of work or labor. In ancient Greece, as in many societies, labor was delegated to alien races and peoples, and to women supposedly disabled for public life by their emotionality and irrationality. The redress of these injustices, which continue in various forms into the modern era, has been a primary theme of liberatory philosophy. Arendt asked a question prior to the question of whether work or labor should be the province of any class, sex, or race: what is the place of work and labor in human life? The very distinction, Arendt argued, between the two different experiences is being lost and with it a recognizably human life. Locke, for example, defends property rights based on private ownership of the body and appropriative labor, rather than on permanent boundaries of private land holdings that separate private from public space. This allows Locke to force open traditional private property to capitalist appropriation (HC 111). Locke's capital property, as wealth in the form of imperishable gold, silver, and coinage, can then be extended indefinitely (HC 109ff). Private spaces—homes, workshops, farms—become commodities to be bought and sold by those with money. As the physical spaces for labor in the household, and work in the family business or workshop, are appropriated, privacy shrinks to a laborer's bare bodily movement, sold for wages. No longer sequestered in a private home or workshop, the laborer or worker is "imprisoned in the privacy of his own body" (HC 118).

As productivity is further increased by automation, mechanization, and the division of labor in capitalist and socialist countries, the distinction between work and labor continues to disappear. Except for the designs of a few engineers and technocrats, there is no more work, only the labor force that fuels production. The shape of goods is determined not by a craftsperson's forms of utility or beauty, but by the motions of machines. In the drive for productivity and a surplus that can be turned into accumulated wealth, durable objects are only a barrier. Consumption is stimulated by the production of disposable goods that are immediately consumable. The difference between the *use* of objects made in work and the *consumption* of services provided by laborers is gone. Removed from physical reality and natural cycles, everyone, except a few directors, goes through automated movements which bring not even the "natural happiness" of labor.

Much as she sometimes seemed to gloss over the fact that in classical Athens, work, labor and politics were defined not only by physical boundaries but also by gender and race, Arendt recognized the "obvious injustice" of confining any group—whether women, slaves, particular races—to labor, "of forcing one part of humanity into the darkness of pain and necessity" (HC 119). She acknowledged that one result of modern socialized production was the abolition of slavery and the release of women from at least some of their forced domestic labor in the household. What Arendt, from the vantage point of her distinctions, calls attention to is the ambiguous results of this "liberation." In capitalist countries, in the place of the private household and the workshop, there is now an administered "society" and "social problems" to be solved by welfare agencies. Women are liberated from private families and private workplaces into corporate and state administrations. Socialism is the completion of their "liberation," as additional state overseeing of production and services is added. In the place of the private satisfactions of work and the natural happiness of labor is now autocracy and direction.

If work dissolves into labor power, advanced technology and the abandonment of habitat earth presents the remote possibility that both labor and work can be eliminated. The "great contradiction" in Marx, Arendt echoed Weil, is that he took labor as the mark of man at the same time as he looked forward to its abolition (HC 104). Arendt, along with Weil, noted the defects in Marx's projected technological utopia. In a cybernetically administered socialist society, liberation from labor produces a disutopia in which life processes and mindless consumption rule. There is no more activity, only "behavior," functionally determined and predictable, processes for which physical survival is the only end. Concern for habitat earth disappears, along with any permanent "home" of cultural objects. "Eventually no object of the world will be safe from consumption and anniliation through consumption" (HC 133). With work unnecessary and the economist's dream of maximum automated production realized, society loses all ability to find meaning. Society can no longer recognize its own futility—the futility of a life which "does not fix or realize itself in any permanent subject which endures after labor is past" (HC 135). In such a world, the one human place left may be the archaic household, shrunk to a few temporary rooms where women continue to perform the labor of maintaining human life. The cost of such an erasure of boundaries can be seen in the breakup of the Soviet Empire. The result of the complete socialization of labor and work was not only the terror of forced collectivization or party purges, but an even more irreparable tearing apart of the fabric of human life. When central administration breaks down, where there had once been values, aspirations, traditions, along with injustice and oppression, there is only incoherent strands of practices and behaviors, no protection against crime, manic entrepreneurship, and racial hatreds. As Weil warned, when the last *metaxu* are gone, nihilism may be the result.

The focus of feminist social theory has been on the injustice that divides people by sex, as well as class and race. Both Weil and Arendt called attention to a prior question. What is or should be the relation between human activity and nature? For non-Western women concerned to protect *metaxu* in the form of indigenous styles of labor, for welfare mothers struggling to maintain their dignity, for working women trying to find satisfaction in their work, the problem cannot be understood solely in terms of inequality and prejudice. Egalitarianism assumes an existing economic/social substratum of institutions and practices *within* which equality is to prevail. Arendt reopens the question of the relationships which constitute those institutions and practices. Many chided Arendt for not sufficiently valuing egalitarianism, but in her view, until the nature of functional and economic relations between human activity and natural necessity are understood, the call for equality can as easily lead to universal degradation of the human condition as to universal liberation.

Her philosophy might be particularly useful for women in developing countries. In terms of much Western social philosophy, the alternatives for such countries have been understood as untenable primitivism, which temporarily protects ways of life as archaic artifacts, and modern Western social structures and economic arrangements. Into this unsatisfactory dilemma Arendt introduces a new line of thought. Starting not from Marx's species-being or Descartes's autonomous subject, but from forms of human activity in relation to habitat earth, the measurement of social progress would not be production, or even elected governments or scientific rationalism, but whether recognizably human forms of life are maintained. Weil looked to nature itself; along with natural necessity, there is a natural but divine point of equilibrium which makes method possible, and which, once made conscious, can be incorporated into human work. Arendt, in the aftermath of Stalin's Gulags and Hitler's Holocaust was unwilling to rely on divine revelation. If human life is to survive inhuman automation and regimentation, separate physical spaces *on earth* have to be preserved or reconstituted for the differing activities of labor, work, and politics.

The Restitution of Private Life

Unlike an object, which can be imagined to have a unique presence of its own, spaces are defined reciprocally, by the boundaries between them. One space requires the other space which defines it. In classical Greece, public citizenship was dependent on private property holdings of families which were not alienable and which gave the standing required for public life.[19] In modern societies, both capitalist and socialist, the boundaries between private spaces of household labor and work and public spaces of political action are erased. Private property, the basis for the household and the workshop, and for the private dignity of work and labor subject to necessity, disappears. In socialist countries, it is nationalized; in capitalist countries, it is appropriated as capital wealth. Houses are no longer permanent family dwellings but sellable commodities, temporary shelters in which to rest from work and consume. Possessions, with no permanent home, have none of the meaning of the furnishings of the traditional household, symbolic of family honor, and reflective of the sacred significance of the hearth. State and corporate workplaces are owned by no one; workers go to them as to hostile camps.

This disappearance of private space means that there is no space, private or public. Instead of a household there are social services. Instead of a workplace, there is production in increasingly bureaucratized corporate units. Instead of politics, there is administration and the registering of the personal and shifting moods in opinion polls and national elections.[20] Property is money, convertible, ephemeral, ultimately meaningless. Private life with no space left to it is internalized, reduced to shifting subjective drives and appetites. Labor with no private space is the sellable commodity of a worker's body. Capitalism maintains productivity by retaining a competitive struggle to survive and provides a choice of pleasures and diversions in the form of a wide variety of goods for sale. In totalitarian Marxism, even that small freedom of choice is gone. The means of subsistence are distributed. The means of production are managed. In communism, the last vestiges of private as well as public space disappear in a homogeneous administered society.

From the perspective of both Marxism and capitalism, economies in which work and labor in private establishments survives are archaic. Households and workshops may survive in inaccessible corners of less developed countries, but there is no reason to think that these economies are viable, or that anyone would choose to live in them if they could progress to the pleasures of urban consumer society. Certainly the delegation of the maintenance of the private spaces of households to women or servant classes is no longer defensible. Arendt's question remains: are domestic labor and work, subject to natural necessity, more appropriately done in private? Even more important, without private spaces for labor and work, is the standing for public appearance possible? If the sense of self and reality necessary to make a stand and appear to others depends on the identity achieved in thoughtful work, as Weil argued, it may also depend on refreshment and reflection possible in homes where physical needs are met. Without permanent private spaces, women and men have no place to think, no integrated self, no reality, no identity from which to come together in public to create a world in common. The familiar objects and decorations of the family home, in which the history and personality of family members is remembered, disappear along with shared public monuments which express common values. There is no past because there is no place to tell the stories of family or community history; there is no future because there is no place to discuss what might be done. The wealth of a few political players allows them the luxury of politics; the majority of women and men are reduced to impulses, sexual and other, and must find an alienated identity in the fictitious symbolic constructs of commercial advertising or in the equally fictitious propaganda of political posturing.

For racial groups that have been identified as servant classes, for women confined to domestic labor in the home, escape from private life into the modern work force has seemed to be the condition for liberation. The capitalist corporation or the Marxist industrial complex are understood as a means of escape from the tyrannies of a patriarchal private household or family business. Arendt calls attention to the mixed results. With no protected private place for the discharge of private bodily functions, the dignity of freely acting in public life may not be possible for anyone. With no secure place to which to withdraw to be alone or with intimates there may be no occasion for the thought which prepares for public life, and the judgment which restrains public action. With work reduced to meaningless programmed motions, the grasp of reality which grounds political positions may not be available to anyone. Their job monitored by managers, their problems administered by social agencies, women may have less autonomy than they did in the home.

For many oppressed groups, the call has been for legal equality in the workplace, but when legal equality is won, the actual situation of disadvantaged groups may not change. Women of color, as well as white women, continue to try to raise children in substandard housing or in no housing at all. African-American young men murder each other in gang warfare. Women of color find work only in menial positions. The answer has typically been socialization. It must no longer be a private matter that the workplace is segregated by gender and race, that pay is unequal, work conditions are dangerous, wages inadequate, products unsafe and the environment polluted. These social matters will be administered by the state, not in private firms or families. But Arendt did not understand human life in terms of the modernist opposition between private, individual choice and socialized, collective, public administration. The corporate workplaces in which hierarchies of gender and race are maintained are not private in Arendt's sense. They are a result of an appropriation of private space. They may be ruled by a few powerful white men, but they are owned by no one and home to no one. The politicizing of the family and workplace only means that one public space, dictatorially ruled, changes to another, at best efficiently administered.

Beginning from her observations of the distinctions between labor, work, and politics, Arendt opens a fresh line of thought in this seeming impasse. If the inhuman leveling and bureaucratization of socialization is rejected, the human distinctions between labor, work, and politics might be maintained, but in nonoppressive forms. Is the private space of the household and domestic labor *necessarily* ordered, as Aristotle ordained, by natural power relations between husband and wife, master and slave, Greek and barbarian?[21] Even if labor— washing, cleaning, cooking, nursing—subject to natural necessity is most humanly done by persons for themselves in private, should anyone be exempt? Was not the mistake made by the Greeks to think that a few men could detach themselves from physical existence? And might it even have been this delusion which led the Greeks to the carnage described by Weil and to the eventual destruction of the Athenian state? If the answer to these questions is yes, then might it be possible to imagine private spaces of permanent households that are not exploitative of women or servants but which are maintained by the joint labor of women and men, heterosexual or homosexual couples, extended families, alliances between friends?[22]

In the modern capitalized or socialized state, people die, give birth, are ill among strangers, with little dignity and according to procedures which they do not control. In a reconstituted household, some of these functions might be returned to private space and the control of families. The private matters of birth and death, over which women traditionally officiate in the household, are a necessary part of human existence. Arendt, herself, reinstated natality at the heart of human life and used it as a metaphor for free political action. Women and men who nurture children in the home, care for the sick, lay out the dead, far from being disqualified for politics, might be more likely than those with no homes or families to have the courage to found something new and to practice the forgiving and promising that makes political action bearable. A reconstituted household in which labor is shared might be a necessary condition for citizens capable of taking part in public life.

Given the complexity of modern production, the difficulty in returning work to private spaces is more challenging. If Arendt is right, and Weil's thoughtful method can never eliminate forceful direction in work and labor, then the private workplace must, to some extent, remain a place of subjection. If work is to be done correctly and diligently, there will have to be foremen, managers, bosses with the authority to give direction and force obedience. There will be divisions of labor, opening the possibility that there will be discrimination on the basis of sex or race. Sometimes, Arendt seemed content to leave it at that, with the proviso that politics be kept separate and free. Another possibility, suggested several times by Arendt, is that a space for policy-making might be cleared within the private workplace. Administrative decisions may have to be made autocratically, but instead of a monitoring of those decisions by supracorporate state administrations, decisions on policy might be made by democratically constituted, nonsexist, nonracist workers' councils such as those which have operated briefly in the course of socialist uprisings. The drive of corporate firms for profit causes a limitless expansion of production and the wasteful and polluting disposability of goods. In workplaces in which policy is freely discussed, some of the village craftsperson's concern for utility and beauty of form might return. The relentless expansion of corporations, described by both Luxemburg and Weil, creates environmental stresses on habitat earth that absentee owners escape by living in high-rent districts protected from toxic waste and pollution. Workers living and working in a community might have a natural interest in ecology, and might make policy decisions that cut into management's drive to make profits at all costs. Arendt noted that the appropriation of private spaces in capitalism released the productivity of labor from traditional forms of work, but once that productivity threatens the habitat earth, it may have reached its natural limit, along with the utility of corporate or state dictation of industrial policy.

A more radical possibility, not explicitly considered by Arendt, is that workplaces might be returned to private ownership. Given the complexity of modern production, it is unlikely that in many cases that ownership could be by single families or individuals, but workshops and plants might be owned collectively and cooperatively by workers in partnership. As in any partnership, relations have to be defined; given the need for supervision and direction, they will not necessarily be egalitarian. The possibility of workplaces privately owned by workers in partnership, problematic though it may be, is all but invisible in the mainstream political philosophies which have defined economic alternatives in the modern period. In the debate between capitalists and socialists, the choice is between state or corporate administration. Weil's ideal of thoughtful, self-administered labor, and Arendt's insistence on the honor and dignity of work in private spaces away from the public eye might provoke study of federated cooperatives or family workshops as alternative economic units.[23]

Feminist social philosophers have typically identified themselves with liberalism or socialism, defined as different adjustments in a standoff between individual freedom and collective administration.

To ground the decision as to which value is more fundamental, both capitalism and socialism defined a human essence: for the capitalist, a Lockean freedom to do as one likes, for the socialist, communality. Arendt's account of work and labor cannot be placed on this conceptual map. She begins not with a human essence but with the fact of human activities characterized by differing human *relations* to the earth. Diverse forms of work and labor for Arendt are not symbolic variation or the result of the materialist workings of history; they are the enduring fact of human beings' differing relations to nature. From this alternative beginning point—valuing human life as it has been lived and might be lived—economic arrangements are no longer to be judged by the capitalist's wealth or the socialist's equality.

When wealth or equality are achieved in a leveling of state or corporate administration in which distinctively human life disappears, the only recourse is to the postmodernist's hyperreal world of symbolic relations. Arendt provides a material alternative: the preservation, reestablishment, and fostering of distinct public and private spaces that support diverse ways of life. These spaces can no longer be places for labor or work that is sexually segregated, or for households in which women are exclusively responsible for domestic labor, but they might be spaces in which women and men experience together the physical satisfactions of labor and the honor and dignity of work in private, and so secure for themselves the standing necessary for participation in public life.

4. Speaking Freely

The Pursuit of Immortality

How can a woman speak out in public so that her words have power to influence others and to bring about change? In what language can she tell truths and create the possibility of new ways of living? The relation of women to language has been a major topic in recent feminist philosophy. Is language a neutral instrument for the expression of a woman's ideas, so that within the logical framework of truth-preserving inference she may say anything she likes? Or are there in the grammar and semantics of a given language, or in any language, constitutive structures which map out concepts in advance of a woman's speaking, and within which her meanings must be framed?

In asking these questions, feminist philosophy of language has followed the "linguistic turn" in the philosophical tradition. With the description of reality, including the reality of sexual difference, increasingly reserved for science, philosophers took as their object of expertise the logical and linguistic structure of any description. Many feminist philosophers followed suit. If Anglo-American philosophers could analyze and neutralize idioms of natural language that seem to posit essences, universals, spirits, ghosts, or mental objects inconsistent with scientific materialism, feminist philosophers could use the same therapeutic techniques on topics like abortion and discrimination to dispel irrational prejudice and bias. If structuralists and poststructuralists can theorize ordered or disordered symbolic complexes built into the semantic structure of languages, postmodern feminist philosophers can borrow their tools of deconstruction and discourse theory to expose and unsettle concepts of sexual difference.

But no matter which branch of contemporary linguistic philosophy was embraced by feminist philosophers, there was one underlying theme. Language imposes limits on speakers. To speak clearly, one must respect its grammar. To speak meaningfully, what is said must be within the conceptual perimeters of rationally or semantically ordered meanings or a disruption of those meanings. Feminist philosophers can either trust that logical analysis will help to restore reason and justice to issues of interest to women; or they can abandon political truth-telling for textual and discourse studies. Arendt's account of political speech undermines the philosophical grounding of this dilemma between feminist strategies. Speaking can be "frozen" in oppositional categories or logical inferences, but neither more logic and structure, nor an opposing textual license can capture the freedom of a speaking-together that changes the course of human affairs.

If Arendt's discussion of work focused on the threatened spaces in which work and labor go on, her discussion of language focused on the places where people speak. As with work and labor, she does not construct a philosophical theory about that one "thing" which language is or must be; she distinguishes different kinds of speaking in relation to active life. For Arendt, the freedom or lack of freedom of what a woman might say or do is not a quality inherent in a class of linguistic objects, but is a function of how, when, and *where* people speak. Talk between people goes on in a variety of settings. Private spaces, such as the home, are places for expressive functions. These can be carried out in gesture, inarticulate sounds, fragmentary interjections, as well as speech, and do not require the distinctively human characteristics of grammar and ordered meanings. Family members share the experiences of their day over dinner, give each other support or reprimands, express to each other joys and sorrows, vent on each other loves and hates.

Arendt distinguishes this intimate expression between lovers, friends, or family members from the communication that goes on in public discussion. Provoked by compassion, love, and even hatred, expression and venting is appropriate in private, but not in public discussion where a woman presents herself for diverse others. "Because compassion abolishes the distance, the worldly space between men where political matters, the whole realm of human affairs, are located, it remains, politically speaking, irrelevant and without consequence" (OR 81). Equally irrelevant for political speech, according to Arendt, are the "language games" useful in the administration of a workplace. A sign language can direct or facilitate labor or work, a symbolic code can be used to order movements as in mathematics or science, but neither involves the self-presentation of political speech (HC 179).

In the modern philosophical tradition, both emotional expression and language games have been models for competing philosophies of language. Rousseau made inarticulate expression the basis of an account of linguistic meaning.[24] Against the romantic idea that words can express private sensation, Wittgenstein used, as the paradigm of language, word games in which grocers sort apples and builders dress slabs of rock.[25] Arendt did not deny that words can express emotion, or that "language games" can coordinate activity. Workers *are* given monosyllabic orders that they have no standing to discuss. Family members *do* grunt, croon, and scream at each other. Because work is ruled by natural necessity, and requires administrative orders and not discussion, a code or signal language is appropriate in the workplace. Because the household is the place of the necessity and privacy of physical life, inarticulate expression is appropriate between family members. Rousseauan or Wittgensteinian theories of language reflect postmodern experience, as workers confined to a hierarchically ordered corporate workplace are solaced by a few intimate moments with "significant others." But although this may be the way people do or are made to speak, in Arendt's view, it is not the only way they can speak.

There is another speaking in public spaces which is not the cathartic expression appropriate between intimates, or the sending of "messages" that manipulate behavior and coordinate activities. Contemporary theories of language which take as their starting point personal expression or language games eliminate from language by fiat what Arendt takes as language's most distinctive human function—the revelation of self. Treating language as a unitary *thing* and ignoring distinctions, philosophers like Rousseau and Wittgenstien succeeded only in describing pathologies: speakers who can express sensations but cannot understand others, speakers who can receive messages and manipulate but have no sense of self.

Arendt returned to her favorite example to explain. For classical Greek orators, politics was neither a venting of emotion nor an exerting of power over others. It was a place to present oneself, and win honor and fame. In the Assembly and Council great deeds were remembered and heroes praised. The subject of public speech was not even the drafting of legislation, which was seen as the work of a legislator or "maker" of the law and so subject to the necessity of natural and social conditions. It was not production or the division of labor, which were seen as the business of each individual family. In the public space created by the politics of Arendt's Greek city-state, men broke free from the necessity that binds work and labor to create reputations, meaningful actions, epic narratives.

One of Arendt's most controversial positions was that political talk is not properly about economic matters.[26] Poverty, she sometimes seemed to say, is a private matter to be dealt with in homes and workplaces, where each person or family provides, well or poorly, for its own physical needs. In *On Revolution*, she compared the excesses of the French Revolution with the success of the American Revolution. The French Revolution, fueled by hunger and a demand for economic justice, inevitably turned to tyranny, as contrasted with the American Revolution, in which natural abundance allowed property rights and self-governance to be the main concern:

> Since (the French) revolution had opened the gates of the political realm to the poor, this realm had indeed become "social." It was overwhelmed by the cares and worries which actually belonged in the sphere of the household and which, even if they were permitted to enter the public realm, could not be solved by political means, since they were matters of administration, to be put into the hands of experts, rather than issues that could be decided by the twofold process of decision and persuasion. (OR 86)

At the same time, Arendt acknowledged that the survival of political discussion depends on economic prosperity. When there is acute hunger or need there will be revolution, and political institutions will be destroyed (OR 110). In the United States, "natural abundance" was a "blessing" that allowed political institutions to survive (OR 219).[27]

Even when there is general prosperity, Arendt insisted, not everyone strives for immortality in public life; only some people are motivated to learn about issues sufficiently to discuss them, or ambitious enough to care whether others make decisions for them as long as their physical needs are met. Every person, including women and laborers, has a "claim" to participate in public discussion, in reality few do so. In classical Athens, gender, race, and wealth determined political participants. In the contemporary United States, the voting populace is increasingly limited to middle-class and upper-class citizens. Those who participate in politics other than to cast an occasional vote are a small minority. A single mother who works in the day and cares for her children at night is unlikely to have either the inclination or the time for politics. She is forced to be content with intimate expression in her family and sex life and with pragmatic "language games" at her poorly paid service job. These "privations," Arendt sometimes seemed to suggest, are personal misfortunes, and not the business of politicians. On the basis of these positions, some saw Arendt as an elitist, promoting the interests of those who had money and leisure enough to pursue their immortality in public life.

Factual Truth

But the distinctions on which Arendt's separation of politics from work and labor rests can be separated from her classicist celebration of the glory of Greek orators seeking fame and her failure to highlight racial and gender barriers to political participation. Different kinds of speaking in different kinds of spaces require different relations between persons. Expression presupposes intimacy and commonality. Language games presuppose working relations between strangers. Refusing Weil's utopian reformulation of technical knowledge accessible to all workers, but drawing on Weil's identification of the problem of labor's relation to natural necessity, Arendt worked to cordon off a space for free speech apart from those human activities subject to natural necessity in which speaking cannot be free. If Weil's enlarged science encompassed free human activity and aspiration, Arendt's insistence was that work and labor ruled by necessity be kept in their place, marked off from a politics in which participation is voluntary, policy decisions are made freely without bowing to technical fiat, and factual truth can be determined.

Questions pertaining to techniques—how something can be made or produced efficiently or safely—are properly addressed in functional language: to accomplish this, do this and that. Directions in the workplace, if they are to be effective, are signals to workers to do certain things. Questions of technique and method are not debatable; on the safe running of a nuclear power plant, there can be no respect given to diverse "opinion." Science is "despotic." For this reason, Arendt argued, there can be no free labor and work. When such a liberation is mandated as state ownership and the attempt is made to fuse politics and work, politics disappears. Questions of technique intrude; politicians are silenced; they let experts decide. Or worse, they decide according to the best judgment which advances their own interests. At its most extreme, a centralized administration of all aspects of life on the Soviet model completely replaces politics.

In contrast to the formulaic representations of experts, the style of Arendt's politics is narrative. In political discussion, people give meaning to their experience, remember the past, and imagine a future. Their diverse accounts add further dimensions to an ongoing story of what happened, providing a medium by which mistakes which have led to disaster in the past are corrected, and a new future projected. In the process, new ways of life are envisioned. If the purpose of politics is taken as utilitarian—to bring about some preconceived end, such as feminist values, the greatest amount of pleasure, God's will, economic equality—the communicative function of speech is lost. One truth must prevail and language is its calculus.

That "stories" told to each other by women and men, about what they are doing, did, will do, and what it means, are the way to truth is at odds with much philosophic reason. "Reason" has been defined by philosophers in different ways: as the quasigeometrical proofs of Plato's philosopher kings, the syllogisms of Aristotle's aristocratic citizens, the consequentia of medieval theologians, the "logical form" of twentieth-century positivists, but always it has been defined against an "irrational" counterpart of literature, poetry, stories. Since Plato, Western philosophers have looked to Reason to replace the unreliable opinions and the subjective, emotionally colored accounts people give of events. But in human affairs, if not in science, Arendt, argued, telling and retelling stories is the only way to truth. This is the political process of truth-telling and story-telling on public issues denied to or refused by women like Rahel Varnhagen.

In *Crises of the Republic*, Arendt reviewed political discussion on issues that were topics for political discussion in the United States in the 1960s, beginning with the war in Vietnam. Certainly in the various government documents on official policy, the manifestos and policy statements of the many groups in opposition to the war, academic treatments of the history and social theory of colonial practice, there was a variety of stories with different villains and heroes. Not only were there different honest versions of what happened in Vietnam, there were also outright lies, as in the government's Pentagon Papers. But this giving of different versions of the truth, and even outright lying, Arendt argued, are the necessary condition of free speech. There is no inner realm of perfect freedom where one might intuit alone Descartes' clear and distinct ideas, nor is a political discussant completely immersed "in her own point of view, embedded in the world." Instead, she finds out the truth when she remembers with others how it was and imagines how it could have been different (CR 5). The necessarily constructive nature of this process is the source of the human ability to lie, just as it is of the human ability to speak out of diverse opinions. In contrast to science, which dictates the means to predetermined ends, factual truth—the truth of what happened, what it means, and how it might be different—is threaded through with forgetfulness, and also with purposeful and unconscious distortion. The only remedy for that ignorance and falsehood is continued discussion.

Arendt rejected the traditional remedy of philosophers who, in the face of the unreliability and mutability of human "opinion," retreated to contemplation of a metaphysical Being beyond appearances. However such a Being is conceived—as logical form, essences, physical structures—in each case truth is banished from the one place where it might be determined. When politics is rejected, as deceitful display, unreliable opinion, and manipulation, the very possibility of establishing factual truth and meaning is eliminated. For Arendt, neither the factual truth of what happened nor the meaning of that truth can be established apart from accounts of participants. "Facts need testimony to be remembered and truthworthy witnesses to be established in order to find a secure dwelling place in the domain of human affairs" (CR 6). Logic and argumentation cannot substitute. As a shortcut around the necessary and sometimes painful process of listening to varied accounts, rationalization is often only another form of lying. Not only did "crude image making" occur in American foreign-policy statements on Vietnam, but also a more sophisticated "reason" was used, in which facts were tailored to fit theories. Such incoherent evasion "often serves no other purpose but to divert the mind and blunt the judgment" (CR 12). In contrast, in narrative discussion facts are durable. They reappear again and again; the only way to be rid of them for good is to kill all witnesses, which is an omnipotence even Stalin or Hitler did not have.

Determining factual truth requires linguistic skills jettisoned in philosophers' timeless pursuit of reason. In her analysis of United States policy in Southeast Asia, Arendt exhibited some of them: insightful sensitive listening, a grasp of historical context, attention to both the aims of speakers and the audience to which they speak, penetration to deeper worries behind surface assertions. Political skills are not the skills of logicians, or of scientists who separate themselves from circumstances and pay no attention to history or context. The use of logic and science in totalitarian ideologies, Arendt argued, can stop thought altogether, and cause people to lose the ability, essential to free speech, to detect lying and to determine truth.[28]

> The purely negative coercion of logic, the prohibition of con-
> tradictions, became "productive" so that a whole line of
> thought could be initiated, and forced upon the mind, by
> drawing conclusions in the manner of mere argumentation.
> This argumentation could be interrupted neither by a new
> idea (which would have been another premise with a different
> set of consequences) nor by a new experience. Ideologies al-
> ways assume that one idea is sufficient to explain everything
> in the development from the premise and that no experience
> can teach anything because everything is comprehended in
> this consistent process of logical deduction (OT 470)

If logic has little role to play in Arendt's politics, neither does science. Knowing how to manipulate events and processes is useful in
management and administration, but it cannot tell people what they
have done, what they are doing, and what they ought to do. Science
takes the formulas by which physical reality is measured or altered,
and projects them as an ideal world of patterns; what it describes is
not reality, but technological devices set up as a screen before the
sensuous world shared with others (HC 266–7). The world becomes
what can be done to the world, with no regard for the meaning or
reality of experience. Arendt agreed with Weil that science is not
representation. She disagreed with Weil that the necessity of how a
thing must be done can be the basis for human freedom. Science may
produce a kind of truth, but it is a truth irrelevant to politics, which
requires the factual truth of what happened, its meaning, and how
it might have been different.[29] None of these are determined without
open discussion between diverse persons that goes on apart from the
necessities of science and logic.

The usual philosophical alternative to the "cognitive" discourses of
logic or science has been emotional "expression." It is into these two
categories—cognitive/noncognitive—that philosophers have typically classified uses of language. If ethical judgments are not cognitive—neither analytic nor empirically verifiable—they must express
emotions of approval. If theological statements are not cognitive,
they express fears of mortality. If linguistic surface structures do
not exhibit propositional form, they are emotional coloring. Truth
is understood as the property of cognitive language, of systematic

propositions that are either true by logical law or verifiable according to scientific procedures. Although expressive uses of language may be therapeutic, they can tell us nothing about reality.

Recent feminist philosophers have pointed to a further element in this traditional philosophical opposition between reason and emotion. In philosophical accounts since Aristotle, emotionality in language has been identified as feminine and rationality as masculine. To the "man" of reason has been opposed the passionate woman, suited to the roles of mother and lover but not, unless she manages to be particularly manly, a philosopher. The horns of a feminist dilemma have been drawn accordingly: should a woman learn the masculine art of cognitive discourse? Should she enter politics, play the game as men do, employ accepted modes of rationalization to achieve power? Or should she valorize her feminine passion, separate herself from the world of men and speak a woman's language of the heart? Arendt, because she does not understand language in terms of the philosophical opposition between reason and the expression of emotion but in terms of relations between speakers and between speakers and the physical world, cuts across these two less-than-satisfactory alternatives.

If there is no place for logic or science in Arendt's public political discussion that creates new relationships and institutions, there is no place for expression of emotion either. Expressions of compassion, resentment, pity, rage are appropriate between lovers and intimate friends, but do not belong in politics, feminist or other. No matter how renovating and recuperative may be the venting of emotional expression in private; it cannot replace a political speaking to others which determines truth and meaning. In *On Revolution*, with special reference to the French Revolution, Arendt pointed out the dangers when passion or sentiment is allowed to overwhelm politics. In the early days of the French revolution, the concern was with forms of democracy. When the Girondistes, however, were unable to form a government and the Jacobins took over, passion became the driving force. Abject poverty in France inflamed public opinion. The new revolutionaries found inspiration in the political philosophy of Rousseau, whose doctrine of natural sympathy and praise for natural man in touch with his emotions made passion the basis for social intercourse.

Pity and rage fueled the violence of the French Revolution and prevented the establishment of permanent democratic institutions. In a regression that Arendt found in many revolutionary movements, reformers inspired by pity or rage are tempted to manufacture new demonic villains and new oppressed victims. Expressions of pity are enjoyed for their own sake, along with a pleasant feeling of moral superiority. A sense of the injustice of suffering inspires violent acts. In France, those held responsible for the suffering of the poor suffered the most barbaric of punishments. Pity canceled itself out, as the rebels became incapable of noticing the suffering of their enemies in their self-righteous zeal. In its last stages, pity turns to rage and the impotence of a vengeance that has no practical utility and no designated object. Arendt contrasted the French with the American Revolution, in which pity for the poor was not the driving force. Because in America there was poverty but not "abject want," there was not the same pressing demand for compassion. The framers of the American Constitution were able to speak calmly of political rights and responsibilities.

Presenting Oneself to Others

If the good fortune of natural prosperity cannot be counted upon, if neither the pity of the well-off for the not-so-well-off, nor the rage of the poverty-stricken or discriminated-against can be the basis of a remedial and free politics, if reason and logic lead to thoughtlessness, what, then, is the solution for inequality and injustice? Luxemburg imagined a socialist leadership standing with working people, shaping their interests and aspirations into coherent and effective policy. Weil imagined a divinely inspired social balance which facilitates responses to calls for justice. Arendt's answer, different in many respects, is similar in one: the remedy for poverty or injustice is not a specific set of policies or institutions but communicative relations.

The standard liberal answer to economic and social disadvantage is typically some form of state-administered welfare, either motivated by compassion for the poor and oppressed and conducted in the style of charity, or administered according to the dictates of social science. In neither case is necessary the speaking together between rich and poor, men and women, Jews and Gentiles, white people and people of color which for Arendt is the essence of politics. Even if charity is beneficent and not grudging and condescending, there is little real talk between the masses to be helped and their benefactors. A dispassionate, scientific, welfare policy may be even less communicative. Social scientists and economists are commissioned to study poverty, racism, discrimination, and other social "dysfunctions"; administrators inform the disadvantaged of the findings and the remedies prescribed for them. Not only may Weil's *malheur* prevent recipients from cooperating as welfare, workfare, medicare programs are put into practice, but the social scientific theories on which programs are based may have little reference to the actual experience of women or minority groups. Social scientists may be able to prescribe ways to force welfare recipients to work or to discourage teenage pregnancy; they cannot elucidate the meaning or the truth of phenomena as they are experienced by sufferers themselves. In scientific treatises on sexism, poverty, drug abuse, or homelessness, the poor and discriminated against have not revealed themselves. They have not participated in generating a common world. An alternate approach is to rely on an extension of rights. Not only do persons have the traditional rights to free speech and the vote, it is claimed, they also have rights to minimum income and health care. Civil rights activists, versed in constitutional law, can inform the disadvantaged of these rights. Again, it is unlikely that their clients have the training or inclination to contribute to the discussion.

Arendtian politics is not a medium by which well-off citizens express their charitable compassion, and deliberate if and how they will "help" the poor and disadvantaged. Nor is it a forum in which the rage and resentment of the poor or discriminated-against can be vented. If, in political discussion, no one's words should have the tyrannical authority of science, nor should they be choked with righteous emotion. It is an open discussion in which different citizens of differing economic means, sexual orientation, race, ethnic origin speak to each other and establish solidarity. In such a politics, disadvantaged groups appear to each other as well as to those who are better off.

In most existing Western political systems, there are few forums for such a politics. Politics is the periodic electioneering of political parties. Aside from a few token women and minorities, the great majority of those elected are white, male, and of a similar age. Once elected, their legislative discussions are aimed at winning the next election and courting powerful constituents. It is unlikely that Arendt's factual truth would result from their deliberations. What is missing are alliances between different oppressed groups and even between well-meaning better-off citizens and poorer citizens as they "establish deliberately and, as it were, dispassionately a community of interest with the oppressed and exploited" (OR 84). The rich can be persuaded on occasion to donate to charity or pay higher taxes out of pity; this may only be a cathartic exercise. The poor can be allowed an impotent venting of emotion, but this may not lead to any lasting change. But once both rich and poor are face to face and present themselves in open political discussion, a plurality of persons begins to establish a common world. In such a political space, a "community of interest with the expressed and exploited" comes not from the findings of social scientists or from metaphysical principles of the "rights of Man," but from the knowledge of facts that results when diverse people speak to each other. Like Weil's obligatory response to the "cry" for justice from the suffering poor, the basis for Arendt's community is mutual recognition, but for Arendt, mutuality does not depend on any metaphysical core of the person where all are the same, it depends on the existence of actual physical spaces in which presentations of persons to other persons can take place.

In those public places, speech is not "for others"—in order to further the claims of some party or interest group with which a politician is aligned—and not "against others"—to discredit others and their position; it is "with others" (HC 179–80). With others, women and men are able to make appearances in the world, not in the sense that they purposefully play prescribed roles but in the sense that they reveal who they are in what they say. Although a natural effect of speaking may be to win agreement or lead others to common action, this is not the primary aim of Arendt's political speaking. People can be manipulative, hypocritical, lying, or empty automatons, but manipulation and persuasion are not a revelation of self. In speaking, a woman shows others "who" she is; she communicates her experiences, beliefs, hopes, concerns, her view of the matter. Because she speaks for others to understand, at the same time she puts herself in their positions, sees herself as they see her, takes their view of her into account. As others in turn reveal themselves, she corrects her views and experiences against theirs, and begins not only to grasp truths but to move into relation with others to generate new forms of action. The understanding gained is an achievement, not already there for the most educated or articulate to communicate, but revealed as people speak to each other (MDT 85).

In such a speaking, what is revealed is not "what" a person is, but "who" she is. A woman does not reveal herself as an object—woman— that can rouse emotion or be manipulated, but as a person or "living essence" (HC 181). When she speaks with others, she weaves a "web" of relationship; this web is not an illusory superstructure reflecting a given material reality, but is real in its own right (HC 183). New revelations fall into old webs of relationships, but they also create new stories and new relationships. Stories change their plot when a diversity of voices contribute. Even a person's own account of herself is dialogic. She is not the single omnipotent author of her own story, nor is there a hidden omnipotent author-God writing a history in which she plays a preassigned role. Because her story always intersects with others' stories, as she listens to others, she must constantly revise her own, and so better come to understand and tell what has happened to her and to them.

The Recovery of Political Reference

What *are* appropriate subjects in this speaking together? Arendt's answers to this question, which was often asked her, were not always satisfying. If defense and aggression[30] are not the only "great deeds" to be spoken of and economic justice is not in issue, is politicians' job then only to enhance their own reputations? Certainly, feminists and others have noted the lack of reference to reality in the agonistic rhetoric which is the legacy of Greek politics and also the prevailing style of much party politics in Western countries. When politics is a means of manipulating opinion, a repertoire of signals designed to win over voters and achieve power and influence, truth and reference to human life are gone from human affairs. Arendt shared Weil's distrust of political parties. Parties, she thought, are hierarchically organized mechanisms for getting members into office. Legislators represent the "interests" of constituents who have little opportunity to form any opinions beyond a yes or no vote. Intraparty politics are largely concerned with tactics; discussion with voters takes the form of arousing positive and negative reactions through images and emotionally charged slogans and symbols. In Western democracies, Arendt charged, party politics loses even its "representative function to the huge party machines that 'represent' not the party membership but its functionaries" (OV 23).

Feminist philosophers have found some inspiration in the postmodern philosophies which reflect the resulting "inscrutability" of political reference, "textuality" of media management, reliance on "symbolic" meaning. Reference is impossible anyway, they argue. No one, man or woman, can intuit in the privacy of the mind ideas which refer to reality. The objects of which a woman or man speaks are always constituted within existing conceptual structures. To claim to describe reality or tell the truth is to claim a tyranny over language and to dictatorially mandate one form of words. In this view, constructive politics is ruled out in principle. No one can speak truthfully about what justice is or might be; the only liberation is in challenging and disrupting claims to truth.

Arendt's distinctions, once the obfuscating example of Greek politicians is cleared away, might provide a further alternative. She agreed that the content of just laws and institutions cannot be authoritatively specified by any solitary thinker, but not for postmodernist reasons.

No lone woman or man can refer to objects of political concern, because referential meaning is necessarily interpersonal. If subjects are plural because we "reveal ourselves as unique persons" (HC 183), so are the objects of their speech. Objective reality exists because people appear in public to others. Reality is the shared world and shared perceptions, which are a function and result of communicative relationships. Because there are others who see and hear what we see and hear, there is a common world to be known (HC 52). Concepts only have substantive meaning as "congealed" experiences in that world. In manipulative uses of language, as well as in social science, political rhetoric, and much ordinary talk, concepts are emptied of meaning; reference is lost and words have only oppositional meaning. "Thought, no longer bound to the incident, as the circle remains bound to its focus, is liable either to become altogether meaningless or to rehash old verities which have lost all concrete relevance" (BPF 6).

Much of what is said in politics is not self-revealing, meaningful, or referential, but only repressive, manipulative, or the repeating of empty formulas that dull the mind. The alternative for Arendt is neither the rationalist's essences nor the idealist's conceptual structures. For Arendt, objects, to which people refer when they speak freely to each other, do not exist independently of their speaking, nor are they already there, constructed in language. They are generated in political discussion. Words have substantive reference in the common world of relations that speakers are in the process of creating. "What" citizens are to talk about cannot be characterized in any universal way, because the objects about which they speak do not predate their discussion. They are objective only because they are things that are of "inter-est," literally "between us," constituted by relationships (HC 182–3) (OR 81). They are not subjective because the relationships that constitute them are real; they are not fixed because the fact that there are objects between people creates new commonality and new objects of interest (HC 58).

Like Weil, Arendt had bypassed the philosopher's "shocked" Cartesian retreat to mental privacy. A shared world may collapse, as did the medieval cosmos in the face of religious rebellion, mechanical science, contact with non-European cultures. But in times of crisis, a common world can be reconstituted only out of new and disparate experiences. When radically new experiences occur, such as totalitarianism, there is a tendency to try to equate what has happened with old experiences—to call totalitarianism tyranny or authoritarianism; confusion results. In new situations, only renewed public discussion can generate concepts adequate to a "common sense" of what has happened. If there is no communicative space for that common sense

to develop, there can be no understanding of a novel political phenomenon, and no hope for future action.

Arendt's historical studies of political concepts reflect her understanding of the communicative, experiential basis of reference. Rather
than consulting social science to define the theoretical objects to
which "authority" or "freedom" refers, Arendt went to original senses
of words in past political discussions. In much of current use, she
thought, the substantive meaning of words like "labor," or "freedom,"
or "authority" is lost, but meaning can be recovered by remembering
the experiences that words in their original political contexts distinguished. This is because reference to phenomena in actual political
discussion is objective, neither conventional nor subjective, neither
a function of an individual's ideas nor a group's agreement.[31]

Postmodern philosophy of language has been alternatively claustro-
phobic and anarchic: either language is a "prison house" of symbolic
structures beyond the control of any speaker or it is a decentered
semiotic field that can be varied at will. If, as Arendt would have
agreed, there are no longer any absolutes that can hold symbolic
systems securely in place, the recourse of postmodernism has been
obedience or refusal. Arendt, by recovering interpersonal reference
and returning words to concrete distinctions embedded in shared
political experience, elides this dilemma between linguistic license
and linguistic imprisonment.[32] Reference is neither to preexisting
objects to be matched with human interests, a reference which must
inevitably fail, nor to objects constituted in language itself, which is
no reference at all. In both these cases, reference has already been
lost in the disappearance of a shared world of common experience
and in the lack of political spaces in which experiences can be communicated to others.

Like Weil's cry for justice, stories must be heard to be understood.
Luxemburg blamed the schematic dogmatism of socialist theoreticians. Weil placed the barriers to hearing in the natural necessity
that rules that people will try to avoid the suffering of others. Arendt
cited the disappearance of the actual spaces in which free referential
speech is possible.

Spaces for Speaking Together

Is it possible to identify, remember, or imagine the conditions that
would make interpersonal political reference possible? Can the spaces
denied to Rahel Varnhagen, destroyed by racist zeal, co-opted in party
politics, eliminated in socialist administrations be restored? The first
condition identified by Arendt, as it was by Weil, is that there be

physical spaces for public speech. If these are lacking, no amount of desire to communicate matters. Spaces require physical location, secure boundaries, and protective institutions that regulate and maintain them: by-laws, a constitution, procedures, law (OR 116). The public spaces of political speech cannot be ad hoc, they must be permanent, transgenerational as well as local (HC 55). Like Weilian social justice, Arendtian politics requires a rooted tradition.

For Arendt as for Weil, politics must be grounded in the distinctive life of a people. In a world government or centrally administered federation that does not respect national traditions, public discussion disappears; there is no depth of experience out of which thought and communication can come, but only a "shallow unity." A transcendental world state would be possible only if truth were a transcendent ideal order that can be known in an absolute sense. Whether or not such absolutes were ever available, it was Arendt's understanding of the postmodern experience that they are now irrevocably gone.

Equally essential to political speech with reference to reality are the private spaces which are the "dark and hidden side" of public space (HC 64). If selves are formed in communication with others, they are also formed in solitary reflection. For public discussion to go on, for there to be something for women to say and a place to say it from, there must be homes and households, secure places for retreat, rest, refreshment, and thought in communion with friends and family. There must be protected workplaces where the making of objects can go away from public life. Arendt echoed Weil's defense of private property. The public life necessary if women and men are to have identity for others is dangerous and exhausting; appearing to others risks rejection and humiliation. These risks will not be taken if there are no private spaces where women and men may reliably care for their physical needs, seek spiritual and emotional solace, gather their emotional forces, reflect, and work. The impermanence of residency, supposedly necessary for modern economies, is destructive of politics. If workers must move wherever there are jobs, giving up homes and communities, private life is lost. Adequate housing and secure, safe workplaces are not only a matter of humanitarian sentiment or even human right; they are essential to the survival of a free politics.

Most important, public speech requires plurality. Within public spaces, differences must be preserved. It is the multiplicity of the perspectives of distinct individuals that, for Arendt, supports a common world, common because it is understood from different vantage points. What generates that commonality is never sameness, but plurality and concern with the same things. To insist on a common denominator in civic life, some "common nature" of woman, man, or human, is to destroy commonality, substituting for it one perspective. Arendt used sexual difference as an example. Plurality is essential "just as men and women can be the same, namely human, only by being absolutely different from each other" (MDT 89). The same argument applies to other differences, differences in sexual preference, in race, in lifestyle, religion. The distinctiveness of persons is not in any sexual, racial, or ethnic essence but in the human condition of natality. Not only are new infants born into the world; women and men in speaking and acting are reborn as they reveal themselves in new ways and "take upon themselves" their pasts, their futures, their appearances in the world (HC 175ff.). The impulse to self-revelation, for Arendt, comes not from any universal biological impulse for survival or from a conditioned response to stimuli, or even from a conscious aim, but from an original impulse of sociability embedded in human sensibility.

Arendt produced few, too few, historical examples of spaces in which political discussion had been possible. Among those she mentioned at one time or another: the Paris Communes in the French Revolution (OR 247), the Jeffersonian Ward system (OR 252), Russian Soviets (OR 250), the Räte councils in Germany in 1919 (OR 260), councils in the Hungarian revolution in 1956 (ibid.), workers councils in Yugoslavia, and cooperatives in East Germany (CR 216). These examples of "counselor" politics she described as "the always defeated but only authentic outgrowth of every revolution since the eighteenth century" (OV 22). The range of her examples showed that the discussions she looked for were not limited to the winning of elections and the making of laws; they could go on in universities, labor unions, town meetings, student groups, activist organizations.

In this free form of participatory politics, talk has a power different from the power of force: a power to initiate action, to convince others to act in concert, to establish a durable web of human relationships, solidarity, and a world in common. Certainly all hope of such discussions is not gone from Western democracies. The slowly increasing participation of women and people of color both in electoral politics and in other venues of political discussion such as unions, university committees and classrooms, and activist groups illustrates the power of Arendt's political speaking. As a result of their participation, the common story of America's past is understood in new ways—slavery, the settlement of the West, family values, all are redescribed by a diversity of speakers grasping together the fact of the American experience. Unrealized still, as it also was in Arendt's revolutionary councils, are the concerted actions that might give permanence to spaces for a continuing free discussion between people who look on each other as equals, value plurality, and nurture the "political virtues" of judgment, trustworthiness, integrity, and courage.

5. Political Action

The Indeterminacy of Political Action

In the workplace, a woman's actions are conditioned by natural necessity; things *must* be done in a certain way to accomplish a given result. In the home, she labors with other family members in rhythm with nature to maintain physical existence. In the public spaces of Arendtian politics, she can act freely, not subject to natural restraint. Political action, Arendt insisted, is not work, not a "making" or a means to any end. When action is mistaken as "making," politics becomes an oppressive attempt to force the world to a given image: the City of God, the ideal Republic, true Communism, an androgynous society. Political action, in contrast to work and labor, is not driven by need and is not the copying of any preestablished form. When a woman takes action, she gives birth to herself, as someone with an identity for, to, and with others. She also gives birth to new relations and institutions.

If knowledge has been problematic in the philosophical tradition after Descartes, so has been action. Once the thinking mind is separated from its physical body, the very possibility of free action is immediately in question. How can a mental event such as an intention or act of will cause a bodily movement and make an action? Philosophers constructed different causal sequences: an idea or thought causes a judgment, which causes an act of will, which causes a action. Or a desire causes a motive, which in turn activates the body. On these accounts, action is a compound of a mental and a physical event. If there is no mental act, no motive or intention, then movement is not action but is arbitrary or reflex. Within this philosophical framework, Arendt's claim that action is unmotivated makes little sense. She was accused of sponsoring a political posturing with only dubious "aesthetic" value, or worse, irresponsible anarchism.

But, for Arendt, action is neither arbitrary nor determined by a mental event or object in the form of a wish, desire, or intention. These "psychological" accounts do not capture the freedom of action. What people do *is* sometimes the result of calculation or impulse; for some people, this may be all that they do, but there is also action, free from motive, not determined by calculation, which has meaning not in private design, but in what it is for others in a web of relationships and institutions that it generates or alters. For Arendt, as for

Weil, freedom cannot be the ability to gratify desires, wishes, or impulses.

Weil's first philosophy preserved some of Cartesian solipsism; as an individual, Weil's worker makes her path in the world. Arendt moved one step further. Free action cannot be the finding of individual paths through physical reality, because freedom requires the participation of others. What allows freedom of political action is neither the exercise of will nor engagement with physical reality, but the ability to initiate and carry through projects with others. A private intention or desire cannot be actualized in the world. Whatever is meant subjectively by an action is irrelevant to its objective meaning for others, irrelevant to what it *is* that has been done. Although people can initiate action that is new, they never act alone. Action in the world is shared with others, and its meaning is not something one person can "make." If a woman thinks she is making meaning, she is most likely killing off and canceling old meanings, and the result is nihilism. The meaning of action is clear only after it has taken its place in human affairs and been responded to, acted on, rejected by others (HC 181–188). Political action has meaning as an element in the story of the actor, but her story is the story of others. There is no one author/maker because it is a shared story, with plots that are never completely determined by any one person's actions. As a consequence, a woman who takes action may not know exactly what it is she is doing, may never know because it may not be clear until after her death.

For Arendt, this was one of the tragedies of revolution; the violence that results is often unintended by its instigators. Regardless of their purposes and aims, the leaders of the French Revolution could not know the meaning of their actions. It would only be for future generations to see the ending of the story they began. In his preface to *Billy Budd*, Melville asked the same question asked in the twentieth century by Marxists faced with the phenomenon of Stalinism: "How was it possible that after the rectification of the Old World's hereditary wrongs ... straightway the Revolution itself became a wrong-doer, one more oppressive than the Kings?" (OR 82–3). Any action, any politics—feminist, socialist, libertarian—may miscarry in ways not envisioned by its founders. A workers' movement may lead to dictatorship, a feminist movement to increased hostility against women, a populist ground swell to fascist racism.

Philosophers tried to escape the uncertainty and frailty of human action with self-undermining results. Marx, for example, looked for a pattern in history to give certain meaning to revolutionary action, but his dialectical materialism only succeeded in making past actions the meaningless motions of historical determinism, the "nails and boards" necessary to build the classless society (HC 78). Kant, Hegel, Sartre, and others tried to find reconciliation in historical processes that would redeem the fact that what is done never matches what is intended. The invisible hand of the economists, the progress of man, idealist essences, all were cited as giving permanence to action. All ended by putting limits on freedom.

Freedom of Will

One popular philosophical recourse was to give up on physical action in the world altogether and refer freedom to an inner freedom of will not subject to any physical restraint. In *The Life of the Mind*, Arendt traced the history of the faculty of will. The questions she asked were not the philosophers' questions: is the will free? or, what is the will? or even: what is the history of the "idea" of the will? Arendt asked instead: what is the *history* of the faculty of willing to which freedom was transferred by philosophers? What, historically, are the experiences to which "freedom of the will" refers?

Will is not found in classical Greek thought. It is not that the Greeks failed to notice an essential human faculty; they did not have the inner "experience" of willing. The will makes its first preliminary appearance in Stoic philosophy as a place of retreat from the Hellenistic world in which freedom and certainty had become problematic to an inner life where peace can supposedly be achieved in an act of willing whatever fate ordains. Willing becomes an important experience in early Christianity. Under injunction to obey the commandments of the Old Testament Father-God, not only in outward conduct but in inner feeling as well, Christians such as Augustine turned inward on themselves. The moral struggle was not to choose rationally between conflicting desires, as it had been for Aristotle, but to invent a faculty that could "will" to obey God against oneself and one's own desires. The theological experience of obedience to the will of God against the self gave experiential meaning to the concept of the will. Action was now transposed to an inner stage. The question was no longer: are actions free?—meaning do we act under constraint? Do we have power in the world?—but: is the will free? Have I succeeded in subduing my appetites in obedience to God?

This pseudo-freedom of will taken up by philosophers supposedly refers to a subjective feeling or event accessible to introspection, but even its innerness is false. The will is not inner in the same sense that heart or mind are real and inner in relationship with what is outer (BPF 146). The inner freedom of the will is a parody, a "politically irrelevant" acting out of acting in the world (BPF 145). From its clear expression in political action, freedom had become an "obscure wood where in philosophy has lost its way" (BPF 145). The will of the philosophers inevitably splits and turns against itself. Inherent in will's Christian origin is not potency but impotency, the sense that, much as one may manage to be chaste in deed, one cannot will to be chaste. The body may be subdued by discipline, but the self is more recalcitrant. "I will" is always at the same time, "I will not," which leads to blockage or paralysis, so that there may be no possibility of action at all (BPF 158–9). Will naturally becomes oppressive as it continually struggles against the "I will not" it inevitably awakens (BPF 162). Unlike thinking, which is split but dialogic, will's splitting is agonistic, aggressive, dangerous, more oppressive than any tyranny of reason (BPF 163). Will becomes Kant's good will, legislating heartlessly according to universal principle, or a will to power fueled by self-destructiveness that vents its violence outward on the world, or Rousseau's sovereign General Will before which minority opinion is silenced (BPF 89). In all these cases, will replaces real freedom, which is power in the world and a place to exercise it (BPF 148).

Worse, in the split between the "I" who wills and an "it" who wills not, will is inevitably tyrannical. In Nietzsche's and Heidegger's treatment of the will, the split between "I will" and "I will not" widens. Nietzsche's will becomes a commanding "I" who rules another self, freedom of the will is "a passionate superiority towards a someone who must obey." In his Nazi stage, Heidegger approved Nietzsche's will to power; then inevitably retreated to Nietzsche's "eternal recurrence," denying the primacy of will in favor of a metaphysical "call of Being." Lost in the "woods" of philosophical theories of the will, philosophers, with the possible exception of Duns Scotus, were unwilling to pay the price of freedom which is the acceptance of contingency in human affairs.

In what Arendt took as its most positive Christian formulation, by Duns Scotus, the will could be a sense of confidence and a source of delight. The destructive splitting of the will could be finally overcome in merger with God, mystical experience, or a foretaste of paradise. These experiences, politically irrelevant in themselves, might even be a source of political energy. But in the godless modern period, the inevitable split in the will is only overcome by fashioning the self into "an enduring 'I' that directs all particular acts of volition" (W 195). The will becomes a *"principium individuationis*, the source of a person's specific identity" (ibid.). This sense of the self as a solitary and autonomous rational decision-maker makes "new and serious trouble" for freedom. The self is now an "I" that is against a "they," against the others that I am not. The prospect of action by such a self is unbearable; first the responsibility is total and unredeemable, second there are no clear standards from which to judge what ought to be done. Not only is freedom of the will not freedom of action, ultimately it makes freedom impossible to conceive. The willer inevitably slips, with Nietzsche and Heidegger, back into some form of metaphysical absolutism or tyranny (W 195–196).

Power of Action

What allows a woman, against the status quo, against those in power, to take political action? Arendt endorses none of the standard philosophical answers. She does not act impelled by a heroic inner act of will; willing only deflects her from action. She does not act out of self-interest, which would be either a reflex or a form of making. She acts as she speaks, to appear as someone for others, and to initiate or carry out a shared project in the world. Freedom, as understood by people of action, is power in the world, power to change and initiate new things, a power which does not have the sovereignty of the will or the force of violence.

To understand the power of action, Arendt drew on political experience, on "original data in the realm of human affairs" (OV 44). One mistake made by philosophers was to equate the power of action with force or rule. Again Arendt made distinctions. Weil's force, Arendt argued, is properly natural force. She sharply criticized the conflation of power and force in "organic" theories of society; to understand relations between persons by way of biological metaphors is to fail to make a distinction between the necessity of natural processes and human freedom (OV 75–5). But if power is not force, it is not willful violence either. Violence can be used to buttress power, but is a sign that power is waning. Except in extraordinary situations, violence is never enough to keep power; only when a population has been atomized, so that no power any where exists, is it possible to institute a rule of terror.

Nor is the power of action in "ruling." This conflation of sovereignty with political power Arendt saw as another common mistake in political philosophy, beginning with Plato.[33] Far from being identical, power and sovereignty are antithetical. "Initiation" and "carrying through," the two reciprocal forms of action, are not ruling and obeying. The initiator needs someone to carry through what she does, the activist needs inspiration and guidance; in contrast, the autonomous "sovereignty" of a ruler—if it is not based on brute force which can never be completely effective anyway—is an illusion. Even an autocrat's decrees depend on the actions of others. Although there is power in leadership, in the ability to move and inspire others, it is not sovereign power, nor does it come from strength or physical force. It comes from a disclosing power in human words and actions that establishes new relations.

If those who initiate are not ruling, those who carry out are not "obeying." This confusion comes from failing to see the artificiality of the traditional opposition between freedom and authority.[34] When freedom is understood as freedom of the will, as inner autonomy and omnipotence, then it must conflict with authority. If the pseudo-idea of freedom is rejected, however, there is no incompatibility between authority and freedom; the two are complementary. Unlike rule, authority is not based on force—but on tradition and respect. Arendt agreed with Weil that tradition is not always the enemy of freedom. It may trap generations in archaic ways of doing things, but can also be "a thread which safely guides through the vast realms of the past," providing a groundwork of permanence and durability which makes action possible. When tradition has failed, as in late twentieth-century experience, or when there is no tradition, the past is endangered and there is no "dimension of depth" in actions (BPF 94). In her studies of political experience, Arendt worked to free action from an obfuscating grid of opposed meanings: power/dependence, force/impotence, strength/weakness. In actual political experience, regardless of the definitions of philosophers, power involves the dependence of others, the use of force signals impotence, a show of violence is a sign of weakness.

Power of action, the ability to act in concert so as to create new relationships and initiate new forms of life, is not something an individual can have but only a number of individuals working together. As a result, action never has a completely predictable result. How, then, is it possible to have the courage to act if it means living with the knowledge that the meaning of what is done may never be known? How is it possible to tolerate the possibility that what is done in good faith may turn out to be evil? Arendt's answer to these questions was bracing. With all "banisters" gone in the postmodern period—tradition, religious authority, absolutes—what redeems action can only be found in action itself. There is no way to armor action in goodness. One of Arendt's most controversial claims was that Weil's goodness has no role to play in public affairs.

Goodness, for Arendt as for Weil, is an inner state of the soul: Jesus' love for his neighbor, Socrates' love of the good, Kant's good will, the innocence of Melville's *Billy Budd*. Goodness is "absolute," "radical," "natural," beyond compromises, discussion, plurality. For Arendt, it is because of this very purity that goodness is dangerous in human affairs. The hanging of the good Billy Budd for murdering the villain Claggert applies the lesson of the French Revolution: any absolute, even if it is the Good, destroys the plurality necessary in public life. Goodness cannot establish lasting institutions (OR 79). It can be violent, just as Billy Budd was violent. It is inarticulate, and cannot "talk *to* someone *about* something that is of interest to both" (OR 81). Goodness is beyond virtue, beyond temptation, beyond the human skills of compromise and negotiation, promising and forgiveness that make action together possible (OR 82). Saints, religious leaders, gurus, reformers, and the innocent, primitive Billy Budd, perhaps even Weil herself, should not hold positions of power.

Lenin, Stalin, Hitler, the saint that we thought would lead us into heaven creates a hell. The voice of conscience that chastised the vices of rulers, once enthroned, orders executions. The reaction is disbelief. They must not have been good; goodness may be hard to detect, but if it had really been there, we would have had heaven on earth. But it was goodness itself, Arendt pointed out, that caused the havoc. The good are angry, violent; they care nothing for worldly institutions or interpersonal discussion. Weil's goodness is out of this world; from its perspective the humble virtues of this world are always compromised.

Arendt agreed with Weil that goodness is not a thing whose qualities can be enumerated or which can be revealed in a Platonic or Christian vision. Once goodness is "shown" or displayed—once the claim is made to know good or have acted out of goodness—goodness is immediately corrupt and perverted (HC 75–6). Its place is in the privacy of the heart where it should remain, not revealed to anyone, even to oneself, made manifest if at all in a religious experience that cannot be spoken. Once the claim is made that an action, a program, a institutional structure is "good," goodness, inevitably compromised, becomes an absolute. Goodness may be part of the depth out of which a woman speaks and acts, and a source of her vital energy, but it cannot "appear" as a quality of that speaking and acting. There is no such thing as a good action. To think there is, is to mistake the status of goodness as an inner state of the soul. When goodness becomes transcendent values claimed as the inspiration necessary in action, those values become mores or customs, and can be changed at will. Righteous insistence on Christian values when fashions change can become righteous insistence on the extermination of witches; insistence on feminine values may result in the persecution of nonfeminists or the alienation of women of other cultures.

Is there no restraint, then, on political action, no moral limits? Are free and heroic acts beyond judgment? Arendt, after the experience of Fascism, was hardly likely to feel comfortable with such a license. But in a world without absolutes, she argued, limits on action can only come from action itself: from "virtues" internal to action, practical skills of speaking, arguing, persuading, listening, promising, forgiving, trusting, judging, taking risks—skills that allow action with others, sustain relationships, and build lasting institutions.[35] These political virtues, unlike Weil's goodness, are not transcendent, absolute, or outside the world; they are inherent in human action itself as self-regulating devices. In promising or trusting, a new relationship is formed; in forgiving, absolution allows people to begin a new life released from the past.

Virtue, in this sense, is not a solitary pursuit of the good, the private business of the Platonic philosopher escaping from the world of the flesh to an intuition of essence or divine equilibrium. Like political speech, political virtue *requires* plurality; there must be others to promise and forgive, trust and judge, others who are different. In promising and forgiving, the unpredictability of what is done is eased. In promises to follow or to implement, a degree of certainty and predictability is possible in human affairs. Alternately, forgiveness redeems the unintended consequences of actions. Someone who takes action is responsible for the consequences—to act is to undertake that responsibility—but forgiveness means that she will not be trapped in those actions forever if they miscarry. She can be freed from the past to do something new (HC 237). Promising and forgiveness make action bearable, but they are no final guarantee; they cannot insure that action will be for the good, they cannot insure that it will have the effects desired. There is no way to evade with justification the essential fragility of human action.

Virtue has its limits. Not all acts are forgivable. Absolute premeditated evil, unlike most unfortunate actions, is not forgivable; this is why, when evil like the Holocaust occurs, there is a crisis. Absolute evil, like absolute good, may require containment, punishment, execution, war, and all the suffering and pain that comes from violence. There is no way to finally protect human action from that possibility. Also dangerous, Arendt pointed out, are the new technologies of science in which actions are created that are not forgivable in another sense. Science's invention of natural processes is one of the only spheres for action left, but in natural processes the self-regulation of forgiveness and promising cannot operate. With nuclear power there are no promises and, in the case of catastrophe, no forgiveness. The outcome of bombings and meltdowns has no "meaning" (HC 322). No stories, no human relationships come from mass destruction. Again the question: how, aware that unforgivable actions have occurred and may occur, with no tradition or authority to follow, is anyone, woman or man, to find the courage to act at all?

Principled Action

This was the unanswered question that pressed Arendt in the last years of her life. Luxemburg relied on theory from the standpoint of working people, Weil on the revelation of a divine equilibrium in human affairs. For Arendt there was no such recourse. What kind of guide is there for action when working-class consciousnesses turns to imperialist militarism? When the sense of divinity has been lost? Like Weil, Arendt read Kant with attention. Kant had been right, she thought; free action is not a utilitarian making, nor is it driven by desire; it is principled. But the principle cannot be Kant's universal law. In his attempt to avoid the determinism that he believed was a necessary presumption of scientific knowledge, Kant removed principles and action from the world. To Kant's practical reason, ruled by the rational principle of consistency, action in the world is irrelevant. The Categorical Imperative might save a woman's soul, but is of little use to her if she is thinking how to prevent evil in the world. Even more serious, with theological warrants no longer credible, Kant's contentless rational principles are likely to dissolve, as Arendt pointed out in *Eichmann in Jerusalem*, into "Kantianism for the little man" or mindless duty to the law. If Kant's "act on the principle you would will to be universal" has no reference to actual human affairs, how are principles to be determined? Why not action on the principle of hatred or jealousy, a possibility which Arendt sometimes admitted? Are not "dignity," "honor," "love of equality," examples Arendt gives of principles "inherent in action," only an individual's own jealously guarded dignity, honor, and advancement (HC 192–8)?

Arendt continued to resist any reversion to universal law or principle. She claimed for her principles of honor, dignity, equality of human beings no transcendental status; she claimed them only as principles necessary for action in the world in solidarity with others, necessary if people are to establish human relationships and form a human community. Relationships depend on plurality, and therefore on respect for one's own and others' honor and dignity. When people accept and are willing to accommodate others' positions, they can enter into relationships. In wealth, status, or talent, people may not be the same, but if in principle they are equal, each has his or her particular place in the world. As Arendt described them, principles of "distinction," "excellence," "glory" do not necessarily call up the image of the posturing politicians striving for immortal fame. Political relations will never be, nor should we want them to be, like the relations in a family where all have become one, where all agree. There are and will be problems, problems that threaten the future of any human relationship. For this reason, public affairs require the excellence of leaders, initiators, and activists who strive for distinction, and who stir and inspire others to action.

In the terms of the utilitarian philosophy which underlies much of modern social policy, it is difficult to understand distinction and excellence in any but self-serving terms. Either we distinguish ourselves in acting out of calculation of self-interest, or we manage to press our desires on others. When, however, distinction and excellence are understood not as expressive of individual self-interest or profit, but as substantive principles internal to action, they play a different role. When admiration is not something to be consumed, something for which a person has a need as he might have a need for food or sex, a principle of excellence can provide a basis for action that is not selfish or paternalistic, but responsive to others. To act on the principle of excellence and distinction is to act as a human being ought to act in the eyes of others so as to deserve respect.

Without any transcendent Form, divine commandment, or Categorical Imperative on which to base a choice between principles, Arendt's principledness is a value in itself. What about evil principles: Aristotle's principle, by no means gone from human affairs—natural rulers should rule natural slaves, men over women, masters over slaves, citizens over laborers, Greeks over barbarians? These, it can be argued, are not principles at all in Arendt's sense. Sexism or racism might be a principle of rule; they cannot be principles of *action*. The Aristotelian "natural master" no longer acts, he "makes." He is alone; his subjects, wives, slaves, colonies are things to be controlled and administered. The slave or the woman cannot act; she can only labor under his direction. Ruling has destroyed the speech necessary to give action meaning. Wives, conquered people, subjects and slaves are reduced to private intimate expression among themselves, and to simple signals necessary if work is to go on. Even the master can no longer speak, because there is no one to whom he can speak. His recourse is to logic, reason, and universal law.

What specifically does an Arendtian politician do when she acts on principle if she does not produce something, or try to bring about an end such as human happiness? This question Arendt never answered satisfactorily. If she is not to deliberate economic or social issues, and if her main concern is not to be the militarist adventures that exhibit aggressive imperialist bravado, then it would seem that an Arendtian counselor has little to do. Maintain the roads. Run the post office. Set up a police force to prevent crime. Establish a court system. Provide for meeting places and procedures. Allow the invisible hand of the market to distribute wealth between rich and poor. Allow traditional authorities in the private spaces of schools, church, and family to decide matters of education and morals. On some of these issues, Arendt found herself in uncomfortable agreement with conservatives. Writing on the violent civil rights confrontations in Little Rock, she did not take the side of civil rights activists, but argued that the schools were private and that civil rights activists should concentrate on miscegenation laws in which there was a public discrimination.[36]

But Arendt's distinction between matters which should be administered and political matters of principle is not the liberal's opposition between private and public. This for Arendt is to misframe the problem. Not only, as Weil understood, is the dividing line between individual right and social jurisdiction indeterminate, and of no sure protection to anyone; free action as Arendt understands it, has been ruled out. An individual by herself can *do* nothing. Nor do administrators *act* as they administer according to expert opinion. As she thought more about the problem, Arendt moved away from her strict sequestering of politics from work. Even though the labor movement often functioned as a special interest group, it could also be a political movement with discussion of general issues and ways to democracy (HC 212–220). She tentatively approved the development of workers' councils and cooperatives in Eastern Europe (CR 216). She argued that, even though in a factory execution has to be administrative, policy might be debated democratically (CR 216). These scattered suggestions of a politics within the workplace suggest another way of understanding Arendt's distinction between administration and politics. Given the earthly condition of human labor and work, if politicians begin to manage the economy, they are no longer actors, they are makers and bosses. They will do it badly, because the political virtues of honesty and integrity are not the managerial virtues of discipline and efficiency. Worse, they will put into effect a process that compromises free action, as principles disappear, and politics becomes the brokerage of economic interests or the administration of a planned economy. But there are issues of principle intertwined with economic life, on which political action must and should be taken.

Questions of administration must be dictated by correct technique, and decided in a more or less dictatorial manner. Arendt cited minimal standards of decent housing, or whether a bridge is safe for traffic, as matters that are not debatable, and therefore not political. What buildings should be condemned or what bridges rebuilt must be decided by engineers and architects (I 318–9). But such issues have a double aspect. What constitutes decent housing is an administrative question; whether or not that housing should be integrated or where a bridge might be located are matters of principle, political questions, which should be debated and adjudicated (I 318). Arendt's distinction between administrative and political carves out a space for free speech and action that is eclipsed by both individuals' willful choices and state administered social policy.

When all social and economic issues are not classed as administrative and decidable in the same way, it is possible to begin to make judgments as to which social and economic issues are political and which are not. Should we take action to redress the hardship and suffering caused by business cycles? Should we initiate a graduated income tax and welfare programs to redistribute wealth? Should there be state-funded medical care? Even if the conservative's free market economics could ensure the greatest happiness of the greatest number, it is a political question how that happiness should be distributed. The question of whether the unemployment and poverty of a few is justified by general prosperity is a question of principle, a question of dignity and honor. The question of whether large holdings of wealth are defensible when there is abject human need, or whether the right to medical care is as fundamental as the right to free speech are questions of principle. In these cases, the "right measures" cannot be simply "figured out" (I 317). Even further, if Arendt is right, and questions of fact, as opposed to questions of technique, can only be settled in narrative public discussion, the fact of whether correct techniques are actually applied by corporations or government agencies is itself subject to debate.

This distinction between political questions of principle to be "acted" on, as opposed to technical problems to be administered, is obscured in both capitalist democratic theory and socialist theory. In capitalism, market forces determine the best outcome, helped along by government regulation and the adjustment of conflicting interests in elected legislatures; in Marxism, state management decides how resources are to be allocated and produced. In neither case is Arendt's distinction between administrative and political acknowledged or implemented. In capitalist democracy, freedoms of speech and assembly leave a remnant of space open for protest, even if few lasting relations result from it. Legislative politics, dominated by economic interests, is in principle open to independents, who on occasion resist pressure and rise to the level of principled speech and action. In Communism, political action is reduced to resistance that either is crushed by terror or retreats underground out of public view. In both cases, with little or no public space cleared for the political, bureaucracies operate without accountability. In capitalist democracies, mass media makes voting, the only political activity left, more and more subject to corporate manipulation. In communist states, justified and unjustified paranoia, the inherited weaknesses of postcolonial socialist economies, and the protection of privilege and corruption make violent reprisals among the administrators of the state the only public activity.

In developing countries, the choice, as it is usually presented, is between the dangerous instability and punishing economic hardships of a primitive free market economy always dependent on established capitalist economies, or state bureaucracies that sustain the power of local elites. Again Arendt's political matters are often not considered: how far is national and regional identity a value? Should freedom of movement and life-style override questions of industrial efficiency? To what degree should consumer preferences for goods be the criteria for production? Should people be allowed to have products that are harmful to them? These, it could be argued, are political questions of principle to be acted upon, rather than problems to be administered.

Questions of principle in developing countries might include the issue of industrialization itself. Should a country preserve traditional production methods which preserve some degree of Weilian thoughtfulness and tradition against large-scale industrial development? Economic theories of international trade, implemented by capitalist organizations such as the World Bank, make this a question of administration. But in free political discussion, citizens might decide that patterns of traditional work have value that overrides the quantity of goods produced. The meaning and value of traditional living spaces and cultural practices, the importance of access to Western consumer goods, the desirability of tourism might all be weighed and considered, and principled action taken. The preservation of traditional communities and forms of life are relevant to "honor" and "dignity," to cite two of Arendt's principles of action. A people's honor might depend on not becoming a client of a great power no matter how well rewarded in foreign aid. A people might decide that their dignity demanded preservation of their culture regardless of the temptation of Western consumer goods.

Even when the traditional venues of politics—counsels, parliaments, committees—are barricaded by privilege against principled action, it may be possible for women and other oppressed groups to clear spaces for political action elsewhere, in households, educational establishments, workplaces, and businesses. To take an example from education: much of what must be decided in a university is administrative: how the buildings are to be heated, how classes are to be taught, how finances are to be organized. These decisions are made by managers, teachers, accountants. But in meetings of a university curriculum committee, action might be taken on matters of principle. The committee members may take the issues as purely administrative, addressing the adjustment of the claims of different departments to a share of the courses taught or required. In that case, members of the committee speak and act not out of principle but out of the self-interest of the department they represent. But it is also possible to make the committee a place for action. What should students learn? How should the course of study relate to professions, citizenship, culture? Should there be a core of knowledge that all students should acquire? Should gender courses or diversity courses be required? Action on these questions of principle is not the "administration" of a campus bureaucracy, but free action that creates new kinds of relations and educational institutions.

Although the actions of a committee may not have the force of law, and can be overruled by administrative veto, their initiatives may also have a founding power and authority that force can never have: the power to create new relationships and new communities of interest. For Arendt, such a politics depends on free action, not predetermined by a calculated plan or a preconceived motive, or even by any coherent idea of what the future should be. We listen to others, we see others act, when it is our turn to act we can never know exactly what it is we are doing. We tell the truth, we present a point of view, we initiate a proposal, we vote yes or no. Inherent in the process is vulnerability, the threat of ostracism, and the fear of being wrong.

Feminist social philosophy has oscillated between two poles: liberal democratic theory focused on rights, and socialist theory focused on government regulation and administration. In both cases, women have been disappointed. In communist countries, experiments in liberalized relations between men and women gave way to a return to the patriarchal status quo. In Western countries, after most of the liberal agenda of equal rights had been achieved, women were still disadvantaged economically and politically. Arendt's conception, fully developed, might be the beginning of a new wave of feminist politics which circumvents and not only subverts the seemingly impenetrable fortresses of institutional power.[37] What she defends as politics is power, not the power of vested interest and custom, nor the power of rule or force, but an originating power of self-presentation to others, and free principled action of initiation and carrying out, in which new relations and institutions take form.

In addition to whatever natural urge there may be to retreat to dogmatism, or to refuse to hear the unfortunate, there is another fact of human life: we have no stable identity except for others. Obscured in the prominence of Luxemburg's socialist leaders, and in Weil's first philosophy, where a solitary self makes pathways in physical reality, this fact allowed Arendt to hold out hope for a liberatory, but not utopian or visionary, politics. A feminist agenda drafted and promoted by lobbyists, intellectuals, demonstrators does not constitute such a politics. In an Arendtian feminist politics, more important than any agenda of employment benefits or abortion rights would be the creation of spaces where diverse women might speak pitilessly and freely to other women, to other oppressed groups, and to men. In that speaking, solidarity might result between feminists and civil rights activists, between environmentalists and peace activists, between idealistic academics and realistic neighborhood activists, between morally responsive members of the middle class and ghetto residents, solidarity which is a basis for political action that creates new forms of life. If feminism has often seemed stalled in adversarial challenge to a male world, Arendt holds out hope for a feminist politics which, from an independent base of solidarity with diverse others, might make a new world.

6. Thinking

Between Times

But how is a woman to have the courage to begin? If she is no one before she speaks out and takes action, then she has nothing to say or do. Where is she to get that grasp of the whole that Luxemburg saw as necessary for intelligent action. Even more important, once she does act, how is she to keep on course in the compromising press of human affairs? How is she to keep herself from being drawn into currents and movements which end in failure or disaster? Given the uncertainty of action, and the unsureness of its justification as Arendt describes it, it is not surprising that many women fail to act.

Reporting on the trial of the Nazi war criminal Adolf Eichmann in *Eichmann in Jerusalem*, Arendt addressed this question by way of an extraordinary case. Eichmann, like so many Germans, had failed to act or speak against the Germans. Instead he had taken the opportunities they offered to advance his career. Here was the man who had organized the Final Solution, perhaps the greatest crime in history, and, contrary to the expectations of his judges, he was not full of malice or obsessed with hatred of Jews. He had simply not thought about what he was doing. He had done his duty as it was defined for him by his superiors. If he and other Germans had thought, would it have been different? If thought cannot discover absolute principles on which to act, might it at least inhibit evil action?

In *The Human Condition*, Arendt turned away from the contemplative life of the philosophers to the active life. Now, observing Eichmann, and struggling with the problem of action in a postmodern period without transcendent principles, the question of thinking reasserted itself. She, herself, was a thinker not a doer, although on occasion she had been pressed into action (D 305–6). In *The Human Condition* she "thought" about forms of human activity. But as a thinker, she escaped her own thought and judgment. What is this thinking that Eichmann and other Germans did not engage in? How is it distinguished from other mental processes like willing and judging? Under what conditions does it flourish? Under what conditions does it become impossible? Most important, what is thought's relation to political action?

In *Thinking*, the first volume of her *The Life of the Mind*, Arendt reviewed "professional" philosophical opinion on thought. Buttressed behind metaphysical fallacies, constantly on the defensive against the charge that philosophy is useless, pressed to claim that insight into a reality beyond the understanding of the masses is possible, philosophers lost touch with the experience of thinking and began from what they had to say to defend philosophy and their professional status as philosophers (T 89, 166). Neither the rationalists' deduction nor the empiricists' induction are thought. Both turn inward, the one on the workings of brains or minds, the other on internal sensations or observations. In neither case is thought *about* anything, because in neither case does thought engage a reality that can be shared with others, the only reality there is.

In order to come to an understanding of thinking, it is necessary to clear philosophy out of the way, a task that Arendt credited Kant with beginning, although he had not been willing to give up the connection between knowledge and thinking, and did not fully realize it. "Metaphysical fallacies" that arise from professional thinking, such as Descartes's autonomous consciousness or the two worlds of reality and appearance, must be explained and dissolved. Thinking has to be liberated both from the science which the positivist mistakes for thinking, and from idealist revelation or intuition as an incommunicable state of the soul. The thinking that can protect against evil is neither the inaccessible formulas of science nor the abstruse metaphysics of philosophers, but a normal part of human life.

Philosophers often made it seem as though a thinker migrates to a timeless world of the spirit to contemplate unchanging truths. Plato's aspirant to knowledge rejected mortality and the senses for a super- natural world of reason where eternal ideas are illuminated by the Form of the Good. Descartes closed his mind to sensory distractions to intuit permanent mathematical structures. Phenomenologists dis- covered essences by bracketing out the experiential world. Empiri- cists isolated from immediate perception artificial sense data to be the basis for scientific representations. The unacceptable alternative was taken to be relativism, the view that thinking is situated and ungeneralizable, a projection of one person's experience at a particu- lar time and place.

Arendt took neither horn of the dilemma. When a person thinks, she draws back from action and experience into the privacy of her mind. She is nowhere, "homeless," out of the world. But that with- drawal is not an absolute removal; it is temporally placed. Thought is not above or out of time but "in between" two times. We think between a past and a future, in the eye of a storm of human events, where trains of remembrance and anticipation cross and recross (T 193). Thinking begins from memories of what has happened and has been done, projected into a future in which we will communicate to others, make judgments, and take action. The formations of mem- ory are already thoughts as they are "imagined" or "desensed" with the awareness that it "could have been different" (T 85). It is not just that anxiety about the past or worry about the future moves or inspires thinking; this would be consistent with traditional accounts of thought. The very movement and substance of thought, for Arendt, is between past and future.

At times, tradition bridges the gap between past and future and makes a smooth transition, so that thought is unnecessary. But when tradition breaks down, as it has in the postmodern period, people are trapped. This, as Arendt saw it, is the tragedy of the late twentieth century: thinking is necessary, but at the same time people have forgotten how to do it. As long as there is a tradition that is trusted and respected, there is little need to think. Only a few professional thinkers need to engage in thought. When tradition becomes meaning- less, thinking becomes vitally necessary. Arendt used Kafka's parable to explain (BPF 9–14, T 202ff.). Without tradition to determine his actions, a thinker is like a fighter who has two antagonists, one the future that presses him back into the past, the other the past that presses him forward into the future.[38] There are three struggles going on at once. The past struggles against the future; the man struggles against the past; the man struggles against the future. In Kafka's version, the man can win none of these struggles. Either he dies of exhaustion and despair, or he leaps out of the line of fire to an unreal metaphysical world apart from human affairs.

But Kafka, Arendt said, misrepresented the man's position. He imagined the conflict between past and future as necessarily rectilinear, which leaves the thinker no place to stand. In fact, a thinker's insertion between past and future can deflect the force of both past and future, so they are no longer part of an unidirectional flow, but meet at an angle. From that angle results a diagonal. Thinking is that diagonal. If the thinker can walk its line in equal distance from past and future, she gives herself room; she is no longer a fighter attacked from both sides, but is able to remove herself from time, at the same time as her thought remains rooted in the present, at the intersection of past and future. From this vantage point, she can judge the past and the future. When she learns to move along the line between past and future, not falling off either into empty rationalization or despair, she has discovered, as Arendt put it, the "region of the spirit."

As practice in thought that might bridge the present's widening gap between past and future, Arendt undertook the exercises in political thought in *Between Past and Future*. In these historical/linguistic/experiential studies, Arendt walked an oblique line between past and future in which criticism and expectation are not separable. Arendt's critical interpretations of past meanings of power, force, rule, and authority were not refutations, but attempts to imagine for a possible future the living experience out of which concepts come. Alternatively, her visions of the future were not fantasies but drew on a past which makes them intelligible and meaningful. She began from her, and our, particular historical situation; by moving out, at the angle between past and future, she finds the vantage point from which to survey both in a thinking that, as she put it, "arises out of incidents of living experience and must remain bound to them as the only guideposts by which to take its bearings" (BPF 14).

The Measure of Things

By "living experience," Arendt meant experiences of objective reality that the thinker "remembers," experiences that are shared with others, recounted by others, preserved in writings and records, and marked in language. But simple memory is never enough for thought; memory cannot activate thought "outside a pre-established framework of reference" (BPF 6). Memories must be named, and names require general concepts under which experiences fall. Thought is never secure "until it is condensed and distilled into a framework of conceptual notions within which it can further exercise itself" (OR

222). This framework, however, cannot be a fixed grid of oppositions that stops thought. Concepts "hold the measure of all things" (TMC 430, T 170),[39] but in philosophical abstractions they congeal, and come to represent "frozen thought which thinking must unfreeze" (TMC 431). The role of thought is not to intuit ideas already there in a pseudo-world of reason, but to continue to develop concepts adequate to changing human experiences. Arendt assumed what much of modern philosophy of language after Descartes takes as impossible: experiences can be named intelligibly because we live in a shared world; we are in direct contact with that shared world through our senses; we can communicate experiences to others.

Meanings cannot be established in definitions. When we simply define our terms:

> We have ceased to live in a common world where the world we have in common possesses an unquestioned meaning-fulness, so that short of being condemned to live verbally in an altogether meaningless world, we grant each other the right to retreat into our own worlds of meaning, and demand only that each of us remain consistent within his own private terminology. (BPF 95–6)

Nominal or semantic definition typically depends on opposition. What is a man? A man is what is not a woman. What is a woman? A woman is what is not a man. In the *Sophist*, Plato initiated the method of philosophy as division into opposed categories. The "true" philosopher successively places an object—in this case the false deceptions of Plato's rivals, the democratic Sophists—into one of two opposing categories, until a final, unflattering "definition" is reached that is consistent with philosophic values.

In contrast, for Arendt, thinking is with concepts derived from "de-sensed" memories of experience in a world shared with others. Again she took neither horn of the philosophers's dilemma: is thinking prior to speaking so that words are conventional names of ideas in the mind? Or alternatively, is thinking internal speech dependent on meanings as they are established in public use? It is not, as Plato believed, that spoken words must be made congruent with clear and distinct forms of thought. Nor does thinking depend on concepts whose meaning is "use"; uses of words can be empty or mistaken. For Arendt, speaking and thinking are independent but reciprocally related. Thinking begins from memories of "common sense." The empiricist's atomic, private impressions of a single sense have no communicative reality for Arendt. Whatever neural event might correspond to a visual or aural sensation, it cannot be put into words that report a thought. What can be communicated is experience of an object grasped by more than one sense and by more than one sensate being (T 50). In thought, memories already shaped by this common experience are "desensed"[40] to make abstract ideas, ideas whose meanings can be questioned, ordered, criticized. The thinker makes sense of what has happened to her in the same way people tell stories about past events; she works what has happened into a web of understanding.

Naming "disalienates" experience (T 100). The language of sense is further extended by metaphor to create abstract ideas and conceptions[41] which are the "unseen measures that bind and determine human affairs" (T 151). Like Weil, Arendt understands abstract meanings as based on balance and equilibrium, but unlike Weil, that balance is not divinity; it is inherent in human sociality. Meanings are not the frozen concepts of philosophers, but moving measures by which to judge what people say and do.

Thinking can only "appear" in speech (T 98). But more than that, even unspoken thinking takes the form of a dialogue with self that mimics interpersonal communication. What creates the need for systems of grammar and meaning is the fact that, in intercourse with others, we have to "come to terms with whatever may be given to our senses." We are required to "give an account of what occurred." Even the "frozen" oppositional concepts of philosophers, remote from ordinary talk though they may have become, are rooted, in so far as they have meaning, in the interchange of speech. Philosophers metaphorically extend concepts to map out a pseudo-solitary inner life of the mind, but even then they cannot leave the real world of shared appearances completely behind. There is no "other world" of reason apart from sense, memory, and opinion, only a reciprocal movement back and forth, between the exchange of concepts in speech with others, and the recreative reordering effort of thought in solitude.

At times, philosophers, in moments of conceptual change and confusion, are able to reach beyond oppositions, asking questions that go "to the heart of the matter" (BPF 38). Like Luxemburg and Weil, Arendt cited Marx's *Theses on Feuerbach*. Marx, describing man as a "natural being" beyond the traditional philosopher's dichotomy between reason and sensuous life, proposed concrete experience as an alternative to the dead end of antiquated idealism and futuristic scientism. Such oblique advances out of the impasse between past and future are achieved not in a Platonic dialectic which manipulates oppositions, but in the dialogical processes of thought and speech. Marx's involvement in labor politics, his journalism, his debates with

Hegelians, anarchists, and socialists alternated with thought in which frozen concepts were reordered and reframed. Such thought is not deductive or linear; it has a double duality: first, a split in the self that allows an internal version of that same conversation which, in turn, has provoked thought; second, a dialogue with self that prepares for a public life in which we will once again be one self appearing to others.

For Weil, there was an essential link between progressive social theory and the use of language. When words become labels, absolutes, or frozen concepts, language no longer performs its proper function. Arendt described that function differently. For Weil, words mark ideals of balance, ratio, equilibrium, out of the world of force, by which phenomena in that world can be measured and judged. Arendt translates these otherworldly relations into this-world relations. Words have value as concepts, in that they mark out objects of interest between people. There is no thinking without language, but language is the medium of a thought that moves in response to what others say and think.

The Two-in-One of Thought

Arendt looked for an object lesson, someone who thought out loud in public, someone who fulfilled the normal duties of citizenship and who made no claim to be a professional thinker. Her choice was the unprofessional philosopher, Socrates.[42] A Socratic thinker, no matter what praise or honors she might win in public, has to face a critic at home. Once alone, her self splits and an interior dialogue begins. When she thinks, she is not lonely because, for better or for worse, she keeps herself company (T 74–5). In contrast to Plato, who began the "freezing" of thought in metaphysics, Socrates was Arendt's model for a thinking in which a person submits everything that she has done and said and will do and say, to "cross-examination" (T 188). The result is the familiar Socratic ethics: it is better to be wronged than to do wrong; it is better to be out of harmony with the whole world than out of harmony with oneself.

Arendt distinguished this dialogic thought from the philosopher's "consciousness" (T 187). Thinking is not the philosopher's reflective doubling of self-consciousness, in which a person is aware of herself as "the same." This view of the self leads to the fallacy of solipsism, a illusory projection of the mind and of thinking as self-sufficient (T 47). Sameness, Arendt argued, cannot establish identity. Identity is always bound up with difference, with being different from other things. The self is no exception. What generates an inner identity, independent of others, that allows innovative action, is difference, the difference between self and others, and also the difference between the two-selves-in-one necessary for thought. When this inherent duality is actualized in self-questioning, there is a mind. To try to solve an "identity crisis" by finding a unitary self is to stop thinking, and thereby to lose one's identity (T 187).

What moves a person to thought? What drives her to begin that often painful and unsettling inner dialogic questioning which insures that her actions will no longer be thoughtlessly dictated by expediency, custom or blind appetite. As always, Arendt looked to history for the answers. The Greeks thought from a sense of wonder and awe, perhaps linked to Weil's revelation of divinity. In the late Roman Empire, the thought of Stoics and Epicurians was motivated by an escape from a world in which there was no more hope or happiness (T 141–166). The example of Socrates suggests another reason. The aim of thinking is to be friends with oneself. When a woman senses she is acting or speaking with others in ways inconsistent with her professed beliefs, she is in contradiction with herself. She has become her own adversary. Either she does not believe what she says she does, or the concepts under which she understands what she is doing are inadequate to her experience. Given that she cannot escape herself, given that doing wrong by her own standards will put her in enmity with herself, she must find some resolution. We think to be consistent with ourselves, to be able to keep promises to ourselves, and also promises to others that are both explicit and implicit in our actions and words.

Although the consistency in speaking and action which is the aim of thinking may be the precursor of logical consistency, it is not logical consistency. In logic, concepts are kept in place by oppositional definitions; the "insight, won from the factual experience of the thinking ego, gets lost" (T 186). Aristotle's original formulation of consistency is Socratic:

> we must necessarily believe it because . . . it is addressed not to the outward word (*exo logos*, that is to the spoken word addressed to someone else, an interlocutor who may be either friend or adversary) but to the discourse *within the soul*, and though we can always raise objections to the outward word, to the *inward discourse* we cannot always object.

This insight into thought, however, is lost in Aristotle's schematized syllogistic logic:

A cannot be both B and A under the same conditions and at the same time. (HC 186)

In logic, the search for consistency which is the impulse to thought becomes legislation which all are required to follow and prohibition that forbids thought.[43] Logic is the form of ideology. An ideology "can explain everything and every occurrence by deducing it from a single premise" (OT 468). The "logic of an idea," projected onto reality, insures that whatever happens is in accordance with law—of History, as in Marxism, or of Nature, as in Fascism. Logic is monovocal, making it certain that there will be no movement in thought that is not a deduction from first premises.

In contrast, although thought is not addressed to any other person, nevertheless, it "points to the infinite plurality which is the law of the earth" (T 187). We become the Socratic two-in-one of thought out of the pluralistic sociability of human life; the two are rooted in the same principle. "I first talk with others before I talk with myself" (T 189). The various kinds of interactions between a woman and herself that occur in thought are derived from the great variety of forms of interpersonal discussion. She questions herself, criticizes herself, exposes the meaninglessness and lack of reference of her concepts, confronts her positions with contrary testimony. When she leaves her solitude and returns to the world, she is one again, consistent with herself. Just as free interaction with others prepares her for thought, so thinking prepares her, as one self, to enter into dialogue again with others. Thinking is a dialogue with self which always involves "an anticipated communication with others with whom I know I must finally come to some agreement" (BPF 220). Thought, like conversation, requires the dialogic skills that Arendt admired in her friend Karl Jaspers. He could listen, he was able to give a candid account of himself, he had the patience to stay with a subject, he had the ability to entice a matter out into discussion (MDT 78–9).

Thinking, like public discussion, is narrative. It begins in memory, in the need to tell a coherent story about what has happened. Because stories often conflict and must be reconciled, in thought we go over and over the story, attempting to capture the perplexing meaning of what happened. What was it that she, he, they, we said—trying to get it right, and each time knowing that the story is not quite right, does not hold together, that we have not yet captured what really happened in preparation for discussion with others, where we must be ready to present one story and one self. The various thought trains of memory, imagination and conceptualization that make up thought cannot be one woman's or one man's. Left only to herself, a woman has no thoughts or memories, no way to generate conflicting points of view, but when she is worried, when things do not make sense to her, and she must sit down to think the problem out, she hears the voices of others conflicting with her own. The ways she answers them and herself in thought, when she sees that she and they do not see things the same way, are similar to the ways in which she might answer in public. Why do you think that? she asks herself. Explain this more? What justifies you in taking such a move? How could you have been so stupid? The complex movements of interpersonal dialogue have a counterpart in the movements of thought in solitude which prepare the self for becoming one again to present and explain itself.

For philosophers, thought has been an internal matter of private ideas. Whatever is seen as their source—reason or sensation—thinking has been understood as the manipulation of those ideas. The postmodern turning operation externalizes those ideas in systems of signs, so that thinking becomes not the manipulation of private ideas but the manipulation of public signs. For Arendt, neither the sorting of private ideas nor the deconstruction of conceptual relations is thinking which, even as it withdraws from the world, has a grounding in experience in the world and a future in returning to the world.

The Uses of Thought

The problem, of course, with such a thinking from the point of view of philosophy is that it has no unitary binding authority. Since Plato's Philosopher Kings, the goal of professional thought has been to grasp a truth so compelling, so certain, that it will set everything straight. For this purpose, Arendt's thought is useless. Its purpose is not to find *the* truth on which we and others must act, to find *the* principle which must guide our and others' judgments, or to know *the* good which politics must institute. How then are judgments to be made? How is one to know what action to take? How are those who think something false to be proven wrong and made to retract? No matter how many people believe something, it may not be true. The Germans, many of them anyway, believed that Hitler was right, and even if all of them had actually thought about Fascism and agreed to it, it wouldn't have made it true that it was right. Just as with action, rational limits seem to be necessary to constrain thought to the truth and keep it from being a frivolous or impotent spinning of mental wheels.

Characteristically, Arendt worked out from the problem obliquely. The solution could not be to find an authoritative representation to buttress belief or action, and make it impregnable to criticism. Instead, she looked at the complex relation between thought and action. This was the crucial question. First, because Arendt now believed that the relation between action and thinking is the key to protecting against evils such as Fascism, and second, because she also believed that the relation between thought and action might explain how actions that create something new are possible, given action's fragility and indeterminacy.

The thinker's role cannot be preacher. Theoreticians, as removed thinkers, cannot tell practical people what to do (D 309–10). Again, the philosophers' reversible opposition between theory and practice does not capture human experience. As Luxemburg pointed out, when thinking congeals into rationalization, or action into practice dictated by theory, both thinking and freedom of action are lost. The relationship between the experiences of thinking and action, as understood by Arendt, is not linear. It is not that what we do is determined by what we think, or that what we think is determined by what we do. The two human activities are distinct, reciprocally and not deductively connected. Thinking prepares for action, as action prepares for thinking, but not in the sense that theory dictates what must be done. In action, we appear to others who are not us. In thinking, we appear to ourselves as another. The condition for each activity is the same: human difference, enhanced and reworked in thought and action. The virtues required are similar—the acceptance of difference, skills of reconciliation and negotiation. Principles, of honor, dignity, equality, internal to action motivate thought (T 71). In promising, the fragility and uncertainty of human action is made bearable. In the attempt of thought to achieve consistency, the same ability to promise is enhanced. If we are consistent with ourselves, we have the ability to keep promises. If we are in the habit of thinking, we have occasion to reflect on our inconstancy.

Arendt moved to the crucial question. Thinking can help people to keep promises but how does it prevent evil? It cannot reveal the good. It cannot determine Kant's universal principle of action. Socrates' inquiries yielded no final result, no definition of the good. His thinking broke down the rigid formula of traditional Greek morality, left his partners in dialectic in confusion, what they thought was knowledge hopelessly compromised by his cross-examinations. The Socratic effect was not indoctrination, but stimulation, awakening, and, in some cases, even the paralysis of uncertainty. There are dangers in such thought; some, like Alcibiades, might slip into nihilism or cynicism, but, Arendt concluded, there are worse dangers when people do not think (T 177). When people act according to convention or rule and those rules are reversed—when the Christian "thou shalt not kill" becomes the Nazis' "thou shalt kill"—people may continue to thoughtlessly obey. But once the thinking process is stimulated and frozen concepts that support policies are undermined, action becomes problematic. Thinkers no longer can be so confident they can save the world, or that they come from a superior race or sex; the absolute which precludes individual judgment falters. In times of moral crisis, those who go home to the Socratic two-in-one may hesitate or refuse to participate in evil. This inhibition of the certainty of action may be a modest benefit beside the promise of the philosopher's absolutes, but it is what, in Arendt's judgement, Eichmann and other Germans lacked, and what was responsible for passive resistance in other parts of Europe.

If thought can cause beneficial doubt and uncertainty about present courses of action, it can also help to understand past action and its meaning. In *Between Past and Future*, Arendt began with a quotation from the writer Rene Char who, like many French intellectuals, joined the Resistance in occupied France: "Our inheritance was left to us by no testament," wrote Char of his experiences in the Resistance. Arendt explained what she understood Char to mean by this "strange aphorism" (BPF 3). In the Resistance, intellectuals such as Char had experiences that were new to them. They had been forced for a brief time to be part of a "public" world in which actions and words had meaning. After the defeat of the Germans, they returned to private life, and to the same tired political ideologies, with a feeling of loss. What was this treasure they had lost? They could not know because it had been left them "by no testament." No tradition had preserved and passed on to them the experience of freedom in a public sphere so that it could be recognized. The bureaucracy of the nation-state, the managed markets of capitalism, the party politics of Western democracies, the academic skirmishing of intellectuals erased even the memories of such a space. What the resistance fighters lost had no name, and so it could not be remembered or preserved.

In thought testaments can be written, inspiring future action. When there have been actions as momentous as those in the resistance to Fascism, the civil rights struggle in the American South, the fight against apartheid in South Africa, the contemporary feminist movement against women's oppression, thoughtful remembrance can bring actions to "completion" (BPF 6). Thought articulates what has been done, forms concepts that name it, places actions in a "framework of reference" that allows the experience of free, principled action to become a "testament" for the future.

Impartial Judgment

In Fascism, the active life Arendt described in *The Human Condition* turned pathological, distorted out of all recognition. It was even possible to see disturbing parallels between Arendt's insistence that politics is a free display of self, unrestrained by external moral limits, and the murderous willfulness of the Nazis. Thought may confuse and paralyze sufficiently so that people hesitate to act, and mass participation in evil is averted. Thought may prepare for promising and forgiveness; it can provide a testament for the future. But it cannot dictate action. Arendt's principles internal to action are no final guarantee against evil. Pressed to relent and accept the presence of universal moral restraints, Arendt continued to refuse. There are no longer any absolutes; if they are necessary, we are lost. It does no good to cry out that we need what we do not have.

The puzzle of political action remained. Unless a woman's thought can form a judgment that has authority, how is it possible to act resolutely? And if no binding judgment is possible, how is it possible to initiate new beginnings when there is no intact tradition on which to draw? How can there be the institution of a nonsexist society, when nowhere in Western history is there a society that has not been male-dominated? How can relations of equality between races be established, if the conceptual structures of Western culture are infected with a racist definition of the Other? How can there be a free politics, when politics has always been parasitic on the exploitation of oppressed laborers and workers?

At the end of her last published work, *Willing*, Arendt turned away from philosophical theories to political actors for an understanding of the thought and action that can found a new order. As she reviewed the great mythic beginnings of Western culture—the founding of Rome, the Hebrew exodus from Egypt, the American Revolution—she found what she called an "abyss of freedom." Between liberation from oppression and the establishment of positive conditions for new institutions, between rebellion and a new constitution, there is a nothingness, a period of aimless wandering in the wilderness that in the past had only ended with the remembering of a previous model: the law of God as revealed to Moses, the restoration of Troy, the City of God. The problem for action in the last years of the twentieth-century West is that there is no longer any model whose remembrance can serve. In practice and in theory, it is clear that the institutional, Western, monotheistic religions are tainted with sexist and racist partiality. Archaeologists and historians have taken any remaining romance from ancient mythic beginnings, as they have documented the aggressive conquest and settlement that accompanied the Israelite conquest of Canaan, the Roman campaigns, and the extermination of indigenous peoples in the Christian conquests of Africa and the Americas.

The postmodern problem of action, as Arendt diagnosed it, is rooted in the situating of action in time. With no viable tradition to smooth the way, action must have natality; it must bring about new things. But no matter how independent of determining causes and intentions a free action may be, in the future, when it is judged and evaluated, it will require justification. How is that justification possible without authority external to action? If feminist thought, for example, denies absolutes, rejects a Father God, refuses symbolic constructions of the Good, refuses even the supposition of any essence of Woman, how can feminist action be justified? And action must be justified because otherwise, it is arbitrary, meaningless, and potentially destructive. There is no guarantee that theory from a given perspective, whether it is of women, workers, or an oppressed race, is reliable. Even when political spaces are preserved where people can present themselves freely to others, they may still appear as master and slave, sadist and masochist, destroyer and victim. They may even establish permanent relations and communities on the basis of these relations. At this point, the very desirability of freedom in a world without absolutes is in question.

For inspiration, Arendt turned again to Kant—her Kant, not Kant the theoretician but Kant the thinker. Kant, she believed, grasped the problem from the beginning. Although he had been sidetracked by transcendental metaphysics, inherent if not explicit in his thought is an "unwritten political philosophy" focused on judgment and not on the rationalist "kingdom of ends" of the *Critique of Practical Reason*. "Practical reason" is useless for politics; few act according to universal principles. As Kant himself admitted, it's even better that they don't because principles are so easy to mistake. Goodwill, abstracted from inclination, takes the moralist off the earth to the contemplation of private heavenly rewards; natural self-interest is a better regulating device for human affairs.

In her last lectures on material prepared for *Judging*, the final unwritten volume of *The Life of the Mind*, Arendt cited Kant himself in support of a creative continuance of Kantian thinking. Alongside the austere autonomy of transcendental and practical reason, Arendt insisted, Kant never completely lost sight of an early unphilosophical conviction that thought and judgment require others.

> While discussing Plato, [Kant] once remarked "that it is
> by no means unusual, upon comparing the thoughts which
> an author has expressed in regard to his subject . . . to find
> that we understand him better than he has understood him-
> self. As he has not sufficiently determined his concept, he has
> sometimes spoken, or even thought, in opposition to his own
> intention."

Arendt concluded: "this is of course applicable to his own work" (T 63).
In Arendt's reading, Kant's thought is open to response and further
extension, open to the possibility that someone else might understand
him better than he understood himself. Pressed into the future by
his contempt for the empty and elitist ratiocinations of scholastic
philosophers, pressed back into the past by his horror at the nihilism
of Hume's scepticism, Kant thought and acknowledged that his thinking could not go on without critical response. His method, as he
described it, was not to reject or refute objections, but to incorporate
them into his thought (LK 42). As Arendt quotes him: "Unless you
can somehow communicate and expose to the test of others, either
orally or in writing, whatever you have found out when you are alone,
this faculty of thinking exerted in solitude will disappear" (ibid.).

Arendt's Kant was not the august authority of the idealist tradition,
but a man thinking about a problem, a political problem, which had
bothered him from the beginning: how is judgment of particulars—
judgment that does not simply subsume a particular under a preexisting universal—possible (LK 10)? And further, how is it possible to
act if there is no judgment that an action is justified? The problem
of aesthetic judgment, addressed by Kant in his "Third Critique," is
analogous. Here also are two standpoints, the standpoint of the artist
and the standpoint of the judge. The critic must have something to
judge, the genius of the artist is worthless without the critic's judgment to keep it in bounds. Genius, to be valuable and meaningful,
must be communicable, must present itself for another's judgment. In
turn, judgment creates the space in which artistic freedom is possible.

Surprisingly, the metaphor for Kant's aesthetic judgment is taste,
the most subjective of senses. Visual models can be the basis for
science; hearing and touch give rise to images which can be examined.
Taste is not representable in any image or model and is inherently
discriminatory only of the particular. Because of this lack of "objectivity," empiricists rejected tastes and smells as subjective "secondary
qualities" that cannot be the basis for scientific knowledge. Then came
the insight of the "Third Critique." Taste is not simply subjective.

In its very subjectivity is a kind of objectivity. Inherent in artistic appreciation is the sense that we appreciate beautiful or good things *with* other human beings. This is not the distanced, rational judgment of practical reason regardless of what anyone else thinks. We appreciate a meal or a beautiful landscape with others because we share common earthly feelings and sensations. Taste, subjective through and through, in contrast to the "imaginary" objectivity of sight, rests on a "common sense" (LK 70–1). We not only taste, we taste as another would taste. We not only appreciate an object of art, we appreciate as another would appreciate it. We not only take pleasure in an act of bravery, we take pleasure in it as another would take pleasure in it. Vision, far from being the most public sense, may be, in fact, the most solipsistic of the senses, in contrast to pleasure, taste, and appreciation which are essentially communicable and shareable.

In the view of empiricist philosophers, taste cannot be communicated because it is not focused on a projected, generalized, scientific object but on a unique, particular happening. But in taste there is something that is not "objective" in a different sense. Taste is mingled with a "common sense" of whether our pleasure in an object is worthy of us, with the question of whether other sensing beings would feel as we do. When we taste, we taste as others would taste, aware that others might take the same pleasure. Mixed with a felt "subjective" approval of a particular is the communicability of that approval. At the very roots of human sensibility is not private sensation that must by some magic be put into words—a process in which the substance of experience is bound to be lost—but communicability. "The nonsubjective element in the nonobjective sense is intersubjectivity" (LK 67). "Common sense," Arendt argued, who had now moved well beyond Kant's own theory of aesthetic judgment, is essential for language. If it is missing, the only recourse is to logic, rationality, or inarticulate expression, and the communicative functions of language are lost.

On the presumption of an essential privacy and incommunicability of sensation, language will always, no matter what theories of language philosophers devise, be incomprehensible. Communication will have to be artificially induced in logic, semantics, grammatical structure, conventions of behavior, which cover over the fact that we cannot, in principle, understand each other. Arendt's Common sense makes such a compensatory "linguistics" unnecessary. Experience of and judgment on a particular event is directly communicable in words because of the intrinsic communicability of sensations, a communicability which is part of the very feel of sensation. Because sensation is accompanied by imagination—we are able to imagine how things might be experienced from other points of view—and by reflection—

we can bracket our own position—impartial judgment is possible that is communicable and therefore persuasive.

> The it-pleases-or-displeases-me, which as a feeling seems so utterly private and noncommunicative, is actually rooted in this community sense and is therefore open to communication once it has been transformed by reflection, which takes all others and their feelings into account. (LK 72)

The *sense* that a feeling or reaction or judgment is worthwhile, and sharable, not ignominious or perverted, for Arendt is the human soul, a soul whose characteristic is not privacy but intersubjectivity.

The founding myth of Western philosophy is that there is a truth and goodness to which thought and action must conform, a truth and goodness opposed to the shifting and uncertain judgments of women and men. The authority on this truth and goodness was to be philosophy, which arranges concepts in correct and unquestionable order, insulated from the confusions of private and uncommunicable experience. Arendt's impartial judgment is in another tradition of thought. Such a judgment is of real particular events; it is rooted in individuals' communicable experiences of those events; it is cognizant of the distinctions marked in the language in which events are discussed. Impartial judgment, determined by no principle or rule, is representative. It achieves generally because the judger—the thinker, journalist, reporter, historian, writer—judges not only from her own position but also from her sense of the position of others. Impartial judgment is not discardable relative expression of personal taste, it is not one perspective among others. Its validity comes not from consensus or majority rule—which can always be wrong—but from the representative quality of a judgment that is enlarged by an imaginative ability to occupy others' situations and grounded in a sense innate to human beings that experience is communicable and sharable with others.

Arendt's impartial judgment is Luxemburg's "view of the whole" from the standpoint of the oppressed, as well as Weil's response to the cry for justice. Working people may not understand their situation. Oppressed people may be too crushed by misfortune to feel, to judge, or to cry out. Arendt's thinker does not depend on any merger of consciousness or symbiosis of feeling, but puts herself in the others' position. Her judgment does not simply reflect others' feelings but illuminates their situation in ways that they have not thought of and cannot articulate. At the same time, it is open and remains open to their response.

A New Foundation

The last unwritten volume of *The Life of the Mind* was to have shown how such an enlarged judgment is related to action. Like Kant, Arendt watched revolutions fail: in Eastern Europe, and in the student movements of the sixties. After her death, there were more failures: the resurgence of ethnic hatreds in Europe, war in the Middle East, in the West a massive redistribution of wealth away from lower-income groups, the continued impoverishment of developing nations. Arendt, like Kant, struggled with the contradiction between a refusal in "dark times" to engage in violent acts, and the removed judgment that change only comes from fomentation and unrest.[44] Like Kant, she spared no dogma from criticism, refused the solace of a school or discipline in which she might have found some respite from thought, at the same time as she also refused to renounce the possibility of judgment with authority for others.

If Arendt was Kant, I am, perhaps you are, Arendt, trying to think "without a banister," convinced that there is no return to the Christian Father-God, or Plato's Good, or Marx's dialectic of history, or the Rights of Man, convinced that these absolutes are now irrevocably compromised by autocracy, sexism, racism, totalitarianism, but also convinced that without the possibility of a just and compelling judgment—without the filling in of that last blank page in Arendt's typewriter—there is no possibility of action that can bring about change. In my "imagination," here is how Arendt might have written on that blank page.

No action carries its own justification with it, but requires others who will judge what has been done. A woman who speaks and acts depends on the spectator's "it-seems-to-me"; she is not her own master, but must act in accordance with what spectators expect of her. "The final verdict of success or failure is in their hands" (T 94). Nor is the spectator insulated in her judgment on action; her verdict is not independent of others, but must take them into account. What restrains action and protects against evil is not sincere good motives, or knowledgeable calculation, or universal principles but a delicate reciprocal relation between action and judgment. If there must be public spaces for action; there must also be public forums for impartial judgment: courts, newspapers, books, news media. Judgment is more than a right of individuals, it defines and protects the very space that makes free action justifiable and therefore possible. If the actions of diverse politicians, leaders, activists, are public and viewable, and if a reciprocal freedom of thought of diverse writers, commentators, thinkers, leads to impartial judgments of the worth of those actions, the abyss of freedom can be bridged.

The justification for progressive action cannot be predetermined by any model or schema, feminist, religious, or Marxist, but depends on the possibility of responsive, concrete, enlarged judgments of particular events and actions that in their impartiality and representability make the responsibility for action bearable. Judgment, in turn, is regulated by no universal principles or logic, but only by the presence of others for whom judgment is made and who will judge in return. No judgment is all-powerful against the force and aggression that brings about evil, but force and aggression have one weakness: they only destroy, and do not create relations. Because their rule is limited, the possibility of free action which founds new relations is always open. Action is for others' judgment. Its meaning and value is in that judgment. When action is insulated from reciprocal judgment, no matter how barricaded in rationality, well-founded in principle, politically correct, or congruent with religious commandment, it is arbitrary, an expression of unidentifiable emotion, a whim, meaningless even to the actor herself. The key to a free politics and to a freedom of thought that can determine truths is in the maintenance of this movement back and forth, between the past and future of thinking and acting.

We remember, think about, and judge the past actions of history, in which many women and men have suffered from sexism, racism, and aggression. In doing so there is a possibility of reconciliation with the past. Even when forgiveness is not possible, the weight of the past is lifted; it becomes possible to begin again, no longer trapped in revenge, resentment, or despair (BPF 391). In the present, presenting herself for the impartial judgment of others, a woman learns to act without depending on the suspect models of the past, without repeating what has gone before. For the future, Arendt projected a further possibility: an "original compact" between actors and thinkers—between politicians, administrators, leaders, managers, and historians, journalists, writers, artists, philosophers, between women and men—a contract in which the sociability and communicability at the root of sensation, thought, action, and judgment becomes a law: a law that acknowledges a shared world where commonality is dependent on plurality and diversity (LK 75).

Conclusion:
A Tradition of Women's Thought

One of the major disputes in recent feminism has been over the nature of femininity. Should women strive to be generic Men, claiming all the rights and privileges that men have claimed as human beings? Or should they proclaim their femininity as a liberatory essence? Are the differences between men and women superficial and irrelevant to social roles and status? Or are there essential differences between the sexes in personality and experience? Feminist visions of change have typically been made to depend on how this question is answered. If there are no essential differences between men and women, then equality and the inclusion of women in all areas of existing society and culture must be the primary feminist goal. If femininity is an essential characteristic, then the feminine in culture and politics should be reempowered, either in a matriarchal new age, or in an androgynous balance of masculine and feminine.

In presenting Luxemburg, Weil, and Arendt as women thinkers, I have not wanted to align myself with either side in this dispute. These are women who take upon themselves the authority to speak for both women and men. They are also women whose thinking differs from the style of most philosophy written by men. I have not meant to argue that their grasp of the human condition is privileged because they are women, any more than I have meant to argue that their neglect of gender issues is unimportant. But there is a sense in which that neglect made it possible for them to address the deepest of human concerns offstage from the drama of Western philosophy. That drama, chronicled in standard histories of philosophy, played out at conferences, disseminated in classrooms, interpreted in research institutions, and perpetuated in philosophic literature, is well known. Those of us who are students of philosophy have been drilled in its plots, characters, crises, and resolutions: the detachment of knowledge from the senses and practical life, the construction of logical techniques of argumentation, the projection of a transcendent realm of the spirit in which an all-powerful God and absolute good reside, the promotion of a mathematical science suited to the needs of modern warfare and industrial production, the extension of science to economics and social theory, and more recently a postmodern crisis of confidence. The names of the major players are familiar. We have been told their stories again and again, happy to discover new minor characters, new motives, new meanings, twists we have missed, intent on exposing sexist attitudes embedded in the most abstract of theories, glad to find theories or concepts that might be appropriated for feminist ends. Like any human story, the story of philosophy is worthy of respect. To ask whether women could have played—would have played if they had been allowed—major roles in this drama is futile. The history of Western ideas has been written by men for male characters; in its narratives women have been occasionally an object of concern but never the agents of change.

Weil, Arendt, and Luxemburg, tell a different story: the problematic origins of Western culture in Greek and Roman imperialism, the changing relations between leaders, rulers, and subjects as the Catholic church attempted to establish the City of God, new theories of knowledge and experience as industrialization changed the ways in which women and men interact with the material world, revolution as a violent attempt to reinstitute social justice, a global economy in crisis which resulted in two world wars. It is not the only story and it is not the whole story; missing, for example, is the persistent thread of sexual oppression that continues to survive political and economic change. But what has interested me in the story Luxemburg, Weil, and Arendt tell is the change in plot and characters. Here philosophers like Kant and Descartes do not play the same parts they play in standard histories of philosophy, traditional or feminist. There is no heroic striving for the certain foundations of knowledge, for communion with an all-powerful God, for the ultimate blueprint for a just state, no sigh of resignation at the end that there is no truth, no reference, no form of the Good but only the tortured turnings of symbolic structure. Philosophers, men or women, struggle more or less effectively with the painful shared experience of the present. From there the movement of thought is back—how did we get here, by what road, and what does it mean?—as well as forward—what must we do next so the Holocaust will never happen again, so that we can recover our roots and our sense of the sacred, so that we can deal justly with each other?

If these are women's questions, they are also the questions for which men are desperately in need of answers. It is not just that traditional philosophy has not answered them, it has seldom asked them. Why they have not been asked, why so many of the motifs and concepts of philosophy have been symbolic representations of constructs removed from material life, are questions currently explored in critical feminist philosophy. The explanations have been various: male hormones, masculine psychological formation, memory of a primal scene of Father-murder, the innate structure of the male brain. It is important to determine if any of these is true. But what I have wanted to show is that the recovery of thought not contained in any dualistic metaphysics, or founded on a primal contrast between masculine presence and female lack, or tangled in a line of floating signifiers, or implicated in institutions that exercise oppressive power is also possible. If I am right in my reading of Luxemburg, Weil, and Arendt, not only may the content of that thought be different than it has been represented in philosophy, but also the nature of thought, and relations between thinkers. The descent from father to son in philosophy has been marked by rivalry, hostility, schism, and merger. Once past his training in dialectical debate, a philosopher claims his identity by rejecting paternal figures—refuting the thinkers of the past—and by identifying with paternal figures—claiming his heritage as a Marxist, existentialist, phenomenologist, deconstructionist. Between Luxemburg, Weil, and Arendt, and between them and other thinkers, are no agonistic contests, disputes, no stunning refutations, no foundational reversals. Weil's and Arendt's treatment of Descartes can be used as an example. Neither attempted to defend or refute Descartes. Weil uncovers the tension in Descartes's early work to put into perspective his and our universal science. Arendt remembers the shock of the scientific discoveries of the seventeenth century to get at the experience behind Descartes's conflation of perception and sensation. Descartes is neither an ally nor an enemy, but a co-worker. No primal father to be murdered or worshipped, his thought is part of a past shared by both women and men.

Judging from the work of Luxemburg, Weil, and Arendt, the framing assumptions of a tradition of thinking in this sense would be different from those prominent in the standard history of philosophy. In contrast to Plato's original separation of those who theorize in the meta-world of knowledge from those who live in the physical world, these women assume that all humans share a common material world and that all thinking begins from that shared condition. Because of that shared condition, others' thoughts are never completely alien; being human, they can be understood. It was Luxemburg's attempt to *under-*

stand Marx that most offended orthodox Marxists. For them Marx
was the father who tells the truth, not a man who struggles with a
problem women share, worse, a problem he was not able to solve.
Similarly, Arendt's liberation from the influence of her powerful
teacher Heidegger, hopelessly compromised by his support of Fascism, was accomplished not in a reversal of his views, but in understanding of the impasse into which he worked himself, an impasse
which she believed had its source deep in the philosophical tradition.
Again the comment was negative: she had recapitulated, refused to
roundly condemn Heidegger's fascism. In these cases, the movement
of thought from thinker to thinker is not linear or combative, but
expansive, a growing, developing understanding of a shared condition
that continues to incorporate more and more stands of experience,
more and more material as it increases in volume.

Inherent in this process is an alternate understanding of knowledge.
For Luxemburg, only human commitment permits a coherent grasp
of social reality. Schema, such as Marx's schema for capital accumulation, can be written down, but there is no reason to think that they
represent reality unless formulas are constantly referred back to experience. Luxemburg's commitment to working people provided the
base that made it possible for her to appreciate the danger in Lenin's
facile repositioning of Marxist schema. Standing with workers in 1914
and 1919, it was clear to Luxemburg that the world no longer made
sense in orthodox Marxist terms. Leninism might be a coherent, logical extension of Marxist logic; ungrounded in reality, it had no claim
to truth.

Luxemburg, like so many other socialists, took for granted the socialist conviction that Western workers' consciousness would lead to
the democratization of work. Scrutinizing more carefully this goal,
Weil called into question not only Marxist science, but any view of
knowledge as a privileged representation, proposing in the place of
the dominant empiricism, a science rooted in bodily interaction with
the physical world. Questioning the utopianism that imagines that
labor or work can be liberated from oppressive direction, Arendt
detached thinking that can establish factual truth from scientific
knowledge. Stepping back from the necessities of physical labor as
well as from ongoing political commitments, she made a space between past and future for a thought which finds other, oblique passages into the future. Such a passage is not available to individual
revelation, but has its source in dialogue: in the discordant voices of
political involvement, in inner conflict.

These different accounts of knowledge have in common a rejection
of knowledge as a privileged representation of reality. Knowledge may

be stored in the form of representations, but to maintain reference it involves active and continuing engagement with physical and social reality. As a result, knowledge is reconnected to concrete commitments in the world, physical activity, interpersonal understanding. The thought that sustains knowledge is a process and an activity, never finally terminated, resulting in no universal system or foundational truth. Unlike the philosophical ideal of the pure knower who, when he finds ultimate Form, can hope to contemplate it in perfect bliss, thought, is never at rest; constantly it is enlivened by commitments, tasks, and relationships.

A crucial area of concern for these thinkers was the current stagnation in social thought. All three of them rejected the standard alternatives of Marxism and liberalism. They did this, however, not by grafting on to either Marxism or democratic theory another theory—of patriarchy, psychoanalysis, discourse, or culture—but by submitting social theory to present experience and to judgments from the larger perspective of the history of the West. This return to the roots of social thought finds the soft common ground of liberalism and Marxism in the global projection of a world which is national and parochial. As a result, neither Marxism nor democratic theory accounts for imperialism, capitalist expansion, or the ongoing global interactions between capitalized and noncapitalized economies, in which women and men continue to suffer. Capitalism retreats to a myth of capitalist stability and prosperity dependent on the exploitation of noncapitalist economies, ignoring the devastation often caused by capitalist development. Socialism, when it is dominated by schematic Leninism, continues on with a rhetoric that, even with the collapse of the planned economies of Eastern Europe, has no basis in economic or social reality.

Weil probed an even deeper contradiction in socialist thought. The professed purpose of Marxist socialism is the liberation of the worker and the democratization of the workplace. At the same time, in socialist states the establishment of "true Communism" is relegated to a distant future, in favor of a "transition stage" in which piecemeal industrial labor is strictly regimented and centrally controlled. Weil begins again from Marx's undeveloped projections of a free unalienated labor, to give a realistic account of the forms of human work and their relation to scientific knowledge. In the process, she asked questions few Communists seeking power have wanted to answer: is the projected goal of Communism possible in fact? Is it really conceivable that the socialist workplace can be democratized? In trying to answer these questions, Weil suggests a new inspiration for liberatory social thought: an ideal of justice that requires radical changes in work methods, in education, in scientific research. Capitalism and socialism, with their rejection of the ideal, put little value on Arendt's habitat earth, or on Weil's "*metaxu*." Both place quantity of production above human liberation; both place efficiency above the development of institutions that encourage the communicative skills necessary for the meeting of obligations and the establishment of objects of common interest. In the course of imperialist wars and industrial development living cultures are destroyed, political institutions are co-opted by commercial interests, the matrixes for networks of relationships that might support the social equilibrium in which obligations can be reciprocally met disappear.

If Luxemburg, Weil, and Arendt were able to tell truths about this process, it may be because their thought is not limited by the oppositional categories of traditional Western philosophy. Luxemburg argued that the *practice* of the masses should not be oppositionally separated from the *theory* of the leaders. Instead, the thinking of leaders like herself has to be generated out of and conditioned by the experience of working people, as they struggle to advance their interests. Weil, in her neo-Cartesian meditations, rejected the opposition of *mind* and *body* on which modernism is founded, arguing that each has identity only in a reciprocal relation. Arguing that *immanent* in the natural world subject to necessity is a *transcendent* beauty and equilibrium, Weil reconceived divinity in a way which does not strain credulity. Arendt confounded the opposition between *reality* and *appearance*, arguing that the philosopher's Being was only a projection of his own otherness onto nature. Actions, for Arendt, are not a construct of two opposed things, a *subjective* idea and an *objective* bodily movement, but events in a common world, whose meaning is determined by other actors and judges. Thought is not a unitary consciousness distinguished from material fact, but a dialogic process reciprocally related to the possibility of political dialogue between persons.

Alternative metaphysical grounding results in different views of both language and ethics. Freed from the project of articulating the imagined logic of an ideal representative science, both Weil and Arendt made a start toward a critical account of language that does justice to language's function in human life. Both noted the degeneration of language, a degeneration which is currently rationalized in philosophical theories of language. Words like "democracy," given a rigid designation in existing forms of government, or nominally defined in interlinguistic relations are drained of meaning. "Democracy is socialism." "Freedom is capitalism." In such slogans, the substantive meaning of "freedom" and "democracy" as ideals or points of aspiration is lost. Even more dangerous, institutions—courts, schoolrooms, workplaces—continue to systematically repress the expressive power of human speech to demand justice. Unlike logic, which can insure agreement by fiat, the deep sources of communicable meaning are in human relationships. More important than any "definition" is the "distinctions" people make in giving an account of their situation to others. In her historical critical linguistic studies, Arendt picked out the complex threads of experience and meaning that distinguish authority from rule, work from action, politics from electioneering. These references are not to a Platonic grid of concepts by which terms are conceptually ordered, nor to "forms of life" constituted by convention, but to the varied experiences of human life, historically conditioned and shaped by people's memories of what is past and their expectations for the future.

Language, when understood in these ways, is not split between cognitive denotation and evaluative connotation. For Luxemburg, the basis for both a coherent factual view of the world and the sense of what ought to be done comes from commitment to and relations with others. Although Luxemburg did not solve the problem of relativity, she gives situational ethics a grounding in both material and interpersonal reality. Weil understood ideals as a different order of reality: a measure or balance possible in human affairs which does not involve a second world of ideal objects, or make the mistake of identifying earthly objects as an absolute good. Arendt cut even deeper into traditional ethical conceptions. Goodness is not any kind of object, but an unshowable source of inner energy that, when claimed as specific ideal or justification, becomes a dangerous absolute. For goodness, she substituted virtue: thoughtfulness, attention, respect and tolerance for others.

The lines of thought pursued by these women are not closed off from other disciplines and forms of knowledge, as traditional philosophy has often been, but are in fertile relation with science, politics, religion, social theory. Inspired by Luxemburg's reflections on knowledge, for example, there might be radical changes in economic science, a field in which, to date, women have had little influence. Expressed in schematic mathematical formulas, resolutely scientific, economics had been the business of men. Enlivened by thought and by the moral urgency that human suffering be alleviated, women economic analysts might address the perpetual exclusion of women's labor from economic calculations and develop methods of economic analysis that elucidate global economic relations. Such an economics would not only "add on" to "gross national products" a calculation of the value of women's labor in the home, but would include among the objects of its critical scrutiny the problem of reference to economic reality, and the relation of abstract schema to human experience. The result might be an economics that addresses the impoverishment of peripheral economies, the threat of environmental collapse, the dangerous frailty of international finance, and the balance between regional identity and larger economic communities.

Similarly, after Weil's rethinking of the modern condition, women scientists and educators, including those who have resisted the feminist claim that science is masculine, might find new ways of doing and teaching science. When science is seen, not as representation, symbolically ordered in gendered categories or sexist metaphors, but as concrete ways of work, the conceptual reversal to a marginalized "feminine" science is unnecessary. Intricate interactions between science and work can be re-examined and reformed, and connections between science and industrial production restored. Feminist epistemologists might find strong and active ties to women and men in the labor movement, in the home, in medicine, in scientific research.

Since Plato, philosophers have prided themselves on their ability to rise above the messy business of practical politics to a higher level of reality. Even philosophers who were actively engaged in revolution, like John Locke, or Marx, are read as theorists whose texts are to be subjected to logical or textual analysis quite apart from business affairs or political involvements. In a thought not closed off to the painful and conflicting experiences which are the source of thought's energy, or to the visions of future action that provide thought's direction, there could be no such separation of thought from human action in the world. If there is no social blueprint in the philosophies of Luxemburg, Weil, Arendt—if Luxemburg failed to specify democratic institutions, if Weil did not make fully intelligible her divine ideals, if Arendt is too admiring of Greek politicians disdainful of women's labor—there are also vital strands of connection to political experience. In the place of necessarily true foundations on which true theory and right action might rest are founding moments of beginning again, to rethink, reconsider, remake the human condition.

In the seventeenth century, reacting to the shocks of the new mechanistic science, stimulated by new wealth in Europe extracted from the Americas and the East, enthusiastic about the consequent victory of progressive mercantilism over archaic feudalism, Locke "began again" from an imagined "state of nature" to rethink the human condition and fashion a modern social world. In the nineteenth century, faced with the horrors of an England industrialized to produce cheap goods necessary to sustain a steady stream of incoming wealth, Marx charted another course. In the last years of the twentieth century, after the Holocaust, the continuing impoverishment of non-Western cultures, the growing racially defined underclass in Western societies, the failure of democracy in capitalism and communism, it is past time for a new founding. If Locke, energized by the conviction that all men had a right to compete for the new riches to be gained in foreign trade and manufacturing, articulated the theory of an emergent mercantilist Europe, if Marx, the Hegelian prophet with a sense of social injustice, projected the theory of a victorious European labor movement, women, in the late twentieth century, are in a position to imagine a world in which the dangers to habitat earth, the disappearance of human *metaxu*, and the subversion of democratic political institutions are averted.

If women thinkers have found some common cause with philosophers like Descartes, Kant, Marx, it is not surprising. The founding principle of philosophy is criticism. Its innovation was the refusal of tradition in dogmatic forms: in philosophy there would be no more slavish handing down of Homeric lore or sacred religious texts to be faithfully repeated and copied. In the place of the same words repeated over and over, the creed of the philosopher is independence, the ability of a thinker to deny his past, subject his teachers to ridicule, reverse the judgments of his predecessors. But, as in all tradition, something is handed down to make the link from generation to generation. What qualifies a philosopher is not faith in any dicta, but faith nonetheless, in a rationality that guarantees the truth of solitary assertion. The logic that defines that rationality changes: from Aristotle's syllogisms, to Ockham's terminism, to Frege's truth functions, to Wittgenstein's grammar, to Kripke's modal logic, but the aim is the same—a self-originating thought that cannot be wrong. Logic, in all its many versions, is the deep sacred text of philosophy, safer from the sacrilege of the infidel than specific tenets, because, hidden behind a liberal plurality of beliefs, it is inaccessible to criticism.

What holds the tradition of philosophy together is not the sex of its practitioners, although men have had their reasons for embracing philosophy, but the various forms of philosophical assertion, barricaded by inference against response, and held apart from the violence of aggression, the economics of poverty, the intimacies of family life. Feminists have noted the arrogance of philosophy, its authoritarian style, its pretensions to be the first word or the last word on all subjects. But that assertion can also be seen, less ominously, as a pretense, a pose all too dependent on the glowing attention of an admiring circle of gawkish young men, students, protéges, followers to whom rewards in the form of academic jobs, publishing, fellowships are doled out, or, as also happens occasionally, played out for some eager young woman, wanting to learn and hoping against hope that she may be taken seriously as a thinker. If this philosopher has now discovered his clay feet in postmodern scepticism, such is the power of the tradition that even his last dying breath is an assertion, as he who claimed privileged knowledge of Being and Truth, asserts—what now would be credible? What but his own death?—the necessary death of the subject, of Being, and of truth. If philosophy is the deep forms of univocal assertion, the new assertion will be that there is no assertion; no one can speak with authority, and any naive attempt at a politics, or metaphysics, or ethics can be exposed, undermined, discredited—by who?—who but the philosophers who know the truth that there is no truth. What might finally seem to be at stake in this last scene of philosophical drama is not the death of the subject but the survival of thought itself. The philosopher's logic claimed to be the essence of thought, the necessary conditions for any thought, but in the attempt to find first principles—necessarily true foundational beginnings for thought—or ultimate truths—a transcendent metaphysics, thought itself stopped dead, fixed in form, unable to operate. Thought, rebuilt from sure foundations, elaborated in logical order, becomes the great celebratory cake of Western reason, ornately decorated with swirls, entwined figures, rosettes, rich filling, many layers, smooth and shining festoons of icing.

What I have tried to show is that if philosophy is just a bit old and stale, and not as nourishing as we might wish, there may be other recipes, other ideas, other ways of thinking, remembered and conserved, able to enliven the heavy stuff of postmodern existence. What, then, might be put in philosophy's place? Arendt's new founding can claim no absolute beginning, no first principles. It begins with questions, possibilities: how should human beings live together? How should we, could we, speak to each other, search for the truth, understand the material reality in which we live, understand the terms of human interrelationship? The only starting point for such a thought is a present braced against lines of understanding that reach out to the past and to the future. Luxemburg, Weil, and Arendt all began again from the material fact of present twentieth-century existence, from a changed relation to habitat earth, from the possibility of methodical work guided by science, from the fact of human sociality, from the memories of a century of barbarity in Europe, from the hope of a better future. What was passed on to them, and what they pass on in turn, is no canonical structure or logic but strains of still-alive thoughts that might be made active in new situations, put to work on new materials, productive of new kinds of nourishment for the self, for the imagination, and for progressive action in the world.

Descartes razed the antiquated structures of medieval theology to begin to build again a structure of thought from his own clear and distinct ideas. Would it be too humble to liken this other thought to the baking of bread? There can be no pretense at an original beginning, or at a loaf that satisfies all hungers for all time. There can be no pretense that a rise cannot fail, collapse, the result turn out to be unworkable, uneatable, wrong. But the redemption of thought is that even in failure, even in lost causes, something is left alive, to be saved, to be used again, in another recipe, with a bit more or less kneading, more care in handling. What kind of knowledge or truth could such a philosophia, without the closure of the masculine ending, produce? How can women thinkers, and their allies, find the stable footing from which to think free of stale old oppressions, to find their source and imagine their defeat, if they have no logic, no definitions, no concepts set out in order, no foundation? They cannot stand out of time, out of their own body, out of their place in the world. How then can they speak for others? Luxemburg, Weil, and Arendt give some possible answers: being human we share our material situation with others; all human beings are the same in their claim to justice; in action with others we can create objects of common interest. None of these are absolute determinants: common causes can be discredited in divide-and-conquer propaganda; claims to justice can go unheard; political institutions can be destroyed.

But thought in the style of Luxemburg, Weil, and Arendt has a kind of immortality. So rarified was the air of the philosopher's world out of the world, it was perhaps inevitable that he would end by turning on himself and his own philosophizing as the only proper subject of thought. But the very thickness and confusion of reality provides new material for this other thought that, like leaven, has its source in material reality and its aim in the preservation and enhancement of human life.

Notes

Notes to Part I

References to Luxemburg's works:

AC   *The Accumulation of Capital* (first published 1913), trans. Agnes Schwarzschild (New York: Monthly Review Press, 1964).

ACAC *The Accumulation of Capital—An Anti-Critique* (also includes Bukharin's critique, *Imperialism and the Accumulation of Capital*), trans. R. Wichmann (New York: Monthly Review Press, 1972).

PW   *Selected Political Writings of Rosa Luxemburg*, ed. Dick Howard (New York: Monthly Review Press, 1971).

RLS   *Rosa Luxemburg Speaks*, ed. M. Waters (New York: Pathfinder Press, 1970).

TP   *Theory and Practice*, trans. D. Wolff. (Detroit, Mich.: News and Letters Comm., 1980).

NQ   *The National Question: Selected Writings*, ed. H. B. Davis (New York: Monthly Review Press, 1976).

L   *The Letters of Rosa Luxemburg*, ed. S. E. Bronner (Boulder, Colo.: Westview Press, 1978).

1. A typical example is this sarcastic response from the Marxist scholar Ryazanov to *The Accumulation of Capital:* "Many thanks for Rosa's book. I have only read the introduction so far. I was stunned and amazed. Such devilish speed with which she produces a book like this, can only amaze a ponderous man like myself. . . . So Rosa has to dash off to her cauldron and brew up some new solutions. . . . Then—May 1912—the brew is ready . . . the epitome of science which has hitherto been hidden from the whole world. . . . Oh fairest muse." From J. P. Nettl's biography,

Rosa Luxemburg (London: Oxford University Press, 1966) Vol. I, p. 834, footnote 1.

2. See Klaus Thewelect's account of the Freikorps in *Male Fantasies*, trans. S. Conway (Minneapolis: University of Minnesota Press, 1987). In the literature, letters, and speeches of the Freikorps the proletarian socialist woman was described as a whore and a demon. Luxemburg was often used as a paradigm case. An example from one of General Maercker's addresses to the Freikcrops: "Rosa Luxemburg is a she-devil. Rosa Luxemburg could destroy the German Empire today and not be touched; there is no power in the Empire capable of opposing her" (p. 76).

3. Quoted by Nettl, *Rosa Luxemburg* (p. 533) from *Leninskii Sbornik* Vol. xxii, p. 46.

4. Monthly Review Press published her *Anti-Critique*, but only with the authorized companion piece by Bukharin, the official Bolshevik economist. Neo-Marxists continue to dismiss her as obviously wrong; see, for instance, Samir Amin whose theory of *Accumulation on a World Scale* owes much to the thesis that Luxemburg pioneered—that capitalism must be understood not as a homogeneous mode of production but as a world system. (*Accumulation on a World Scale: A Critique of the Theory of Underdevelopment*, Vol. I and II., [New York: Monthly Review Press, 1974] pp. 96, 1223, 488). One exception is Joan Robinson's *The Accumulation of Capital* (London: Macmillan 1969) which draws on Luxemburg's critique of equilibrium models. Robinson produces models for equilibrium but points out that these depend on a "state of economic bliss" which even if realizable is highly unstable, given that the assumptions on which the models are constructed are counterfactual. Equilibrium is "a mythical state of affairs not likely to occur in any actual economy" (99). Her conclusion: even if capitalist accumulation is miraculously possible and the state of economic bliss is somehow realized, this only means "that there is an increase in output of saleable goods which are not co-extensive with economic wealth, let alone with the basis of human welfare" (386). See also Robinson's introduction to Luxemburg's *The Accumulation of Capital*.

5. *The Presuppositions of Socialism and the Tasks of Social Democracy* (Hanover: Social Democratic Party Congress, 1899).

6. Democracy functions in capitalism, Luxemburg argued, to unite the nation-state. Once the central bureaucracy and state apparatus are in place, democracy can atrophy, be taken away, or become a meaningless ritual. Hitler's disbandment of parliament a few decades later proved the soundness of this prediction.

7. *Theses on Feuerbach*, Karl Marx and Frederick Engels, in *Collected Works*, Vol. 5 (New York: International Publishers, 1976) pp. 3–8.

8. See, also *The German Ideology*, Karl Marx and Frederick Engels, in *Collected Works*, Vol. 5 (New York: International Publishers, 1976) p. 39. "[Feuerbach] does not see that the sensuous world around him is not a

thing given from all eternity, remaining ever the same, but the product of industry and of the state of society; and, indeed [a product] in the sense that it is an historical product, the result of the activity of a whole secession of generations, each standing on the shoulders of the preceding one, developing its industry and its intercourse, and modifying its social system according to the changed needs. Even the objects of the simplest 'sensuous certainty' are only given him through social development, industry, and commercial intercourse."

9. In *Capital*, Marx turned to locating economic mechanisms that necessarily govern capitalist development, mapping a supposedly inevitable and necessary historical course to the final impoverishment of workers and socialist revolt.

10. *Materialism and Empiriocriticism*, in V. I. Lenin, *Collected Works*, Vol. 14 (London: Lawrence & Wishart, 1962), hereafter (ME).

11. Nationalism and its relation to economics had been of concern to Luxemburg from the early days of her doctoral thesis at the University of Zurich, on the economy of her native Poland. Already, in her thesis, she took a stand unpopular with many of her Polish comrades: Poland, at that time part of the empire of the Russian Tsar, should not attempt independence. Luxemburg argued that the industrial development of Poland had been based on exports to Russia, that the historical roots of Polish nationalism were in the nobility's regressive resistance to progress, and that independence would retard development and so not be in workers' interests.

12. Collected in Horace Davis' edited volume, *The National Question*, this series of writings is one of Luxemburg's most impressive works. Not only does she demystify with incisive analysis and historical example the muddled debate on nationalism that went on in the prewar years in socialist circles; her account of the history and the prospects for European nationalities is timely even in the late twentieth century, as the Soviet federation breaks apart and rival nationalities in Eastern Europe assert their right to autonomy.

13. Some examples given by Luxemburg are Napoleon's "democratic" inflammatory use of the plebescite to get support for his imperialist adventures, and the capitalist claim that "equality" demands there be no legal protection for workers as they contract with employers.

14. Again Luxemburg warned of dangers to come. In fascist ideology, German soil and the German folk were cited as the substance of the superior German race.

15. This was not the menshevik insistence that in each country the revolution must follow the same course. Luxemburg had already begun her rethinking of the Marxist assumption that capitalist or precapitalist economies could be understood as autonomous and homogeneous national systems that change according to a predetermined sequence of internal contradictions.

16. From her prison cell, Luxemburg wrote several articles detailing her criticisms of bolshevik policy. One article was printed in the *Spartacus Letters* after a good deal of hesitation on the part of the editor. A second was sent but rejected. Paul Levi traveled to Breslau to convince Luxemburg to respect the Spartacus policy of noncriticism of the Russian Revolution. Bowing to party discipline, Luxemburg agreed to refrain from public comment. After Levi's visit, however, she drafted a pamphlet, *The Russian Revolution* (RLS 365), again outlining her objections and sent it to Levi, but it was not published in her lifetime. See Nettl's account of these negotiations in *Rosa Luxemburg*, pp. 695–698. The later softening of her antibolshevik line was apparently motivated not by any acceptance of their principles, but by the realization that the Bolshevik's autocracy was at least partly a result of Russia's isolated position, and that the best remedy was a socialist revolution in the rest of Europe, especially in Germany.

17. Although finally, after much pressure was brought on her, Luxemburg abstained from public criticism of the Bolsheviks, there is no evidence that she changed her mind in substance on any of these questions. The question as to how far Luxemburg retreated from her support for parliamentary institutions has been much debated. The Bolsheviks were eager to claim that she had admitted her "error" and returned to orthodoxy. (See Nettl, pp. 716–718, for a discussion of the weak arguments on which this claim was based). She agreed that Soviets, or workers' councils, were the proper organs of socialist democracy; at the same time she continued to argue that a "Workers' Parliament" should be broad-based, including rural as well as urban workers, state employees as well as industrial workers. For a brief period during the German revolution, with reservations, she supported the Spartacus policy of boycotting the National Assembly. At other times, she opposed leftists in the new German Communist party who thought the party should not participate in elections to the National Assembly, arguing against "a radicalism that is a little too quick and easy." (See the discussion at the founding Congress of the Communist party in Germany, *The German Revolution and the Debate on Soviet Power: Documents 1918–1919*, pp. 172–182.) When German Workers' Councils, dominated by conservative Social Democrats, voted overwhelmingly to support the National Assembly and in the meantime to give supervisory power to the existing government, Luxemburg continued to oppose any policy of nonparticipation in elections or voting. Win or lose, she argued, this is the way the masses are educated in political action.

18. The invitation to the Soviet-dominated International came to the German Communists three days before Luxemburg's murder. In the midst of much controversy, she managed to convince her overenthusiastic colleagues that the new International was premature. It should not be formed, she argued, until there were other established Communist parties, otherwise it would be dominated by the Russians. After her

death, Eberlein was mandated to go and either convince the Russians to wait or walk out. After her death, in respect, if not in agreement, the Bolsheviks bowed to her wishes, but only temporarily. The International was soon formed under Russian control, and the German Communist party made subject to the Cominterm. (See the various accounts of these maneuvers in *The German Revolution: Documents*, pp. 454–6).

19. In Germany, for example, Karl Korsch (*Marxism and Philosophy*, 1923) argued that traditional Marxism had underestimated the role of ideology, subjectivity, and culture. Georg Lukács, (*History and Class Consciousness*, 1922) worked out a theory of "false" working-class consciousness that understood its interests in the frame of the existing system instead of projecting a vision of the totality of society. In Italy, Antonio Gramsci, a student of the idealist Benedetto Croce, developed his theory of bourgeois cultural hegemony (*Prison Notebooks*, 1926–37), and Wilhelm Reich, the Austrian psychoanalyst, launched his Sex-Pol movement (*Sex-Pol Essays*, 1924–34) based on a mixture of Freud and Marx.

20. Lenin's writings on imperialism, which came well after Luxemburg's, were later cited as scripture to prove Luxemburg's mistakes. Even though she had begun to write about imperialism years before Lenin, loyalists have claimed that she should have realized her "error" and waited for the authoritative pronouncement. Lenin is continually cited to refute Luxemburg's obvious mistakes, although Lenin's two articles on imperialism written in 1916, "Imperialism as the most recent stage of Capitalism" and its updating "Imperialism as the highest stage of Capitalism," offered no original thesis, but only use the issue to batter his old revisionist enemies in the German Social Democratic party. The problem as Lenin saw it, was that deviationists like Kautsky had been corrupted into supporting capitalism's interests and not following the Bolshevik party line. Lenin had a tendency to see events not from the narrow perspective of capitalist interests but from the even narrower perspective of a power struggle between socialist factions.

21. The labor theory of value is accepted by both Smith and Ricardo. Partly in response to Marxist arguments, it was eliminated in the late-nineteenth-century neoclassical synthesis of Say's empiricist law of markets and Ricardian equilibrium, which replaced labor value with marginal utility—a measurable interpretation of subjective satisfaction—as the basic unit of value.

22. The dispute concerning the relation between abstract economic modeling and reality is in no way resolved. Establishment economics is committed to increasing complexity in mathematics and computer programming, and the resulting econometric models are either articulated without reference to any data, or verified by pretailored measurements doctored to fit. There also continues to be dissent; for instance, the Nobel-prize-winning economist Wassily Leontief, who was one of the first to work with computers and mathematical input-output systems, or Oskar Morgenstern, who was the coinventor of games theory, both

criticized the growing preoccupation with an imagined reality rather than actual economic processes. See for example Morgenstern's *On the Accuracy of Economic Observations* (Princeton: Princeton University Press, 1963).

23. From the first chapter of Luxemburg's textbook on political economy, derived from her lectures at the party school. Unfortunately, only part of the book survived and was published in 1920 in a version edited by Paul Levi, and again in 1951 in a version supposedly more faithful to the original.

24. The tendency to take production as the ultimate determinant of economic reality is inherited by Marx from classical economics. When Marx looks for the reason for the expansion of capitalism, he looks within production for a falling rate of profit and not at the contradiction between social distribution and production as does Luxemburg. When monopoly and price control make a falling rate of profit no longer inevitable, there is no way to explain imperialism. The tendency for economics to focus on production is at its most extreme in late-twentieth-century "supply-side" economics, in which production is supposed to create its own demand.

25. In volume II of *Capital* (trans. E. Untermann, Chicago, 1907), pp. 590–610, Marx continued to try to work out the difficulty. If manufacturers of commodities must buy an increase in producer goods then where will they get the money to pay for them? They cannot lower workers' wages below subsistence. It cannot come out of the capitalists' consumption because then there will be an unsold surplus in another place. Marx's final answer, in volume II, is brief. The problem is monetary. When there is an increased supply of goods at constant prices and a fixed supply of money there will be a failure of demand. The remedy is in gold production, which infuses the system with an increase in money supply and supplies commodity producers with sufficient funds to buy new producer goods. But, notes Luxemburg, this is a solution that Marx had already branded as "absurd" (AC 154). The contradiction in the system is deeper than the adequacy of the medium of exchange. Regardless of available funds to buy producer goods, what inducement does the capitalist have to expand his production if there are no new consumers in sight?

26. When economists were finally forced to admit that there are business cycles, equilibrium was reasserted. Economists insisted that cycles would always turn around in the "long run" so there would be "overall" equilibrium. In the crisis of the great depression, government was given a role in smoothing these imbalances by creating greater liquidity in the money supply—a remedy whose superficiality Luxemburg had already exposed—and by a temporary suspension of some aspects of the free market.

27. See Luxemburg's example of obviously false mathematical reasoning in ACAC, pp. 69–70.

28. Contemporary neo-Marxists still insist faithfully that internal accumulation is possible. For example, Paul Baran and Paul Sweezy (*Monopoly Capital* [London: Monthly Review Press, 1967]) argue that foreign investment and foreign sales cannot be the external solution to the problem of accumulation because they only create more profit and therefore more difficulty in finding investments. (Luxemburg never argued that foreign exploitation was a permanent solution but rather that, as the opportunities for expansion diminished, capitalism would be in increasing crisis.) Baran and Sweezy explain the possibility of accumulation by citing wasteful expenditures in advertising and sales that, along with liberal credit from modern banking institutions, keep consumption at a high level. Even they, however, admit that this is not sufficient to absorb surplus production but must be supplemented by government spending, especially military spending. Their account of the reason for this spending is Luxemburgian: to protect capitalist markets abroad from socialist encroachment.

29. For a contemporary version of a global economics that analyzes the interaction between capitalist and noncapitalist economies, see Samir Amin, *Accumulation on a World Scale: A Critique of the Theory of Underdevelopment*, Vol. I and II (New York: Monthly Review Press, 1974). Amin reviews the history of exploitation from the mercantile period until the present, distinguishing economic development from the economic indicator, "growth." Underdevelopment is, in fact, caused by growth—measured in production of raw materials for an external capitalist market and imports of goods from capitalist manufacturing. Development, on the other hand, requires an integrated economy, responsive to the needs of local inhabitants and local production. Amin also points out permanent structural relations of dependency which might suggest that Luxemburg's prediction of deepening crisis is unfounded. See, for a historical account specific to Africa, Walter Rodney, *How Europe Underdeveloped Africa* (Washington, D.C.: Howard University Press, 1982). Rodney emphasizes the economics of the slave trade that prepared the way for colonial conquest of Africa and the accumulation of European capital.

Notes to Part II

References to Weil in the text:

AD   *Attente de Dieu* (*Waiting on God*) (Paris: Fayard, 1966). My translations.

EL   *Ecrits de Londres* (*Writings from London*) (Paris: Gallimard, 1957).

FLN   *First and Last Notebooks*, trans. R. Rees (London: Oxford University Press, 1970).

FW   *Formative Writings*, trans. D. T. McFarland and W. Van Ness (Amherst: University of Massachusetts Press, 1987).

GG   *Gravity and Grace*, trans. Emma Craufurd (London: Ark, 1987).

IC   *Intimations of Christianity among the Ancient Greeks*, trans. E. C. Geiss-buhler (Boston: Beacon Press, 1958).

LP   *Leçons de Philosophie*, presentées par Annie Reynaud (Paris: Plon, 1959).

NR   *The Need for Roots*, trans. A. F. Wills (London: Ark, 1987).

O   *Oeuvres Complète*, Tome I, volume 1–2 (Paris: Gallimard, 1988).

OL   *Oppression and Liberty*, trans. A. Wills and J. Petrie (Amherst: University of Mass. Press, 1973).

SE   *Selected Essays*, trans. R. Rees (London: Oxford University Press, 1962).

SNG *On Science, Necessity, and the Love of God*, trans. R. Rees (London: Oxford University Press, 1968).

SL   *Seventy Letters* trans. R. Rees (London: Oxford University Press, 1965).

WG   *Waiting for God*, trans. Emma Craufurd (New York: Harper & Row, 1973)

1. The reference is to Parmenides, who condemned what he called "mortal opinion" for following the contradictory way of "what is and what is not," and who identified a unitary homogeneous "Being" as the proper object of philosophical knowledge. See A. Nye, *Words of Power: a Feminist Reading of the History of Logic*, chap. I, (New York: Routledge, Chapman & Hall, 1989) for a historical analysis of this denial and its various subsequent forms.

2. It is difficult to translate *malheur* in a way that preserves Weil's meaning. Literally, the meaning is unhappiness or misfortune. Weil uses it in a more specific sense for a permanent condition in which the inner self is wounded. As such, it can be distinguished from physical pain or common misfortune, which are almost always transitory and can be handled in one way or another.

3. Weil's attention to *malheur* points to the weakness in liberal welfare programs in which uncooperative recipients are often blamed for their ingratitude, stupidity, and laziness. "When we do a service to beings thus uprooted and we receive in exchange discourtesy, ingratitude, betrayal, we are merely enduring a small share of their affliction. It is our duty to expose ourselves to it in a limited measure just as it is our duty to expose ourselves to affliction. When it comes we should endure it as we endure affliction, without referring it back to particular people. . . ." (GG 25).

4. See, for example, *Economic and Philosophical Manuscripts*, Karl Marx and Frederick Engels, *Collected Works*, Vol. 3 (New York: International Publishers, 1975) (Hereafter CW), pp. 270–7.

5. A full description of her impressions of prewar Germany are recorded in "The Situation in Germany" (FW 17).

6. Weil advised French workers to have nothing to do with the Communist party: she told the party to break its ties with Russia. Weil argued that

the Soviet state was the opposite of what Lenin had intended: there was no free speech; the Communist party had become a privileged administrative bureaucracy; there were no Soviets and no worker's councils with any power; the secret police was independent of popular control. She was equally critical of the socialist "New Deal," managed economy in the United States and the technocratic economic theories on which it was based. Control of production by managers and technocrats under state direction, she argued, could be as or more oppressive to workers than traditional capitalism (OL 8, 15, 17, 27).

7. Paragraph one: *The Germany Ideology*, CW Vol. 5. Paragraph two: *Capital*, Vol. 1, trans. Samuel Moore and Edward Aveling, ed. Frederick Engels (New York: International Publishers, 1976) p. 44.

8. See, for example, Engels's *Origins of the Family, Private Property and the State*. Engels argues that primitive Communism was interrupted by an assertion of ownership by men, a move which brings about radical changes in society, including the patriarchal family and the "universal downfall" of the female sex.

9. Like Luxemburg, Weil favorably compared the Marx of the "Theses on Feuerbach" (CW, Vol. 5: 3–9) to Lenin in *Materialism and Empiriocriticism* (CW, Vol. 14 [London: Lawrence & Wishart, 1962]). Lenin, she charged, was only interested in maintaining dogma against opponents, whereas Marx was struggling with the problem of materialism and idealism (OL 29ff.). Marx did not choose materialism over idealism, as Lenin did; instead he suggested a synthesis of idealism and materialism in which thoughts are not "reflections" of reality, but ways of acting in the world (OL 31).

10. Weil's beginning preserves Cartesian solipsism in one respect. Weil's self may not be detached from the physical world, but she is alone in respect to other people. In Weil's primal scene, others exist only as resistant objects. "To be in direct contact with nature and not with men is the only discipline. To be dependent on an alien will is to be a slave" (GG 141). This causes Weil to have difficulty explaining how nonoppressive social relations are possible, and necessitates the later move to a supernatural source of virtue. Feminist philosophers after Weil have taken the revision of Cartesianism one step further, drawing on object relations psychology to describe the evolution of a self in relation to others. See, for example, Nancy Chodorow's classic *The Reproduction of Mothering* (Berkeley, California: University of California Press, 1978).

11. "The problems that arise in such situations of interaction may be reduced to problems of use and enjoyment of the objects, activities, and products, material and ideological ... of the world in which individuals live." "Numerical determinations first arose as means of economic and effective adjustment of material ends to material consequences in qualitative situations marked by deficiency and excess." John Dewey, *Logic: The Theory of Inquiry* (New York: Holt, Rinehart, and Winston, 1938) pp.

60, 397. However, there are conflicting tendencies in the thought of Dewey which might be profitably explored in the style of Weil's study of Descartes. In *Logic*, Dewey begins by referring to the necessity that living organisms maintain a balance in their internal and external relations with their natural and social environment, arguing that inquiry, both common sense and scientific, develops out of those interactions. Immediately, however, he reverts to operational language, speaking in terms of "use and enjoyment" and identifying true judgements as what "works" or "reaches the end intended." Although for Dewey intended ends are never set or final ends, their validation is ultimately rooted in organic processes of consumption, avoidance of pain, power, and control which for Weil are destructive to a natural ideal of equilibrium. This problem of grounding scientific method in evolved biological processes is also inherent in contemporary versions of Dewey's naturalized epistemology, such as Quine's.

12. With the discovery of non-Euclidean geometries, philosophers of mathematics were forced to find new accounts of the foundations of their discipline. Some turned to arithmetic grounded in set theory as the basis for mathematics (Cantor), some to a fundamental intuition of natural numbers (Brouwer), and some to metamathematical proof of consistency (Hilbert). None of these attempts were successful. Russell's paradox eventually exposed the deficiency of set theory. Brouwer's constructionism—all mathematics must be constructed out of natural numbers—eliminated many standard proofs as invalid. Metamathematical proof leads to a formalism in which mathematics seems to be only an empty game.

13. See Descartes, *Meditations on First Philosophy III* (Indianapolis: Hackett Publishing Co., 1979) pp. 23–24. "Surely, in this first instance of knowing, there is nothing else than a certain clear and distinct perception of what I affirm. Yet this would hardly be sufficient to render me certain of the truth of a thing, if it could ever happen that something that I perceive so clearly and distinctly were false. And thus I now seem to be able to posit as a general rule that what I very clearly and distinctly perceive is true. Nevertheless, I have previously admitted many things as wholly certain and evident that nevertheless I discovered afterward to be doubtful."

14. This is the standard empiricist answer which has many versions from the phenomenalism of Locke and Hume to the logical positivism of Carnap and Ayer. The attempt to identify the stable sensory building blocks of knowledge ranges from Hume's definition of impressions as more lively and forceful than ideas, to Russell's atomic propositions known by acquaintance.

15. This is the Kantian synthesis. We can have no experiential knowledge of the metaphysical postulates of scientific representations, but principles such as "every event has a cause" are necessarily true because they are the condition for the possibility of scientific knowledge.

16. See the contemporary scientific realism of W. V. Quine or Saul Kripke, who tend to accept the established procedures of scientists at any particular time as validating knowledge. Weil's description of present-day science brings out some of the problems in passing responsibility from philosophers to scientists," scientists of the same specialty, although dispersed around all over the world, constitute a tiny village. . . . The villagers seldom leave the village; many scientists have limited and poorly cultivated minds. No one has ever been particularly concerned to develop their critical spirit. . . . The state of science at a given moment is nothing but this; it is the average opinion of the village of scientists. This opinion, it is true, is based upon experiments, but the experiments are conducted only in the village, with no outside control, and with costly and complicated apparatus, which is found no where else; and the experiments are prepared, repeated, and corrected only by the inhabitants of the village and, above all, are interpreted only by them" (SNG).

17. It is analyses like these which have prompted Wittgensteinians like Peter Winch to take an interest in Weil. Although there are surface similarities between her thought and Wittgenstein's, there are also important differences. Wittgenstein can either be interpreted as a conventionalist—even in the domain of necessary truth, meaning is generated by constitutive rules that define "forms of life"—or, focusing on a few remarks in *Philosophical Investigations*, as a naturalist—language games are rooted in primitive expressions. Weil was neither a naturalist or a conventionalist. She does not think of mathematics and science as conventionally constituted "forms of life," but as methods of systematically interacting with and transforming physical reality. The problem of understanding how there can be any critique of "language games," with which Winch himself has struggled, and not completely successfully, does not therefore arise for Weil.

18. Weil's nondualist metaphysics might be an alternative way of founding an ecology movement. Traditional philosophy offers either a utilitarianism calculation of ecological breakdown, and, therefore, pain in the future or a holistic approach in which humans are seen as unprivileged parts of the universe. A Weilian philosophy of ecology would go deeper to reform the substance of relations of individuals with the physical world in productive work.

19. See for example, Charles Stevenson, *Ethics and Language* (New Haven: Yale University Press, 1944) for a postpositivist emotive theory, or R. M. Hare, *The Language of Morals* (Oxford: Clarendon Press, 1957) for an imperative theory.

20. Weil gives a mythic history of this misunderstanding of God in a novel retelling of the story of Noah and his sons. Noah, who first "planted the vine," had a Dionysian vision of God. One son, Cham, who founded Egypt and Phoenicia, accepted his vision. The other two sons, Japhet and Sem, founders of the Greeks and of the Semites, refused it. The Greeks then "came ignorant into Greece" and were reeducated via the

Egyptian influence in Pelasgian, Cretan, and Mycenean thought. The Israelites, on the other hand, refused the vision of Noah in favor of a national God that would advance their military interests in Canaan.

21. As scholastic theology, inspired by Greek philosophy but faithful to the scriptures, tried to find unanimity, the conflict between the two traditions continued to produce many puzzles. How is the idea of an all-powerful creator God consistent with evil in the world? Can God do what is logically impossible; if not, it would seem that there is a limit on his power. Can God create a man that does not have the essence of a man? How can free will be compatible with God's omnipotence? See, for example, the logic of Ockham, which is an attempt to devise a language that leaves intact God's power, in Nye, *Words of Power*, pp. 103–124.

22. Her argument is as follows: each culture pronounces in its own words the name of God; there is no one religious language that can be counted on to indubitably and certainly deliver understanding of divinity. Even in Old Testament Judaism, where Weil believed the vision of God is particularly defective, there is a degree of truth; at the same time, all expressions of God are to some degree imperfect. For these reasons, it is better to stay with one's native religious language, the mother tongue of one's first aspirations to the divine, and not add to the difficulty of religious understanding the difficulties of learning a new language (AD 176). For Weil, if missionary zeal is misplaced, so is righteous refusal of Christianity and conversion to a foreign religion. In these cases, the convert is in the unfortunate position of a writer writing in a foreign language. She is apt to be clumsy and inept, and wastes her energies.

23. Weil's family was Jewish but did not observe Jewish religious practices. Her rejection of Judaism for Christianity, her apparent insensitivity to the Nazi's persecution of Jews in France, her insistence that she was not a practicing Jew have been much criticized, with some claiming that she was anti-Semitic. In her defense, she was not the only one who found it hard to grasp the full enormity of the Nazis' Jewish policy. Her criticism of Old Testament Judaism is motivated not by prejudice but by a critical reexamination of the Judeo-Christian heritage.

24. In an interesting early writing, "On Freud" (O I:278–280), Weil explicitly makes the analogy between the longing for perfect goodness and the return to the infant's fusion with the mother. The good mother, like God, withdraws and refuses out of love for the child. Related is her discussion of sexual love. Weil, although she adopted chastity for herself, did not see sexual union as necessarily impure. Sexual union is analogous to fusion with the mother or with God, and so is divine. "*La reaction, le respect de ce qu'on aime constitue l'essential de la pudeur. Ce qu'on aime est sacre*" (O I:278). Sexual love is pure when there is respect for the other person, when she is loved as a whole person, and when there is mutual pleasure. "All perversion consists in ceasing to consider the loved

being as a person, in considering him as an object, and notably an object divisible into parts" (O I:279).

25. The other experiences she speaks about to Father Perrin in *Waiting for God* were in 1937—an unspecified happening in a chapel that made her go to her knees; and in 1938 at Solesnes—an experience of divine love inspired by the metaphysical poetry of George Herbert (AD 43).

26. See their respective introductions to her religious works. Father Perrin, in *Waiting for God*, Thibon, in *Gravity and Grace*, Eliot, in *The Need for Roots*. Thibon, the editor of *Gravity and Grace*, interrupts her text with a footnote when he judges that things have gone dangerously far from tradition. For example, when she says "God has committed all phenomena without exception to the mechanism of the world," he adds, "she thus overlooks the margin of indeterminacy and spontaneity which God has left in nature and which allows for the introduction of liberty and miracles in the world" (GG 94). For her chapter heading "The Meaning of the Universe," he cautions, "The identification of the soul with the universe has no connection here with pantheism" (GG 127).

27. The function and location of holy places in Mediterranean popular religion can also be contrasted with institutional Christianity. Household shrines, often by the hearth, display religious symbols that represent the presence of the sacred in family life and in domestic work. Public rites in village churches celebrate the natality and mortality of physical existence and the seasonal turning points of the communal year, such as Easter, New Years, Assumption, and Epiphany. Chapels in remote locations serve as places of pilgrimage, reflection, and sacrifice. Family meals and rituals celebrate holidays and feast days. Weil wrote of such domestic sacraments in her last days, as she was dying of starvation and tuberculosis: "From this alliance between matter and real feelings comes the significance of meals of solemn occasions, at festivals, and family in friendly reunions . . . the joy and the spiritual significance of the feast is situated within the special delicacy associated with the feast" (FLN 364).

28. An example is Weil's treatment of sacrament. It is not that God is in the Eucharist's bread and wine as in Catholicism, or even the symbol of God as in Protestantism. Both understandings of sacrament are mistaken according to Weil. A sacrament is only a "hypothesis" that represents a harmony which is not in any particular content of the sacrament but is in the conventionality and therefore order and form of the practice. The bread and wine themselves cannot be good: it is the repetition of the convention of the Eucharist that is the source of purity (WG 183–4). When sacraments are seen in this way, there is a natural tolerance for a variety of religious practices. If God is in the Eucharist's bread and wine, it is blasphemy to attend or support any other sacrament. But if the conventionality of a sacred practice is only one way to approach an always otherworldly purity, then the conventions of many sacraments and liturgies are legitimate approaches to God.

29. Some commentators have described Weil's ethics as Kantian. There are important differences, however. Kant's "treat each person as an end not a means" is an alternate way of stating the categorical imperative: I should not act individually, but only in ways that I could will to be universal. Such an attitude does not recognize the other's will in the way that Weil prescribes. What one person wills to be universal is not necessarily what another might will.

30. "*To kalos*," usually translated as the "Good," which plays such an important role in Plato's philosophy as the highest Form, has no English equivalent. In Greek it means both beautiful and good, reflecting a pre-Platonic nondualist metaphysics which Plato did much to supplant. Our vocabulary reflects his success. The word "beautiful" refers to the physical quality which is the object of aesthetic judgment, the word "good" refers to a nonphysical quality which is ideal—to think otherwise is to commit the "naturalistic fallacy."

31. Diotima's nondualistic philosophy has been misinterpreted in most classical scholarship as a version of Plato's theory of Forms. See my articles, "The Hidden Host: Irigaray and Diotima at Plato's Symposium," *Hypatia*, Vol. 3, No. 3, Winter, 1989; "The Subject of Love: Diotima and her Critics," *Journal of Value Inquiry* 24: 135–153, 1990; "Rethinking Male and Female: The Prehellenic Philosophy of Mortal Opinion," *Journal of the History of European Ideas*, Vol. 9, No. 3, 1988, for a discussion of the ways in which Diotima's teaching differs from Plato's. Diotima and Weil agree that everyone strives for beauty and goodness and that this striving is the motive force for all human activities. The problem, as both Weil and Diotima describe it, is not that some desire evil, but that few know how to properly pursue beauty. Most are deflected to a striving for wealth or power, or remain obsessed with sexuality. Love, for Diotima and for Weil, in all its forms, is an aspiration toward the divine. It is for this reason, and not because of divine interdiction, that, for Weil, sexual sins are so serious. Sexual sins, like seduction or rape, involve a forcing of sex without consent. Even the agreement to engage in a simple exchange of physical pleasure constitutes a kind of force exercised on another because it involves accepting consent from a "low part of the soul," rather than from the whole person. If the aspiration to beauty in any form, including sexual attraction, is a movement to God, this forcing of consent is blasphemous; it is to make physical pleasure a God (AD 163).

32. This is an interesting if eccentric reading of the Persephone myth. The focus is usually taken to be on the divinity of the goddess, Demeter, who bears the grief of her daughter's abduction by the Lord of Death, Hades, and through the power of her suffering restores her daughter to life. Demeter is completely absent from Weil's account. Here Weil herself may be still captive to the masculine imagery of traditional Christianity, in that it is the masculine divinity of Hades that she recognizes, and

not the grieving Demeter's attention to the suffering of her vanished daughter, which is a divinity more in keeping with her own philosophy.

33. Commentators have accused Weil of a pathological masochism and claimed that she dissolved the self into brute physical process, but the acceptance of pain, for Weil, is related neither to hatred of the body nor to obedience to God's commandments, but rather to contact with reality and solidarity with the unfortunate. Weil explicitly rejects self-immolation. There is always enough pain of others available to share without inflicting it on oneself, and there is an absolute obligation to reduce pain in the world. Martyrs who seek out pain for themselves or others, and who take joy in a painful death, worship a false, manufactured God (GG 76). When, however, it is possible to experience pain not as an unfair imposition, the beauty and necessity of the world are not contemplated or represented as in art or science, but enter directly into the body. Pain is the "nail of necessity" in our soul, the place where "blind force enters brutal and cold." "Nailed in the center of the universe" (AD 120), we feel directly God's love.

34. Weil much admired the medieval Albigensian civilization of Languedoc ("A Medieval Epic Poem," "The Romanesque Renaissance," SE) not just for its rejection of the God Jehovah of the Old Testament and Roman Christianity, but because the religion of Catharism had infused a whole culture with spirituality (SL 129). In Weil's Oc religion was not a supplement or an addition to practical activities but infused political institutions, social relations, work methods, living patterns with spirituality. In contrast with closed militant Catholic Europe, Oc was open to the currents of thought from Egypt, Persia, Greek philosophy, the Pythagoreans, the early Christian Gnostics and a continuation of the old Mediterranean culture which had been open to a wide variety of religions and ways of thought. Weil speculated: if the Albigensians had not been crushed by the Inquisition would another Europe have resulted?

35. Although *Ecrits de Londres* has not been published in English as a separate volume, some of the papers have been translated and included in collections such as Rees, ed. *Selected Essays*, and Miles, ed., *Simone Weil: An Anthology*.

36. See also her analysis of Hitler's propaganda in EL, "Sur la supression generale des partis politiques."

37. Weil's apparent endorsement of censorship was shocking to some. She argued that if anyone publishes in order to persuade of the truth of his or her position and not just to express a personal opinion, then false views can be censored, and, after publication, punished. Weil was not just thinking of libel, but gives an example from academic scholarship. If a historian, for example, misrepresents the past, and it is an avoidable error, he should be punished (NR 36–7ff.). Characteristically, what Weil emphasizes is not a *right* to say what one wants, but an *obligation* to tell the truth.

38. See a collection of her writings on war, in *Formative Writings*, pp. 227–278.

39. This approach might be fruitful also for Islamic women, returning to the indigenous Mediterranean sources of Islam, or for Jewish women restoring passages in the Old Testament which indicate the inclusive ways of worship condemned by militant Hebrew prophets demanding the destruction of Yahweh's rivals.

Notes to Part III

References in the text are to the following of Arendt's works (see bibliography for complete citations).

OT   *The Origins of Totalitarianism*

HC   *The Human Condition*

OR   *On Revolution*

BPF   *Between Past and Future*

MDT   *Men in Dark Times*

CR   *Crises of the Republic*

T   *Thinking*

W   *Willing*

TP   "Truth in Politics"

I   "Public Rights and Private Interests," M. Mooney and F. Stuber, eds. *Small Comforts for Hard Times: Humanists on Public Policy* (New York: Columbia University Press, 1977)

TMC   "Thinking and Moral Considerations"

LK   *Lectures on Kant's Political Philosophy*

RV   *Rahel Varnhagen*

1. Arendt argued that logical operations—deduction from self-evident premises, subsumption under general laws, the construction of consistent chains of conclusions—show the structure of the human brain (HC 171). With the common world gone, the empty forms of the shared structures of the brain may be all we can agree on (HC 274). Arendt's claim that logic is a simulation of brain movements gives an interesting perspective on current cognitive psychology based on a supposed similarity between computer functioning and the brain. From Arendt's point of view, increasingly complex models for brain function tell us nothing about the process of thinking but only about physical structures of the brain.

2. Arendt cites the Swiss zoologist and biologist Adolf Portmann for evidence that "the facts themselves speak a very different language from the simplistic functional hypothesis that holds that appearances in living

things serve merely the two-fold purpose of self-preservation and preservation of the species" (T 27). The almost universal acceptance in the nineteenth and twentieth centuries of the view that struggle to survive explains all biological processes might also reflect the experience of industrialization and the reduction of public space, as all human relationships are reduced to the single one of getting a job and surviving in a world where human relationship and community have disappeared.

3.   See Helen Longino's *Science as Social Knowledge* (Princeton, New Jersey: Princeton University Press, 1990) for an example of the kind of discussion of the objects of science that might go on in politics. Longino argues through a number of examples that evidence is never purely logically related to hypothesis; and that social knowledge is required to judge whether data actually tells us about the phenomena in which we are interested.

4.   Arendt accuses philosophers of failing to distinguish between mind and soul or self. The soul or self is anchored in the body; it is the inner source of one's appearances to others as a self. Thinking, on the other hand, is a process, an activity. It is something that we do, not an existing place or substance. The independence of thinking, its withdrawal from reality, is the basis of the philosophical "fallacy" of a separate world of the mind and reason and an autonomous self constituted by self-consciousness. But, Arendt points out, there is no reality that is not an appearance to someone or something. Descartes is the paradigm case of this failure to distinguish, with his "I think, therefore I am," but philosophers of the body like Merleau-Ponty also make the mistake (T 30–35).

5.   Arendt uses as an example the philosophical dispute between Socrates and Machiavelli over the moral status of hypocrisy. Socrates argued, against hypocrisy, that we must be true to ourselves, and become inside how we wish to appear to others. Machiavelli argued, for hypocrisy, that all that can be required of us is that we act virtuously outwardly. Both Socrates and Machiavelli are right. Machiavelli saw no need for inner dialogue because he believed that God told people what to do, but he is right that we are responsible only for our appearance, for what we do and say in public. Socrates is right because to be sincere is to sustain the consistency of our appearances in a Socratic withdrawing and thinking about what we are doing.

6.   Compare B. Honig's deconstructive "reading" of Arendt in which she identifies Arendt's presentation to others with "performative" actions that "subvert identity," "explore its heterogeneity," "dislodge or disappoint its aspirations to univocity," "proliferate its differentiated possibilities" ("Toward an Agonistic Feminism" p. 230).

7.   In 1966, Arendt reviewed Nettl's biography of Rosa Luxemburg for the *New York Review of Books* (reprinted in MDT 33–56). She approved Nettl's choice of topic. Noting that Luxemburg's socialism might be thought one of the failures of history, Arendt asked: "Can it be that the

failure of all her efforts as far as official recognition is concerned is somehow connected with the dismal failure of revolution in our century? Will history look different if seen through the prism of her life and work?" (34)

8. See Arendt's discussion in "Organized Guilt and Universal Responsibility," in *The Jew as Pariah: Jewish Identity and Politics in the Modern Age*, ed. Ron Feldman (New York: Grove Press, 1978).

9. See Arendt's extended discussion in "The Concept of History" (BPF).

10. This was Arendt's first project after she completed her dissertation with Jaspers; she worked on it intermittently from 1929 to 1938; it was not published until 1957.

11. Arendt's comment on the "Women Problem" as it was relevant to Varnhagen's life: "The discrepancy between what men expected of women 'in general' and what women could give or wanted in their turn, was already established by the conditions of the era and represented a gap that virtually could not be closed" (RV xiii).

12. See the report of Jaspers's comments on the manuscript while it was in various stages in Dagmar Barnouw's *Visible Spaces: Hannah Arendt and the German-Jewish Experience* (Baltimore: Johns Hopkins University Press, 1990) pp. 30–71.

13. Compare the reading of Joanne Cutting-Gray, "Hannah Arendt, Feminism, and the Politics of Alterity" who argues that Arendt sees Rahel as "triumphing" because in the end Varnhagen realized that she could not escape her Jewishness. This is, I believe, a misreading of the lesson Arendt takes from Varnhagen's life. In the end Varnhagen does see that an existence as pariah Jew is better than the masks of assimilation, but this cannot "in a serious historical sense" save "the image of her soul." Her "place in history" is guaranteed only through Heine, the political activist, on whom she bestowed "the history of a bankruptcy and a rebellious soul" (RV 227). Although the first step in developing a political practice may be to stop trying to escape one's personal history, a stable sense of self is only won in the actual public appearing to others as oneself which was denied to the Jews in Europe. Rahel's abandonment of assimilation was a legacy for the future, but could not repair her own damaged life.

14. Arendt was often criticized for her failure to focus exclusively on the evil of innocent Jews' oppressors. The most controversial sections in *Eichmann in Jerusalem* were her descriptions of the assistance given Eichmann by Jewish leaders. Nor did she tell the story of Varnhagen's life as the story of an innocent Jewish woman crushed by evil men. This would be to ignore the actual conditions of anti-Semitism which, for Arendt, are not in any psychology, demonic or angelic, but in the real substance of history: human actions, the spaces in which they can occur, the relations which they generate.

15. Compare Michele Riot-Sarcey's and Eleni Varikas's use of Arendt's pariah identity to understand feminist history in "Feminist Consciousness in the Nineteenth Century: A Pariah consciousness," *Praxis International,* Vol. 5 No. 4 (January 1986) pp. 443–465. They argue, using examples of nineteenth-century women's movements in France and Greece, that a perception of exclusion precedes the establishing of a feminist identity.

16. See, for example, Arendt's "Imperialism: Road to Suicide," in *Commentary* 1 (February 1946) pp. 27–35. Arendt drew on Luxemburg's economics to argue that Marx and Marxist writers, "except for Luxemburg," "concealed" the "political pattern of imperialism." Restricted by the category of class, they ignored the character of the typical colonizer, who was neither an industrial worker or a capitalist. More than Luxemburg, Arendt emphasized racism, arguing that the European anti-Semitism which laid the groundwork for racism in Africa and other colonized areas was conditioned by capitalism's creation of a "mob" of rootless and desperate men, driven from ancestral lands.

17. This was a mistake that Arendt believed is perpetuated in the policies of the new state of Israel when it refuses a pluralistic secular state for a "tribal identity" which excludes Arabs from citizenship. See her various writings on the question in *The Jew as Pariah.*

18. One of the most disturbing features of Arendt's discussion of labor in the Greek household is her seeming lack of attention to the fact that this "realm of darkness" is predominately female. Not only were women sequestered in the household, but the majority of domestic slaves were women taken as spoils of war. Like so many classicists, Arendt treats the Greeks as an absolute beginning, ignoring the older Mediterranean culture that preexisted the Hellenic invasions, and in which women played very different roles. Because her "memories" of work and labor are taken exclusively from male philosophers, such as Aristotle and Plato, who had their own agenda, her account does not reflect any actual consensus even among the Greeks. Current research in ancient Greek history, inspired by feminist attempts to recover a nonpatriarchal past, shows that even in classical Greek society the rules of women were not as restricted as Aristotle might have thought appropriate.

19. A better example of the division of private from public space than aristocratic Athenian society as described in Aristotle's *Politics* might be the traditional village community that still survives in Greece and in other rural parts of the Mediterranean, the community that the centrist government and imperial rule of Athens did much to destroy. As the city-state consolidated its power, traditional holdings which passed in the family, often matrilineally, and which were not sellable or devisable outside the family, were co-opted by large landowners. Trade and imperial conquests made money available for high-interest loans which, combined with poor harvests, forced many villagers into debt and foreclosure and, in some periods of Greek history, slavery. In the city-state, instead of property being the basis for citizenship, citizenship was often the

basis for an appropriation of property, as citizens passed legislation that helped them to increase their holdings in the surrounding countryside.

20. See Arendt's discussion in *On Revolution*, pp. 272–3, of the deficiencies of politics in capitalist democracies. Citizens in the U.S., she argues, are represented, but it is their "interests" and not their opinions that are represented. Instead of opinions they have "moods" and "tastes" which are tapped into political handlers. This should not be confused with public discussion.

21. Nowhere does Arendt express agreement with Marx's assumption of an original division of labor between men and women. See Karl Marx and Frederick Engels, *Collected Works* (New York: International Publishers, 1976) Vol. 5, p. 44. ". . . the division of labour, which was originally nothing but the division of labour in the sex act."

22. A classic text on nontraditional households is Schulamith Firestone's radical feminist tract, *The Dialectic of Sex* (New York: Bantam Books, 1971), in which Firestone proposes a variety of freely formed households no longer structured around women's reproductive labor.

23. My interpretation of the direction that an Arendtian feminist politics might take is based on an intuition of a solution not explicit in Arendt's writings. Another possible interpretation is that of Nancy Fraser in "The Struggle over Needs," in *Unruly Practices: Power, Discourse, and Gender in Contemporary Theory* (Minneapolis: University of Minnesota Press, 1989). Fraser begins from Arendt's distinction between private and public, but argues that within the "social" which replaces the private sphere there is not only process but also dispute, which allows some discussion of needs. Fraser concludes, however, that she herself prefers the more clearly political vocabulary of rights. Or see Nancy Hartsock, *Money, Sex and Power: Toward a Feminist Historical Materialism* (New York: Longman, 1983), pp. 210–223, who argues that Arendt gives an original reading of Greek politics in which competition is transformed into a communalism similar to that in socialism.

24. See Rousseau's "Essay on the Origins of Language" in *First and Second Discourses* (New York: Perennial Library, 1986). The expressive view of language was further developed in the nineteenth century by romantics such as Coleridge.

25. Wittgenstein, *Philosophical Investigations* (Oxford: Basil Blackwell, 1958), sections 1–21.

26. Not sufficiently noted by Arendt are the economic concerns that drove much of Greek politics. In Athens, the wealth that maintained the private households of citizens, and that was used to purchase slaves or to mount military expeditions that brought back slaves as war booty, was the business of politics. Citizens did not so much freely appear to each other as they appeared to each other to advance their mercantile or landowning interests. Many of the "glorious" deeds of Greek politicians involved war. As Athens struggled to expand and then defend her empire

in the Aegean, these wars were not so much for the glory of Athens as they were for wealth gained from colonies abroad, control of trade routes, confiscated lands, war booty, and captured slaves. The celebrated "world" of Athens, the great monuments, the Parthenon, the temples of Delphi, the theaters, were symbols of power and superiority that justified imperial power and compensated working classes for the taxes and military service that supported the empire. Pericles' Funeral Oration, cited by Arendt, is elucidative: the point of establishment of the *polis* was to insure that those who "forced every sea and land to become the scene of their daring" would be remembered.

27. Unfortunately, the material prosperity of United States could also be seen not as luck but as violent plunder, as colonialists took over territory from indigenous peoples.

28. This rejection of logic and rationality is the basis of Habermas's dismissal of Arendt's politics (*Social Research* 44:1977). Habermas argues that the constituent rules of speech acts as expressed in pragmatic rules of debate—consistency, for instance—allows a rational consensus between disputants. An Arendtian response might be that to embed logic in the constitutive rules of speech acts imposes on speech an even greater tyranny than the frozen categories of philosophy which can always be metaphorically extended.

29. Arendt spoke of the distinction between different kinds of truth in a number of ways. In *Thinking* she made a distinction between truth, which is the province of science, and meaning, which is the province of thought and judgment. In "Truth in Politics" she speaks of different kinds of truth: scientific truth, logical truth, factual truth. In the *Lectures on Kant*, the distinction is between the cognitive propositions of science, which compel consent, and thinking, which leads to persuasive judgment and sound understanding (LK 72).

30. Whatever glory there may have been in the heroic acts of Greek warriors, Arendt suggests it may be missing from modern warfare: "without the disclosure of the agent in the act, action loses its specific character and becomes one form of achievement among others. It is then indeed no less a means to an end than making is a means to produce an object. This happens whenever human togetherness is lost, that is when people are only for or against other people, as for instance in modern warfare, where men go into action and use means of violence in order to achieve certain objectives for their own side and against the enemy" (HC 180).

31. In support of her distinctions, Arendt cited etymologies in various languages. Some examples: In Greek, *ergazesthai* is distinguished from *ponein*, in Latin *labore* from *facere*. Typically, the words for labor connote physical effort and pain. The French *travailler*, for example, is derived from *tripalium*, which is a kind of torture (HC 80). See Hannah Pitkin's critique of some of her etymologies ("Are Freedom and Liberty Twins?" *Political Theory*, 16:1988). In part, Pitkin's more extensive historical

researches into the meaning of words are an extension or elaboration of Arendt's method. There is a difference, however, between Pitkin's Wittgensteinian methodology of mapping grammar in usage and Arendt's attempt to recover the concrete experiences words distinguish. Arendt did not think that meaning is "use," or imagine "language games" in which words acquire meaning by convention. Instead, she practiced a critical reading of past texts which recovers lost meanings and exposes empty "uses" of words.

32. Mary McCarthy tried to capture the combination of liberation and stability in Arendt's thinking in a metaphor: In the "space that Hannah Arendt creates in her work and which one can walk into with the great sense of walking through an arch . . . within this free space—each distinction was like a little house. . . . And I think that the chance of invigoration and oxygenation does combine with some sense of stability and security . . ." (I 337–8).

33. Arendt asks whether there is an actual political experience behind the idea of the rule of the philosopher kings. Probably not, is her answer. The Greeks had no experience of rule; tyrants were always evil. The experience, she argued, behind this new concept is not political, but the philosopher's ambivalent attitude to human affairs. On the one hand, the philosopher condemns human affairs as beneath him; on the other he dreams of a return from his ideal world to the world of men where he will be in charge (BPF 113). Plato, she claimed, was the first to confuse political power with ruling when he attempted to "drive the wedge" through leading and ruling, by separating the Guardians from the masses and having the Guardians be makers who fashion the shapes of eternal Forms on earth. Political philosophy continued in that tradition, giving a variety of prescriptions for the "making" of the good society.

34. See Arendt's meditation on authority in BPF and her article, "Authority in the Twentieth Century," in *Review of Politics* 17:1956. One consequence of the loss of the meaning of authority is the failure to make distinctions, such as the one between authoritarian regimes and totalitarian regimes. Authority in the Catholic church, for example, has a pyramid structure with levels of authority; action in such a system is still possible, whereas it is not possible in totalitarianism. Both the liberal who says that less freedom leads to totalitarianism and the conservative who says that less authority will lead to totalitarianism are right.

35. Arendt did not count love among the political virtues. Like compassion, love erases the distance between people that makes public relationships possible. Like goodness, it is inner, private, and cannot be "shown" without perversion (HC 52). But love also involves a specific vision of "who," and not "what" a person is, which is essential to promising and forgiving, and to the speaking between equals that must support political action and give it its meaning (HC 242). Loving, then, plays an indirect role in preparing us to forgive and promise.

36. See her article on desegregation, "Reflections on Little Rock," in *Dissent* 6:1959. She reconsidered this position later, when black activists brought to her attention the differences between the situation of Jews in Germany and blacks in the U.S. In "The Crisis in Education," in *Between Past and Future*, she argues that the schools are not public, but they are "between private and public." Although education is conservative and requires tradition and authority, it must also prepare children for public life by teaching them that the "setting right" of the world is possible.

37. There have been a number of recent attempts to try to accommodate Arendt's work within the confines of currently popular postmodernism or deconstruction. For examples see Joanne Cutting-Gray, "Hannah Arendt, Feminism, and the Politics of Alterity," or B. Honig, "Toward an Agonistic Feminism." It is my view that Arendt's treatment of the self, reality, politics, language is distorted as a result. Some of the conflations and leveling in Honig's article: 1) Arendt's variety of languages in different spaces becomes language as understood in a univocal theory of speech acts with propositional cores derived from John Austin via Derrida; 2) Arendt's private/public distinction is taken as a "binary opposition" to be deconstructed rather than a relation between two different spaces; 3) Work subject to natural necessity is seen as an "attitude" rather than as a material condition of human life; 4) Arendt's unique notion of a relation between the "inside" of the body and the "outside" of appearances to others becomes the predictable "opposition" between mind and body; 5) Postmodern jargon such as "master signifier" is read onto Arendt's description of the necessity of bodily processes and needs; 6) The private is taken as a personal sexual relation rather than the actual space of the household. In my view, these examples illustrate the problems of interpretation that occur when women thinkers are read through the prism of men's theories, in this case the theories of Derrida and Foucault.

38. Arendt does not explain exactly why it is that the future presses us back and the past forward rather than vice versa. To attempt a possible interpretation: the problems and guilt of the past press forward; the strangeness and fearfulness of the future press back. It is not clear whether Arendt wants to argue from this parable that insertion in events actually deflects the future or the past. This might have been disclaimed when she says: "to avoid misunderstandings: the imagery I am using here to indicate metaphorically and tentatively the contemporary conditions of thought can be valid only within the realm of mental phenomena. Applied to historical or biographical time, none of these metaphors can possibly make sense because gaps in time do not occur there." In support would be her position that thought is not instrumental, but has to do with meaning.

39. Arendt cites not Plato but Solon another nonprofessional thinker (T 170). Happiness, justice, and so on, are the "non-appearing measure" which "holds the limits of all things."

40. Arendt never explains in detail the process of "desensing." When we remember something that we have experienced, we do not remember it in the way it appeared to the senses. Instead we use our imagination to put it in "desensed form" (T 85).

41. Like some poststructuralist philosophers, such as Derrida, Arendt insists that all philosophical thought, indeed all thought, is metaphorical, but for very different reasons. For Derrida, metaphor has reference to a nonlinear signifying chain of meanings constituted in intertextual processes. For Arendt, the necessary metaphorical nature of thought has reference to thought's source in experience: "the words we use in strictly philosophical discourse are also invariably related to the world as given to our five bodily senses, from whose experience they then, as Locke pointed out, are "transferred"—*metapherein*, carried over to more abstruse signification" (T 31).

42. Arendt makes a distinction between the historical Socrates and Plato. This must be, to some degree, her own construction, as we know about Socrates mainly through Plato's reporting. My own view is that Socrates' discussions as they are reported by Plato, whatever they may have been in fact, do not result in communicative truth or meaning but are disguised lectures in which logic is used to discredit the voices of others. See my discussion of *The Sophist* in *Words of Power*, pp. 23–40.

43. All thinking, Arendt thought, is "after-thought," dealing with "desensed" experience. The only exception is logic, which has "cut all strings to living experience." But it can only do this by taking premises as self-evident; in other words by forbidding thought about them (T 87).

44. Kant responded with ambivalence to the great political event of his time, the French Revolution. On the one hand, applying his categorical imperative, rebelling had to be wrong because it cannot be made universal. (Arendt commented that Kant may have made a mistake here by assuming that any rebellion was a coup d'etat. Other forms of rebellion, such as democratic movements in Eastern Europe, might be universalizable.) But in terms of human progress, Kant decided, the French Revolution was progressive. Kant would not have *acted* as rebel; on the other hand, his *judgment* on the revolution was positive. His judgment as a spectator and as a political actor differ, which shows the asymmetry between thinking and action. The judgment of a thinker does not determine a given action; anymore than action forces any judgment. The standpoint of the actor is not the standpoint of the judge; the activities are independent. Because of that independence, there can be reciprocal relations between the two.

Selected Annotated Bibliography Of Works in English

I. Rosa Luxemburg

A. Books by Luxemburg

On the Industrial Development of Poland (first published 1898), trans. T. De Carlo, introduction by Lyndon LaRouche, Jr. (New York: Campaigner Publications, 1977). Luxemburg's doctoral thesis from the University of Zurich, which was published as a book. This short work exhibits Luxemburg's early mastery of economics, and is an example of her "case by case" approach to national independence.

Reform or Revolution reprinted from *Rosa Luxemburg Speaks* (1898, 1899) (New York: Pathfinder Press, 1973). This is a reprint of Luxemburg's milestone pamphlet against Bernstein's reformist socialism, with a historical introduction by Mary-Alice Waters which places the dispute in the context of prewar European politics. This edition also includes the concluding chapter of Bernstein's *Evolutionary Socialism* for comparison.

The Accumulation of Capital (1913), trans. Agnes Schwarzschild (New York: Monthly Review Press, 1964). Luxemburg's major work. Marred somewhat by the haste with which Luxemburg wrote, and dealing, not always completely intelligibly, with difficult technical arguments, the main argument of the book is clear: the economic core of Marxist theory is flawed by an inadequate explanation of the accumulation of capital. Luxemburg traces the history of the theories of capital accumulation, showing the inadequacies and evasions in classical economics, both bourgeois and socialist, and outlines the international imperialist relations that are left out of both.

The Accumulation of Capital—An Anti-Critique (1921, written 1915) trans. R. Wichman (New York: Monthly Review Press, 1972). In this slightly more readable version of the argument in *The Accumulation of Capital*, Luxemburg turns from the history of economic thought to answering the objections of critics. This volume also includes Bukharin's tract, *Imperialism and the Accumulation of Capital*, which was written after her death as the official Bolshevik response.

B. Collections of Papers and Speeches by Luxemburg

Marxism and Social Democracy: the Revisionist Debate (1898), ed. H. Tudor and J. M. Tudor (Cambridge University Press, 1988). Extensive introduction on Bernstein's socialism and the fierce controversy it occasioned among socialists, followed by a collection of articles and comments from various parties to the debate, including Luxemburg's *Reform or Revolution* and other of her political writings.

The National Question: Selected Writings (1908–9), ed. H. B. Davis (New York: Monthly Review Press, 1976). Translations of Luxemburg's Polish writings on nationalism, which make clear the difference between her and Lenin on the national question. Davis' skillful editing makes this collection a coherent argument in book form. As Luxemburg masterfully analyzes muddled socialist thinking on the emotional issue of national independence, her insight into the dangers of nationalism gives an important perspective on the later break up of the Soviet empire and the rise of factionalism and separatism in Eastern Europe.

Theory and Practice (1910), trans. D. Wolff (Detroit, Mich.: News and Letters Comm., 1980). A reprint of the article that caused Luxemburg's final break with Kautsky over the mass strike and the nature of party leadership. It expresses Luxemburg's growing impatience with the Social Democrats' acceptance of imperialism and their use of Marxist schema that have no relation to historical realities.

The Russian Revolution, and Leninism and Marxism (1917), intro. by B. Wolfe (Conn: Greenwood Press, 1981). Collected in one volume, Luxemburg's critical analyses of the Russian Revolution, including her arguments against Lenin on democracy and the national question.

Selected Political Writings, ed. Dick Howard (New York: Monthly Review Press, 1971). A collection of Luxemburg's major papers on reformism and party organization, with an interesting introduction which relates her positions to the New Left movement of the 1960s. In an attempt to find a new voice for socialism, the editor prefaces each paper with an introduction that puts the issue in perspective in relation to the complex debates in German socialism. He also includes useful explanatory footnotes for each article.

Rosa Luxemburg Speaks, ed. M. Waters (New York: Pathfinder Press, 1970). A collection of Luxemburg's major papers on reformism, the mass strike, militarism, war, and the Russian Revolution, with a bibliographic introduction. Each individual paper is also preceded by a preface which explains the specific issues in historical context. This collection also includes one of Luxemburg's papers on literature: "The Spirit of Russian Literature: the

Life of Korolenkno." Appendixes contain tracts against her positions by Lenin and Trotsky.

C. Collections of Luxemburg's Letters

Comrade and Lover: Rosa Luxemburg's Letters to Leo Jogiches, ed. E. Ettinger (Cambridge, Mass.: MIT Press, 1979). In Luxemburg's letters to her lover and collaborator in socialist politics, the full range of her personality is evident: the force of her mind in contrast to Jogiches practical political skills, her ruthless honesty when dealing with her friends, the emotional range of her consciousness. The complex dynamics of their nontraditional relationship provide an interesting study in gender relations.

The Letters of Rosa Luxemburg, ed. S. E. Bronner (Boulder, Colo: Westview Press, 1978). A selection from the whole range of Luxemburg's extensive and lively correspondence, including letters to colleagues and editors, to political allies and enemies, and to friends and lovers. Especially useful are the editor's footnotes, which identify the references in each letter. The collection is preceded by a short but excellent introduction which marks out the various voices to which she responds, and outlines the disputes to which the letters refer.

D. Books about Luxemburg

Abraham, Richard. *Rosa Luxemburg: A Life for the International* (New York: St. Martin's Press, 1989). Uneven, anecdotal treatment of Luxemburg's life and work. Some interesting material on her personal life, her relations and reactions to feminism, and her various political alliances.

Bronner, Stephen Eric. *Rosa Luxemburg, A Revolutionary for Our Times* (New York: Columbia University Press, 1987). A portrait of Luxemburg which brings out the charm of her personality, her relationships with friends, and her interest in poetry, botany, and literature, as well as her political theory. A corrective to one-sided polemical distortions of Luxemburg's positions, this short book is an intelligent, incisive introduction to her work, which stresses the relevance of Luxemburg's socialism to contemporary events such as the Polish independence movement.

————, *Socialism Unbound* (New York: Routledge, Chapman and Hall, 1990). Excellent background in socialist history and theory. Chapters on orthodox Marxism, Leninism, and revisionism lead up to a concluding chapter identifying Luxemburg as one of the major founders of an alternative socialist tradition.

Cliff, Tony. *Rosa Luxemburg* (London: Bookmarks, 1959). A testamentary pamphlet that very briefly reviews Luxemburg's positions for a popular audience.

Dunayevskaya, Raya. *Rosa Luxemburg, Women's Liberation, and Marx's Philosophy of Revolution* (New York: Humanities Press, 1982). Disappointing splicing together of three different pieces by Dunayevskaya: a superficial overview of Luxemburg's positions—Dunayevskaya, for example, discusses *The Accumulation of Capital* in one sentence, citing an orthodox Marxist authority for the fact that Luxemburg made an obvious mistake—a dated and schematic treatment of socialist feminism, and a somewhat simplistic tract on Marxism. She includes some interesting documentation on Luxemburg's ambivalent response to Clara Zetkin's women's movement but fails to convincingly connect Luxemburg's position with feminism, or to bring out what is distinctive about Luxemburg's socialism.

Ettinger, Elzbieta. *Rosa Luxemburg: A Life* (Boston: Beacon Press, 1986). Readable popular biography that highlights Luxemburg's personal life but does not deal with her thought in depth.

Frolick, Paul. *Rosa Luxemburg: Her Life and Work*, trans. E. Fitzgerald (New York: H. Fertig, 1969). This account of Luxemburg's politics was first published in 1939 by a German emigrant who had been working in Germany to bring out a collection of Luxemburg's works. Frolick, writing from a committed Marxist perspective, afraid that texts would not survive either rightist or leftist repression, attempts to preserve Luxemburg's legacy.

Geras, Norman. *The Legacy of Rosa Luxemburg* (London: NLB, 1976). A collection of four carefully argued essays on the political thought of Luxemburg, two reprinted from the *New Left Review*, 1973 and 1975, that aim to correct misapprehensions about her work (for example, the charges of catastrophism and spontaneity).

Nettle, J. P. *Rosa Luxemburg* (London: Oxford University Press, 1964). An abridged two-volume translation of Nettl's monumental biography of Luxemburg. Although Nettle is not always objective in his analyses, this is the first and major source for detailed information about Luxemburg's life.

II. Simone Weil

A. *Books by Weil*

Formative Writings (written 1929–1941), trans. D. T. McFarland and W. Van Ness (Amherst: University of Massachusetts Press, 1987). This collection includes Weil's thesis on Descartes, which gives important insights into the philosophical foundations of her social and religious thought (first published in France in a collection of Weil's writings on science, *Sur la science*, 1966), her *Factory Journal*, the record of her experiences as an industrial worker and her description of *malheur* (*La Condition ouvriere*, 1951), and some of her early writings on pacifism and war. The introduction by Dorothy McFarland includes useful information on the early intellectual influences on Weil, especially her relation with the philosopher, Alain.

Lessons in Philosophy (notes from Weil's lycée classes, 1933–34, *Leçons de Philosophie*, présentées par Anne Reynaud, 1959), trans. H. Price (Cambridge: Cambridge University Press, 1978). These notes are useful for an understanding of the philosophical dimensions of Weil's early work. Weil discusses theories of reality, perception, knowledge, truth, and the self. Introduction by the philosopher Peter Winch puts this relatively unknown work into perspective.

Oppression and Liberty (written 1937–1941), trans. A. Wills and J. Petrie (Amherst, University of Massachusetts Press, 1973). This is Weil's critique of orthodox Marxism, along with a number of other early political writings. Topics include her rejection of Marxist determinism, her critical comments on Lenin's *Materialism and Empiriocriticism*, and also her theory of power and her understanding of the ideal of liberated work.

Intimations of Christianity Among the Ancient Greeks (written 1941–2) (from *La source Grecque*, 1953 and *Intuitions precretiennes*, 1951), trans. E. C. Geissbuhler (London: Routledge & Kegan Paul, 1957). This volume includes several of Weil's most interesting writings: her interpretation of the Iliad as "the poem of force," her attempts to find "intimations of Christianity" in various works of Plato, and, most extraordinary, a dense gloss on the Pythagorean fragments which Weil understood as an early source of spiritual revelation. The latter is one of the clearest statements of her understanding of the relation between material necessity, science, and divinity.

The Iliad, or the Poem of Force, trans. M. McCarthy (Pendle Hill, 1956). A separate edition of the piece of the *Iliad*.

Waiting on God (written May to January 1942) (*Attente de Dieu*), trans. Emma Craufurd (N.Y.: Harper and Row, 1973). These are the writings in which Weil tried to explain to her spiritual advisor, Father Perrin, her refusal to join the church. In a series of letters and essays she explains her rejection of institutional religion and religious dogma, and describes the series of religious revelations that lead her to a new understanding of divinity and devotion. An introduction by Father Perrin gives insight into the differences between them.

Gravity and Grace (excerpts from Weil's notebooks, *Le pesanteur et la grace*, 1947) (London: Ark Paperbacks, 1963). In a distinctive, epigrammatic, prophetic style, this book is a sampling of Weil's distinctive views on God, love, natural necessity, the nature of the spiritual life, and the relation between the ideal and human society. The documentary introduction by Gustave Thibon, Weil's friend and employer for much of her agricultural work gives an intimate view of the conflicting emotions Thibon felt when faced with her uncompromising spirituality and her strong personality.

The Need for Roots (written 1943) (*L'enracinement*, 1949), trans. Arthur Wills (New York: Ark Paperback, 1987). This is Weil's report to the French Resistance on the principles that should govern the reconstruction of Europe. In it she develops her controversial vision of a rooted society that is structured by equilibrium, that fulfills the needs of the soul as well as the body, and that is infused with spirituality. Preface by T. S. Eliot shows the respect and the caution which her powerful writing inspired in a conservative Anglican convert.

B. Weil's Notebooks

First and Last Notebooks (1933–4, 1942–3), trans. R. Rees (London: Oxford University Press, 1970). This volume includes Weil's prewar notebook, written for the most part in 1933–4, while she was working on her lectures in philosophy in her lycée classes, and in which she begins to sketch out her materialistic metaphysics and epistemology. It also includes her New York Notebook, written during the war while in exile in the United States, waiting for a chance to return to France. The latter is an important source for her mature religious thought. The volume also includes her last fragmentary notebook, written in London. Weil's notebooks, readable in their own right, show the fomentation of her extraordinary mind.

The Notebooks of Simone Weil (1940–42) (from *Cahiers* 1970–4), trans. A. Wills (London: Routledge & Kegan Paul, 1956). These notebooks from the early years of the war and the period of Weil's greatest output of work, show the fertility of her mind as she strains to deepen and extend her understanding of social oppression in a study of Western history, as well as to develop a metaphysics that takes account of the transcendent and its relation to human experience.

C. Collections of Essays by Weil

Selected Essays (1934–43), trans. and ed. R. Rees (London: Oxford University Press, 1962). A collection of essays on a variety of topics. It includes several of Weil's last writings on society, including "Human Personality," in which she rejects the idea of individual rights as a guarantee of justice, and several of the historical writings, in which she identifies positive (the civilization of Languedoc) and negative (Hitlerism) social models.

On Science, Necessity and the Love of God (1940–42), trans. R. Rees (London: Oxford University Press, 1968). This collection is in two parts. The first comprises the writings on classical science and quantum mechanics from *Sur la science*, 1966, without the "Thesis on Descartes" (The thesis is published, 1988, in *Formative Writings*). The second part includes a mixed collection of writings on God, vaguely influenced by Plato, rather more inspirational than theoretical.

Two Moral Essays: Human Personality, and On Human Obligation (Pendle Hill, 1981). Two of the most important of Weil's late articles from *Ecrits de Londres* are reprinted in this volume, in which Weil argues that the protection of the rights of the individual cannot guarantee justice or peace. In order to say what might, Weil develops distinctive accounts of the nature of the self and the nature of moral obligation.

Simone Weil: An Anthology, ed. Sian Miles (London: Virago, 1986). With a short but evocative biographical introduction, this is one of the most representative selections of Weil's writings. Prefacing each with an explanatory paragraph, Miles includes articles from different periods of Weil's life on work, the soul, Fascism, the *Iliad*.

D. Articles by Weil

"Are We Struggling for Justice?" (from *Ecrits de Londres*), trans. Marina Barabas, in *Philosophical Investigations* 53 (January 1987) 1–10.

"The Legitimacy of the Provisional Government" (from *Ecrits de Londres*), trans. P. Winch, in *Philosophical Investigations* 53 (April 1987) 87–98.

E. Weil's Letters

Seventy Letters, trans. R. Rees (Oxford: Oxford University Press, 1965). A selection from Weil's extensive correspondence. Highpoints include: letters to factory managers who had shown some interest in factory reform under Weil's auspices, accounts of her travels in Italy with special attention to art, researches in the origins of mathematics, and references to her interest in and eccentric interpretations of ancient religious sources.

F. Books About Weil

Anderson, David. *Simone Weil* (London: S.C.M. Press, 1971). This short volume is one in a series of inspirational portraits of great thinkers.

Blum, Laurence and Seidler, Victor. *A Truer Liberty: Simone Weil and Marxism* (New York: Routledge, 1989). A skillful and exhaustive treatment of Weil's early political thought, which suffers from neglecting the relation between her later view of society and her reworking of Christianity.

Cabaud, Jacques. *Simone Weil: A Fellowship in Love* (New York: Channel Press, 1964). A readable biography with nontechnical expositions of her major works.

Coles, Robert. *Simone Weil: A Modern Pilgrimage* (Reading, Mass.: Addison-Wesley, 1987). Coles addresses the controversies surrounding aspects of Weil's life and thought, such as her supposed "anorexia" and her "anti-Semitism," from a psychologist's perspective.

Deitz, Mary. *Between the Human and the Divine: the Social and Political Thought of Simone Weil* (New Jersey: Rowman and Littlefield, 1989). Insightful interpretation of Weil's social philosophy with attention both to its political contexts and gender issues.

Dunaway, John. *Simone Weil* (Boston: Twayne Publishers, 1984). In the quasi-testamentary style of so many books on Weil, Dunaway includes a short bibliography and nontechnical descriptions of some of her major themes.

Fioni, Gabriella. *Simone Weil: An Intellectual Biography*, trans. J. R. Berrigan.

(Athens, Ga.: University of Georgia Press, 1989). Novelistic biography which is a splicing together of testimony from those who knew Simone Weil, excerpts from Weil's writing, interspersed with comments from the author. Although this book sometimes succeeds in evoking the feel of Weil's life, it does not succeed in giving an intelligible view of her thought.

Hellman, John. *Simone Weil: An Introduction to her Work* (Philadelphia: Fortress, 1982). Simplistic summary of Weil's work, with emphasis on religion.

Little, J. P. *Simone Weil: Waiting on Truth* (Oxford: Berg, 1988). A brief biography and a summary of major themes in Weil's writing. Little presents Weil both as a maverick who was not and refused to be the founder of a "school," and as part of a universal mystical tradition in which he includes a wide assortment of religious and philosophical thinkers.

McFarland, Dorothy. *Simone Weil* (New York: Frederick Ungar, 1983). A brief, somewhat schematic treatment of Weil's work which attempts to correct the impression that she is only a religious thinker. McFarland shows the interconnections between Weil's spirituality and her social thought, and relates Weil's studies in Western culture and her social philosophy.

McLane-Iles, Betty. *Uprooting and Integration in the Writings of Simone Weil* (New York: Peter Long Pub., 1987). An extended discussion of all aspects of Weil's philosophy, organized around the metaphors of uprooting and integration. Especially useful are McLane-Iles's references to sources and influences, and her interpretations of Weil's relation to thinkers such as Alain, Valery, Mounier, Giraudoux, William James.

McLellan, David. *Utopian Pessimist: The Life and Thought of Simone Weil* (New York: Poseidon Press, 1990). Excellent biography of Weil which focuses on her thought rather than on her personal eccentricities. McLellan studies the rich ideological matrix of her thought in theology, myth, and philosophy, both Eastern and Western. With insight and erudition, he integrates his discussion of events in Weil's life with detailed interpretations of her philosophy, including full attention to her later social philosophy.

Perrin, J. M. and Thibon, G. *Simone Weil as We Knew Her*, trans. E. Craufurd (London: Routledge & Kegan Paul, 1953). Fascinating documentary assessments of Weil from the priest who tried to convert her to Catholicism and the employer, and later friend, who agreed to oversee her agricultural work.

Petrément, S. *Simone Weil: A Life*, trans. R. Rosenthal (New York: Pantheon Books, 1976). Written by Weil's schoolfriend and comrade, this is still the most complete and the best of the biographies of Weil. Not only does Petrément give a detailed account of events in Weil's life, she admirably traces the close nexus between Weil's philosophical positions and her experiences and commitments. The result is that both Weil's extraordinary life and her thoughts are made intelligible.

Springsted, E. O. *Simone Weil and the Suffering of Love* (Cambridge, Cowley, 1986). A nontechnical and inspirational interpretation of Weil's religious thought.

White, G. A., ed. *Simone Weil: Interpretations of a Life* (Amherst: University of Massachusetts Press, 1981). A interesting collection of papers which give various impressions and reflections on Weil and her life from diverse perspectives.

Winch, Peter. *Simone Weil: The Just Balance* (Cambridge: Cambridge University Press, 1989). Although marred by Winch's determination to find in Weil a fellow Wittgensteinian, and by lengthy expositions of Wittgenstein's positions, this is the most interesting and complete philosophical treatment of Weil's epistemology and metaphysics. Instead of passing over the early work in philosophy, Winch shows how it is related to her later political and religious writing.

G. Articles About Weil

Allen, Giogenes, "Incarnation in the Gospels and the Bhagavad Gita," in *Faith Phil.* 6, 241–259, July 1989. Giogenes uses Weil as the model for a new kind of study of religion that, instead of trying to understand other religions from within their own frame of thought, looks for common "Christian" themes.

Milosz, Czeslaw, "The Importance of Simone Weil," in *Emperor of the Earth* (Berkeley, California: University of California Press, 1977). Czeslaw cites Weil as injecting a "new leaven into the life of believers and unbelievers" (98) in a Poland split between rival camps of nationalistic Catholics and atheistic Marxists.

Springsted, Eric, "The Religious Basis of Culture: T. S. Eliot and Simone Weil," in *Religious Studies* 25, 105–116, March 1989. Springsted argues that, given his interpretation of the religious base of culture, Eliot can only be critical of present society as a backward-looking, regretful conservative. In contrast, Weil is able to offer a positive vision of a future spiritual society rooted in work.

Tauber, Susan A., "The Absent God," in *Journal of Religion*, Vol. 35, No. 1, January 1955. Tauber's thesis is that Weil is a mystical atheist who expresses the twentieth-century experience of the "death of God." Apparently hampered by a very limited access to Weil's works, Tauber asserts that Weil believed there is a complete absence of justice and goodness in the world, and promoted "total surrender to brute actuality."

Teuber, Andreas, "Simone Weil: Equality as Compassion," in *Philosophy and Phenomenological Research* 431, 221–238, December 1982. Teuber's argument is that, although it is impossible to derive a theory of obligation from Weil's account of compassion as the basis for equality because there are no principles to decide in cases of a clash of claims, Weil's account is useful as a supplement that gives "depth" to a rational frame of abstract rights. This dual-track morality, faintly reminiscent of Carol Gilligan's *In a Different Voice*, does not do justice to Weil's vision of the possibility of a material relational base for equality, rooted in a human community.

III. Hannah Arendt

A. Books by Arendt

Rahel Varhagen: The Life of a Jewess (written in 1929–38, first published 1957) (New York: Harcourt Brace Jovanovich, 1974). In this powerful early work, Arendt tells the story of the life of an early-nineteenth-century Jewish woman as it is reflected in her letters and writings, and meditates on the philosophical and historical consequences of assimilation. Rejecting her history as Jewess, restricted in her life as a woman, neither romantic sentiment or Enlightenment reason helped Varnhagen to create a viable self or a coherent life.

The Origins of Totalitarianism (first published 1951) (New York: Harcourt, Brace and World, 1966). Arendt's classical study of the "conditions" that crystallized into the catastrophic event of Nazism, which she understood as signaling the dissolution of Western culture.

The Human Condition (1958) (Chicago: University of Chicago Press, 1958). Arendt's treatment of the "*vita activa*," in which she distinguishes three distinctive forms of human activity, labor, work, action, and marks out the private and public spaces in which they occur.

Between Past and Future (1961) (London: Faber and Faber, 1954). In this fascinating sequence of writings, Arendt both explains and practices what she understands as thinking. Citing the contemporary failure of tradition, which has left us with no absolutes or standards of conduct or judgment, she explicates and exemplifies a thought "between past and future" in a series of exercises that attempt to recover the past at the same time as they anticipate the future.

On Revolution (New York: Viking Press, 1963). This is Arendt's critical analysis of revolution. In the course of her comparison of the French and American Revolutions, she develops some of her distinctive positions on the nature of politics: including the exclusion of goodness, pity, and questions of economic justice from political discussion.

Eichmann in Jerusalem: A Report on the Banality of Evil (1963) (New York: Penguin, 1964). Arendt's fascinating and controversial coverage of Eichmann's trial, and her resulting reflections on the nature of evil and the possibility of judgment.

Men in Dark Times (1968) (New York: Harcourt, Brace & World, 1955). Portraits—Lessing, Rosa Luxemburg, Pope John XXIII, Jaspers, Isak Dinesen, Hermann Broch, Walter Benjamin, Bertold Brecht, Waldemar Gurian, Randall Jarrell—that illustrate Arendt's principle of natality. The dark times of the twentieth century are lit by the "light" that comes from exceptional individuals.

On Violence (New York: Harcourt Brace & World, 1969). An unjustly neglected study of the uses of violence, prompted by the student rebellions and the

Black Power movement of the 1960s. Arendt makes careful distinctions between power, violence, force and authority, arguing that although violence is not necessarily irrational, it has no "power" to create new social relations.

The Life of the Mind Vol. I, *Thinking* and Vol. II, *Willing* (New York: Harcourt Brace Jovanovich, 1978). The first two volumes in Arendt's last unfinished work, *The Life of the Mind*, published posthumously, uneven in quality and often misunderstood. Arendt reviews the history of philosophy from Plato to Heidegger, searching for "experiences" that inspired professional, that is, philosophical, views on the nature of thought and will. She ends with the conclusion that professional thinkers are not the best sources for either because they have regularly been willing to sacrifice freedom for an essentialist metaphysics. At the end of *Willing* she restates the problem of freedom as the problem of founding a new political order that does not repeat the past, and suggests that the answer to the question as to how this is possible is in *Judging*, which was to have been the topic of third and last volume.

Lectures on Kant's Political Philosophy, ed. and with an interpretative introduction by Ronald Beiner (Chicago: University of Chicago Press, 1982). Although Beiner presents Arendt's lectures as a way to reconstruct what she would have said about judging in the last volume of *The Life of the Mind*, they stand by themselves as an interesting projection of an unwritten Kantian interactive political philosophy not based on the rationalist "community of ends" of the *Critique of Practical Reason*.

B. Collections of Articles by Arendt

The Jew as Pariah: Jewish Identity and Politics in the Modern Age, ed. Ron Feldman (New York: Grove Press, 1978). This is a collection of Arendt's papers on the Jewish question, written between 1942 and 1966.

Crisis of the Republic (1972) (New York: Harcourt Brace Jovanovich, 1972). A collection of Arendt's writings on political issues of the 1960s in the United States, such as government policy in the war in Vietnam, civil disobedience, mass versus high culture, and education.

C. Articles by Arendt of Philosophical Interest

"What is Existenz Philosophy?" in *Partisan Review* Vol. XIII, No. 1 (Winter 1946) 34–56. Arendt reviews the history of continental philosophy—Husserl, Marx, Heidegger—as a series of unsuccessful attempts to reestablish a Hegelian unity of Thought and Being. This article includes her critique of Heidegger as promoting a pernicious solipsistic view of the self which can only find reconciliation in a totalitarian Overself.

"Imperialism: Road to Suicide," in *Commentary* I (February 1946) 27–35. Arendt cites Luxemburg as the only Marxist who had not "concealed" the destructive "political pattern of imperialism." Arendt emphasizes the racist dynamics of imperialism as an extension of the anti-Semitism of the classless "mob" of men uprooted by European capitalism, who, in alliance with capitalists, carried out colonization.

"Understanding and Politics," in *Partisan Review* 20 (1953) 377–92. In this article, Arendt reflects on her "understanding" of totalitarianism as a phenomenon, distinguishing understanding from social science, which uncritically assumes categories or "natures."

"Authority in the Twentieth Century," in *Review of Politics* Vol. 17 No. 4. (October 1956) 403–17. Arendt brings out peculiarities of the new phenomenon of totalitarianism, distinguishing it from authoritarianism.

"Reflections on Little Rock," in *Dissent* Vol. 6 No. 1 (Winter 1959) 45–56. Arendt's controversial argument against forced segregation in the schools emphasized the quasi-private space of the schools and the necessity to protect children from political violence.

"Truth in Politics," in *New Yorker* (February 25, 1967). After the controversy surrounding her reportage of the Eichmann case, Arendt turned her attention to thinking and its relation to politics. In this exploratory reflection, she focuses on the fragility of the factual truth.

"Thinking and Moral Considerations," in *Social Research* Vol. 38 No. 3 (Autumn 1971) 417–446. (Reprinted Vol. 38 No. 1, Spring/Summer 1984). In this article Arendt explains the indirect relation between thinking and action. "Conscience" is a side effect of thought, with the result that, in extreme cases, a person may refuse to participate in evil.

"Martin Heidegger at Eighty," in *New York Review of Books* October 1971 (reprinted in Michael Murray, ed., *Heidegger and Modern Philosophy* [New Haven: Yale University Press, 1978]). This is the famous/infamous article in which Arendt "forgives" Heidegger for his bad political judgment, which she understands as a "*déformation professionelle.*"

D. Books About Arendt

Barnouw, Dagmar. *Visible Spaces: Hannah Arendt and the German-Jewish Experience* (Baltimore: Johns Hopkins University Press, 1990). A review of Arendt's work on the Jewish question, including an interesting discussion of *Rahel Varnhagen.* Barnouw argues that unthinking criticism by Jews of Arendt's positions on Zionism and anti-Semitism fail to do justice to the principles and insights that underlie her judgments. Barnouw roots Arendt's view of political action in her German-Jewish experience, and shows how her positions on the Jewish state in Palestine and the Nazi war crimes evolve with her philosophies of history, the individual, responsibility, and morality.

Bowen-Moore, Patricia. *Hannah Arendt's Philosophy of Natality* (New York: St. Martin's Press, 1989). An expansion of Arendt's metaphor of natality that traces its sources to Arendt's responses to St. Augustine and Heidegger and describes how it is applied in Arendt's later philosophy of politics.

Bradshaw, Leah. *Acting and Thinking: the Political Thought of Hannah Arendt* (Toronto: University of Toronto Press, 1989). A study of Arendt as the initiator of a new kind of political theory which preserves freedom. Includes useful discussion of contemporary critical commentary on Arendt's philosophy, and an interpretation of Arendt as a pessimist who, in the end, suggests that our only freedom is in the life of the mind.

Canovan, Margaret. *The Political Thought of Hannah Arendt* (New York: Harcourt Brace Jovanovich, 1974). Canovan focuses on the historical and experiential analyses of political concepts rather than philosophical underpinnings to produce an impressionistic account of Arendt's insights and sources of inspiration.

Dossa, Shiraz. *The Public Realm and the Public Self: The Political Theory of Hannah Arendt* (Waterloo, Ontario: Wilfrid Laurier University Press, 1989). Uneven, not always accurate study of Arendt as providing a political "theory," no matter how "literary" Arendt's style.

Kateb, George. *Hannah Arendt: Politics, Conscience, Evil* (Totowa, N.J.: Rowman and Allanheld, 1984). An in-depth study of Arendt's controversial banning of goodness from politics. Kateb cites grave dangers in Arendt's refusal of moral limits or moral inspiration in political action, in Arendt's rejection of representative democracy, and in her attempt to establish an ethics internal to action. His often admiring exposition does justice to the complexity of her positions.

Parekh, Bhikhu. *Hannah Arendt and the Search for a New Political Philosophy* (Atlantic Highlands, N.J: Humanities Press, 1981). Excellent comprehensive review of the major themes in Arendt's political thought, with special attention to her distinctive notions of public space, society, political action. Parekh compares Arendt's positions with traditional political theory, organizes her various arguments into a coherent philosophy of politics, and probes the contradictory tensions in several of Arendt's arguments.

Whitfield, Stephen. *Into the Dark: Hannah Arendt and Totalitarianism* (Philadelphia: Temple University Press, 1980). Whitfield sets Arendt's work on totalitarianism in the context of sixties and seventies debates on the relation between Stalinism and Fascism, and shows how Arendt's thought continued to evolve past these disputes.

Young-Bruehl, Elizabeth. *Hannah Arendt: For Love of the World* (New Haven: Yale University Press, 1982). This is the major biography of Arendt. Young-Bruehl, a philosopher and thinker in her own right, relates the evolution of Arendt's ideas to events in her life.

E. Collections of Papers on Arendt

Bernauer, James, ed. *Amor Mundi: Exploration in the Faith and Thought of Hannah Arendt* (Boston: M. Nijhoff Pub., 1987). A collection of papers predicated on the supposition of a implicit religious substratum in Arendt's thought. Commentators cite Arendt's politicization of biblical themes, her interest in theologians such as St. Augustine, and her love of the world. Also includes two unpublished lectures by Arendt, "Labor, Work, Action" and "Collective Responsibility."

Hill, Melvyn, ed. *Hannah Arendt: The Recovery of the Public World* (New York: St. Martin's Press, 1979). An excellent collection of articles on Arendt. Includes: Mildred Bakan, "Hannah Arendt's Concepts of Labor and Work," an interesting comparison of Arendt and Hegel on the origins of consciousness in interaction with the physical world; Bhikhu Parekh, "Hannah Arendt's Critique of Marx," in which Parekh sorts through Arendt's criticisms of Marx, separating out those that are just from those that are not; Kenneth Frampton, "The Status of Man and the Status of His Objects," an application of Arendt's distinction between labor and work to architecture; Robert Major, "A Reading of Hannah Arendt's 'Unusual' Distinction between Labor and Work," an interesting comment on ways of misreading Arendt, including the ways she misreads herself; Spyros Draenos, "Thinking without a Ground," an insightful description of Arendt's thought between past and future; J. Glenn Gray, "The Abyss of Freedom—and Hannah Arendt," a sensitive and illuminating reflection on Arendt's "blank page" and "impasse" which occasioned it.

Kaplan, G. T. and Kessler, C. S. *Hannah Arendt: Thinking, Judging, Freedom* (Sydney: Allen and Unwin, 1988). A collection of impressionistic rather than technical studies of Arendt's thought on various issues, including a section on the Jewish question and Arendt's *Rahel Varnhagen*. Of special interest is Maria Markus's "The 'Anti-Feminism' of Hannah Arendt," in which Markus argues that Arendt should not be neglected by feminists because she provides a politics of difference, a study of conscious pariahism relevant to oppressed groups, and challenging criticisms of the weaknesses of a "women's" movement.

Schurmann, Reiner, ed. *The Public Realm: Essays on Discursive Types in Political Philosophy* (Albany, N.Y.: State University of New York Press, 1989). A collection of essays not on Arendt's work directly but which take off from various issues she raised.

F. Special Issues of Periodicals Devoted to Arendt's Work

History of Political Theory, Vol. 16, No. 1 (February 1988). The papers focus on philosophical issues raised by Arendt's account of *The Life of the Mind*. Includes, among others: Seyla Benhabib, "Judgment and the Moral Foundations of Politics in Arendt's Thought." Charging that Arendt's account of thinking is not always coherent, Benhabib purposes to "think with Arendt against Arendt" to establish an Arendtian morality generated in action. Suzanne Jacobitti, "Hannah Arendt and the Will." Jacobitti blames weakness in Arendt's account of the will on a incoherent pluralistic notion of the self. B. Honig, "Arendt, Identity, and Difference." Honig argues that *Willing* is not a departure from Arendt's early work, that Arendt does not claim that the will is free, and that Arendt's view of action requires a plural self.

Social Research, Vol. 44, No. 1 (Spring 1977). Testaments, exegeses, appreciations of Arendt's work. Jurgen Habermas, "Hannah Arendt's Communications Concept of Power," is of special interest. Habermas finds Arendt's politics relieved of economic and administrative issues ridiculous, and charges that Arendt had to retreat to the "life of the mind" because she did not see that rational argument can make a link between knowledge and opinion. Also included are: Hans Jonah, "Acting, Knowing, Thinking." Jonah opens with some interesting recollections of Arendt in which she expressed her view that men are the weaker sex, more removed from reality and more deceived by concepts than women; Ernst Vollrath, "History and Political Thinking," trans. Hans Fantel: a useful analysis of the ways in which Arendt's method of understanding transcends the split between theory and practice.

G. Articles About Arendt

Beiner, R., "Judging in a World of Appearances: A Commentary on Hannah Arendt's Unwritten Finale," in *History of Political Thought* 1: 117–135, Spring 1980. A discussion of Kant's Third Critique and a somewhat disapproving description of Arendt's attempt to find in it an unwritten Kantian politics.

Benhabib, Seyla, "Judgment and the Moral Foundations of Politics in Arendt's Thought," in *Political Theory* 10: 1 (February 1988). An indictment of Arendt for separating politics from morality.

Canovan, Margaret, "Politics as Culture: Hannah Arendt and the Public Realm," in *History of Political Thought* 6: 617–642, Winter 1985. Canovan attempts to explicate the artificiality and spatiality of Arendt's public life by way of an analogy with cultural "worlds."

Cutting-Gray, "Hannah Arendt, Feminism, and the Politics of Alterity," in *Hypatia* 8: 1 (Winter 1993), 35–54. An interpretation of Rahel Varnhagen as providing the conceptual frame for a "politics of alterity" that is not based on a "sentimental sisterhood."

Deitz, Mary, "Hannah Arendt and Feminist Politics," M. L. Shanley and C. Pateman eds., in *Feminist Interpretations and Political Theory* (University Park: Pennsylvania State University Press, 1991), Deitz compares positive and negative feminist responses to the work of Arendt, arguing that Arendt brings out the weakness in a feminist politics based on reproduction. Deitz projects an "Arendtian feminism" by an attention to gender.

Dossa, Shiraz, "Hannah Arendt's Political Theory: Ethics and Enemies," in *History of European Ideas* 13: 4, 1991, 385–398. A defense of Arendt's politics against Benhabib's (1988) charge of immorality. Arendt's politics may be inadequate, Dossa argues, but have an "internal morality" and therefore are neither amoral or immoral.

Honig, B., "Toward an Agonistic Feminism: Hannah Arendt and the Politics of Identity," in Judith Butler and Joan Scott eds., *Feminists Theorize the Political* (New York: Routledge, 1992). A deconstructive and revisionist reading of Arendt which attempts to transplant what is taken as Arendt's "performative" politics into the private sphere.

McKenna, George, "Bannisterless Politics: Hannah Arendt and her Children," in *History of Political Thought* 5: 333–360, Summer 1984. An attack on Arendt's concept of freedom as encouraging an empty anarchistic radicalism. McKenna cites Arendt's support for the "unprincipled" student rebellions of the 1960s as evidence.

Pitkin, Hannah, "Are Freedom and Liberty Twins?" in *Political Theory* 16: 523–552, November 1988. A meditation on and proposed correction of Arendt's etymological method using the example of "freedom" and "liberty." As a Wittgensteinian, Pitkin suggests that Arendt should have looked closer at the way words actually were and are used.

———, "Justice: On Relating Private and Public," in *Political Theory* 9: 327–352, August 1981. An attempt to redirect Arendt's public action away from elitist display and back to justice as defined by Aristotle.

Ring, Jennifer, "The Pariah as Hero: Hannah Arendt's Political Actor," in *Political Theory* 19:3 (August 1991) 433–452. Ring argues that critics have "overvalued" Arendt's Greek model of politics and suggests that Arendt's "pariahs" may offer alternative models.

Wolin, Sheldon, "Hannah Arendt and the Ordinance of Time," in *Social Research* Vol. 44, No. 1 (1977) 91–105. Wolin argues that there is interdependence and not separation between Arendt's private and public, but Arendt neglects both justice and the influence of the institutional.

Index